BORDERLINE AND
ACTING-OUT ADOLESCENTS

BORDERLINE AND ACTING-OUT ADOLESCENTS

A Developmental Approach

Gary Nielsen, Ph.D.

Child & Adolescent Secure Treatment Program,
Oregon State Hospital, Salem, Oregon

HUMAN SCIENCES PRESS, INC.
72 FIFTH AVENUE,
NEW YORK, N.Y. 10011

Copyright © 1983 by Human Sciences Press, Inc.
72 Fifth Avenue, New York, New York 10011

Printed in the United States of America
3456789 987654321

Library of Congress Cataloging in Publication Data

Nielsen, Gary E., 1939–
  Borderline and acting-out adolescents.

  Bibliography: p. 237
  Includes index.
  1. Adolescent psychopathology.   2. Personality, Disorders of.   3. Acting out (Psychology)   I. Title.
RJ503.N53   616.89   LC 81–20223
  ISBN 0–89885–109–2   AACR2

To Judy, Darren, and Derek for their patience.

To all the young people who worked so hard to help me see what was there all the time.

CONTENTS

INTRODUCTION

This book is about severe behavior disorders of adolescence and a model that attempts to explain some of the phenomena associated with the problem. It is perhaps presumptuous in its scope, and I have also taken some liberties with diagnostic labels but given the confused state they are in, as far as adolescence is concerned, I have few apologies on that score.

My incentive for writing this book came from the fact that the majority of adolescents who are exhibiting severe problems, if they are dealt with at all, are the responsibility of individuals who are working without an adequate model for understanding or decision making. Yet these people are faced with daily decisions that may have horrendous implications for the young person.

My conclusions are to a large extent based upon my clinical research with adolescents in a residential hospital setting. I am deeply indebted to the young people, the staff, and the administration of the Child & Adolescent Secure Treatment Program at Oregon State Hospital for allowing me the opportunity to carry out this work. The treatment program was a closed system, a culture in and of itself, where my initial approach was more that of a cultural anthropologist than a psychologist. I was equipped with a few working assumptions about psychotherapy, child development, and adolescence in general, but I hope as few biases as possible. The program offered a cross section of problems of adolescents and socioeconomic status. I was amazed to find out how much the young people would accept an adult who understood their world and how much they wanted psychotherapy. The more you correctly confronted their defenses and perceptual distortions, the more they would keep coming back to you despite any initial angry responses. It became evident that the more the ambivalence and borderline personality characteristics of the adolescent, the more inclined they were to classify therapists into those who knew what they were doing and those who did not. This dichotomy was entirely based upon whether they thought you perceived the ambivalence of their perception and could step "through the looking glass" into their world.

I have presented little that could be called "how to do therapy" with the adolescent. Such an endeavor would require another volume to do properly, and, more important, you cannot understand the process of therapy unless you understand what it is you're doing therapy about—in other words, the psychodynamics of the adolescent. Nothing will alienate the young person more than therapeutic process without content that demonstrates an understanding of their world. This content of psychotherapy must be the ability to perceive the ambivalent confusion. I have been asked many times, how do you do a confrontational therapy approach with adolescents? The question should be, what is it that you confront them about? Once you have convinced them that you understand the basic dynamics of content, you have engendered enough trust in the relationship that the borderline adolescents will quickly let you know by their behavior when your perception has gone astray.

During the course of our study of 150 severely disturbed adolescents in residential treatment, we gathered a large amount of information on many pertinent factors, such as family dynamics, early development, social history, the adolescents' perception of acceptance and rejection, course of treatment, and what happened after they left the program. The information was sorted and compiled as to what factors related to what outcomes and into a model that would explain this data. It is this two-factor model of acceptance and rejection that is offered as the most likely explanation. Any theoretical model is of course nothing more than a number of hypotheses that should be subjected to a validation process.

My background and training has included learning theory, early development research, some psychoanalytic training, and outpatient work with borderline adults, before beginning work with adolescents. Many years ago it became clear to me that the ambivalence and complexities of the mother/child relationship was not going to be explained by some of the assumptions that were taught at the time. Early development investigators would study almost any aspect of development except the emotional domain, because there were no accepted models of emotional development comparable to Piaget's intellectual schema. Psychological researchers in particular were reluctant to investigate anything that could not be directly observed, operationally defined, or quantified in some way. There was much clinical evidence of inappropriate parenting and unusual interactions between parent and child, but little to explain how such an aberrant situation came about.

I became very interested in the work of Dr. John Bowlby, because of the relevance to the population with which I was working. There was clearly a relationship between separation anxiety and later problems, although the clinical implications were not understood. What was puzzling to me was my observation that in the more borderline adults oftentimes there was no separation from either parent—the home was intact. It was here that I became interested in the developmental theory of Dr. Margaret Mahler. Her approach seemed to offer a viable model that would explain the aberrant development and relationship between the mother and child as I observed it.

As I began to work more with adults in psychotherapy the term "borderline personality" was just coming into use but was poorly understood, with little diagnostic agreement. Most recognized treatment emphasized a psychoanalytic approach, but often psychoanalysts use little developmental specificity and do not follow the Bowlby or Mahler models of development. Coming across the works of Dr. James Masterson was very significant to me because his approach to treatment of the borderline was solidly based upon the developmental approach of Mahler and could easily accomodate Bowlby's work. In addition, his approach centered around a more direct confrontational approach, which I found matched my own style of therapy.

I owe much to Dr. Masterson's support and his efforts to assist me through conferences, seminars, personal discussion and written communication. I have often found it heartening that those who are outstanding in their fields are often the most open and helpful to talk to personally—Dr. Masterson is certainly no exception to this rule. Throughout the course of this writing he has influenced me around certain issues and in a theoretical sense, but the responsibility for the model as presented here is entirely my own.

I must also add that throughout the course of the development of this material I have read so widely, done so many workshops, and held so many discussions with a variety of individuals that I can no longer be certain just who should rightly be attributed to as a source of a particular idea. I may have incorrectly claimed something as being original with me when in fact the seed was planted by someone else long before; to the extent that I have made that error I apologize.

The information presented was largely taken from the evaluation of treatment of severely emotionally disturbed adolescents. These young people were placed in a secure treatment program because they were thought to be dangerous to themselves or others. One must be cautious about generalizations from this circumscribed population. On the other hand, I have tried this model and approach in a variety of other settings. This has lead me to the conclusion that there is relatively little difference between the residents in my population and the majority of acting-out adolescents who present severe problems in the community.

I have not attempted to substantiate conclusions with statistical data from the study; the model as presented will have to stand on its own merits and potential value to the clinician and youth worker. There will be a volume in the future devoted solely to the follow-up study itself, and final conclusions about the role played by various factors must await that outcome.

I would like to thank James Masterson M.D. and Donald

Rinsley M.D. for their independent and thorough reviews of this manuscript. They were the first to offer critical appraisal.

And finally I would like to thank Susan Latham, my co-researcher on the adolescent study, without whose unstinting dedication to the task there would have been no data and no book. Much appreciation also goes to Patti Goldblatt who prepared and typed all of the early working papers that eventually lead to the final manuscript.

Part I

SEVERE BEHAVIOR DISORDERS OF ADOLESCENCE

Chapter 1

PERSPECTIVE ON ADOLESCENCE

Anthropology has shown us (Meade, 1928, 1930, 1935) that the problem of adolescence is largely relative to the degree that a culture allows for transition to adulthood. In our society the stress often placed on adolescents can result in a major disorder (Offer, 1975, 1979 and Esman, 1975). In this context it may be presumptuous to write about severe behavior disorders of adolescence when we have no model that places the problems of growth and development in a cultural perspective.

Problems are largely defined in terms of the behavior of the adolescent; that is, their inability to conform to social norms and expectations. To a considerable extent, it is to be expected that the transition to adult status be made long and arduous. We do not provide for an easy transition in the sense that the onset of a powerful sexual drive is beginning somewhat earlier than in previous generations, while adolescence itself is being made longer as a transition period for economic reasons.

The adolescent is faced with an apparent contradiction in our culture that is in so many ways oriented toward youthfulness and perpetuating a state of adolescence. One need only view advertising on the one hand, and on the other, take a tour of a local nursing home for the elderly to understand our fascination with youthfulness. We are in effect saying that adolescence is wonderful providing that you are 30 years old and can afford it. Youth means material things, adult benefits, and denying ready access to those who are adolescents only chronologically.

In this context, then, we shall see that some recent interpretations of the borderline condition can be understood in part as a problem of separation from the parents, independence, and ego functions. Likewise, the problems with many of the parents can be seen in terms of a failure to have successfully gotten through adolescence to the point of having achieved an integrated, independent sense of self. The borderline personality is first of all a failure to successfully separate and individuate during the first three years of development because of ambivalent or insufficient libidinal supplies from the mother figure. Problems that originate during adolescence itself may more appropriately be thought of as problems of emancipation without the same pathological significance.

My work is really addressed to the mental health professionals, social workers, caseworkers, school counselors, and residential counselors who must deal with severely disturbed adolescents and their families. Professional training programs often do not provide effective skills and practical training in understanding adolescents. Experience is often confined to the most superficial or artificial set of conditions. Anyone working in the field can tell you that phobias, minor obsessive-compulsive behavior, and the like do not represent the bulk of the problems.

I can remember working in an outpatient setting when high status as a professional meant that you did not have to see the 13- and 14-year olds but could assign them to someone else. It was not until I had had many years of practice that I realized how much most severely disturbed adolescents want psychotherapy, but only under certain conditions; mainly this involves wanting a therapist who can understand what is going on in their perceptual world. Trust is a precious commodity and not readily given by the adolescent. It becomes increasingly important, as we move into the borderline condition where one must be able to cross through the 'looking glass,' so to speak, to understand the world as the borderline adolescent perceives it.

DIAGNOSIS AND OTHER LABELS

A diagnostic label is based on descriptions of complex behavior patterns that taken as an entity is given a name. While some underlying causal state is inferred, there is as yet no acceptable model of abnormal behavior in adolescence that can be put into developmental perspective. Diagnostic applications, such as 'reactions to adolescence' or 'personality disorder' may be accurate, but tend to be of little value in understanding the origin and probably future direction of a behavior pattern. The term "borderline personality" is another such label, but it does have the benefit of a useful developmental and theoretical model that does not depend on a descriptive symptomology but has a strong intrapsychic basis (Masterson, 1976; Kernberg, 1968, 1978; Rinsley, 1971, 1980; LeBoit & Capponi, 1979).

WHY THE BORDERLINE CONCEPT?

I became interested in the borderline personality concept because of its broad appeal and explanatory potential and its treatment implications. I have taken great liberties with the term in my attempt to develop a descriptive and somewhat mechanistic psychological model of severe disturbances in adolescence. It can be defined as a problem of separation from the parent, identity, ego development as an integrated whole, and fear of abandonment all of which stem from early development. It is both a behavioral and an intrapsychic problem. The internal structure of split object relations and split ego functions of borderline adolescents can be seen mirrored in their behavior; especially in acting out to defend against internal representation of stress and in their relations with others. Adolescence in general is a process of developing an ego identity, which to some extent can compound the borderline problems (Erikson, 1968). It has even been suggested that borderline problems in adults are problems of adolescence in the sense that ego development and separation issues were never adequately completed because of the failure to properly separate during the early developmental period.

PERCEIVED REJECTION

What most severely disturbed adolescents perceive is not a separation problem, as such; they are perceiving a degree of rejection and acceptance from loved objects and are feeling a commensurate degree of fear, abandonment, anger, and stress. By this definition the borderline condition is a conflictual situation resulting in high stress from the ambivalent situation with the parents. It is conceptually easy to move the perceived acceptance and rejection along a hypothetical continuum and produce a set of predictable clinical manifestations. Clearly stress has both its internal and external manifestations and the validity of each depends upon where one happens to be looking. While my objective is to develop a descriptive psychology of severe disturbances of adolescence, Masterson's (1976) intrapsychic approach offers the most singularly effective approach to psychotherapy of borderline conditions in adolescents.

CLINICAL MANIFESTATIONS OF AMBIVALENCE

The hypothetical continuum, where total acceptance or rejection can be seen as the extreme ends, allows us to view the borderline condition as the ambivalence of both. It is in fact the closeness of these two diametric opposites that creates maximum stress. The borderline personality is characterized in part by the inability to completely internalize the problem into a psychotic state, whereby they must act out the stress.

In clinical terms the borderline problem shows up as severe ego disturbances and distorted perception. The result is depression, highly variable behavior in keeping with the relative distance between perceived acceptance and rejection, acting out to defend against the depression, and often inward or outward directed aggression. The distorted perception that is necessitated by the nature of the adolescent's psychological reality is such that certain logical rules no longer strictly apply. The therapist must be able to move between two sets of logic as it were; theirs as the objective observer of the world and the one represented by the adolescent's perception. It is this situation that makes a behavioral analysis of the borderline condition difficult at the present state of the art.

Interestingly, as you move toward either end of the continuum of acceptance and rejection the situation becomes increasingly logical in that the adolescent's perception is likely to conform to your perception. There is ordinarily more ego-intactness, less emotional lability, greater perceptual stability and, above all, less stress. The adolescent is operating in a more perceptually comprehensible world. This does not mean that the ego is not pathological, but only that it is integrated relative to the split-ego functioning of the borderline condition. The relationship between behavior and consequences becomes more clearcut at the extremes of the continuum and, in fact, becomes an even more essential part of treatment of the adolescent.

A Two-Factor Model

A two-factor model of acceptance and rejection is a mechanistic view of human behavior in one sense. I have intended it to be comprehensive and as such it is quite general and cannot account well for many specifics. My concern is whether or not it gives the clinician any better understanding of the problem adolescent they have sitting in front of them.

When an earlier stress or drive reduction model was proposed (Dollard, J., Miller, N., Doob, L., Mowrer, O. and Sears, R., 1939) the work of psychology was heavily influenced by cultural anthropology; an influence long since lost. It is indicative of that time in which the authors wrote that credit was given to the influence of Freud upon their thinking, along with the debt owed to the learning theorist, Clark Hull. They tended to dismiss much of Freud's later writing, such as the death instinct, and praised his earlier work. It is interesting that some of the modern writers in the area of borderline personality and other character disorder problems do likewise. What they are all adhering to is the psychodynamics of stress and internalization that is produced by the forces of the child interacting with his immediate environment, as opposed to some preordained pattern of abnormal development that stems from instinctual drives.

ACTING OUT AND STRESS

There are no satisfactory external behaviors by which to measure the intrapsychic structure of the adolescent. This is never more apparent than when we are talking about the adolescent with borderline characteristics, where acting-out behavior takes on special significance because of the depression. The apparently illogical, self-destructive and self-defeating behaviors that do not respond to immediate consequences merely reflect the nature of the internal structure of the adolescent.

Running from the family home would appear to be almost epidemic, although it is certainly a time-tested method of dealing with adolescence. However, when viewed in the context of other behavior patterns it may be related to the ambivalent acceptance and rejection pattern much more than to pure forms of either acceptance or rejection. Thus it can be one form of defending against the effects of that stress. I might add that it can also result from a low-rejection borderline pattern where symbiosis and engulfment between mother and the adolescent has been the pattern. Here the adolescent is trying to escape these ties and the feelings of responsibility that go along with them; they are not battling perceived rejection, but are the ones experimenting with doing the rejecting.

Other acting-out behaviors, such as substance abuse, can often be regarded as symptomatic of a borderline, ambivalent rejection pattern. It is self-medication for dealing with the depression. It is no doubt true that most use of drugs and alochol by the teenager has nothing to do with the borderline condition, per se. The essential difference is that when it is being used to relieve depression it must be nearly continuous otherwise depression sets in and may promote suicide ideation. Self-destructive behaviors, including self-mutilation and drug overdosing, are also more symptomatic of the high-stress ambivalence than any other pattern of acceptance-rejection.

Delinquent behavior by the adolescent can be used as a defense against depression. It can also represent an indirect attention-getting device in the more severe rejection cases. Most delinquent behavior is goal directed and a resolution to stress conditions, and a learned behavior through an indulgent parenting pattern. It is usually associated with a low-rejection family situation that is characterized by delinquent modeling, indulgence, benign neglect, a lack of appropriate limits, and vicarious reinforcement by the parent. This may be interpreted as a rejecting family by some, but the delinquent adolescent has little doubt about the acceptance of at least one of the parents—usually the mother—in that he can demand or coerce behavior he desires.

I will use an example of stealing cars to illustrate the different forms of delinquent behavior. In one case an adolescent stole a car and parked it near a police station with his wallet inside. He had been subject to severe abuse and total rejection from his family for years. He viewed institutions as his only family and he would do what he had to do to return. However, he could never admit his true motivation for stealing and always wanted to play the long-suffering victim role. In another instance an adolescent with a borderline history stole in excess of 25 cars during one cross-country spree. He called me on the phone in the midst of this and stated that he did not have to deal with his feelings and depression as long as he kept stealing cars and driving, and that furthermore this method of resolving stress and depression was more fun than mine.

There is often great difficulty finding residential placements for the severely disturbed, acting-out adolescents in part because they frequently do not stay where they are placed. I have noticed a relationship between the acceptance and rejection pattern and the type of placement that works. The majority of adolescents who are successfully housed in group homes and open-treatment centers appear to be the relatively low-stress, severe-rejection adolescents, where achieving a degree of resolution to the stress is easier. The more ambivalent rejection or borderline the pattern, the less inclined they are to stay in out-of-home placements.

Aggression and violence toward others is more related to acceptance than to rejection, per se. In order to carry out severe aggression the adolescent needs a high degree of resolution, or motivation, depending upon what one wants to call it, which ordinarily does not occur with greater degrees of rejection. Aggression is not generally found throughout the entire acceptance-rejection continuum but is confined largely to two bands. This includes borderline symbiotic relationships that can produce violence within the family and low-rejection, high-indulgence patterns in conjunction with severe pathological rejection that produces violence directed outside the family.

In terms of the model presented here, psychoses can be regarded as a resolution to a set of highly stressful conditions. While I do not believe that there is a simple answer as to which adolescent will develop a psychotic resolution to stress, we can draw some general conclusions. Psychotic behavior tends to be associated primarily with two positions on our continuum. First, severe rejection associated with abusive environments can produce a degree of paranoia and perceptual distortion. Because of the threat, there is a need for the adolescent to internalize the fear and grossly distort the environment even when it is no longer fear-producing. This same situation produces a sublimation of aggression which can be redirected away from the family as sexual aggression (which is displaced aggression aimed at the mother) or firesetting which has much the same connotation. However, the paranoid condition from severely rejecting and punitive environments is questionable because the fear is to considerable extent well-founded in reality and not delusional.

On the continuum of acceptance and rejection there is in one sense little difference between the borderline condition of ambivalence and a certain schizophrenic-producing pattern. When high acceptance is a major part of the perceived ambivalence from the family, you may force almost total internalization and guilt, such that the schizophrenic adolescent feels not only responsible for his own behavior but also that of his parents. The more typical borderline adolescent has more room to manuever between the contradictions, and more basis in perceiving rejection from the family, and thus reacting with their own rejection and anger; a luxury the schizophrenic would not have without tremendous guilt. The literature suggests (Wolman, 1976) that the schizophrenic-producing family is highly rejecting, but I do not think that is the case. It is a case of the observer saying it looks rejecting because it produces schizophrenics. Relative to many other types of families, they have many positive and caring qualities. If they did not, the adolescent would not be as likely to assume the responsibility and guilt for all that has gone on. Real rejection provides you with a degree of pragmatism and grounding in reality if it does nothing else.

Chapter 2

PERSPECTIVE ON THE BORDERLINE CONDITION

Historically the area of severe emotional disturbances in adolescence has been a neglected field of study with some notable exceptions (Erikson, 1968; Masterson, 1972; Blos, 1979; Rinsley, 1980). Analytically oriented authors have provided the sole force of theory behind most of our thinking about adolescence. In recent times the management-oriented treatment and intervention approaches have had a strong impact based upon learning theory (Patterson, 1971), rational-emotive (Ellis, 1973), or reality therapy (Glasser, 1965). Such treatment approaches have provided a consistency and some uniformity to our intervention methods, but they have also lacked a theoretical basis or understanding of severe disturbances. This has particularly been a problem when we are talking about the more borderline, ambivalent acceptance and rejection conditions of adolescence, which tend to deny our straightforward perception of reality and treatments based around it.

If we turn for a moment to the area of psychiatric diagnosis in adolescence there is little comfort in the plethora of terminology, without adequate basis in theory, that can adequately explain one category from another. Masterson (1968) was one of the first to point out the inadequacy of the diagnostic procedures and labels in his follow-up of adolescent cases. He noted that regardless of the psychiatric diagnosis given, the adolescents, contrary to popular belief, did not 'outgrow' the problem in adulthood. As a matter of fact they would often become worse. One of the more popular terms in use at the time was personality disorder. It is basically from this broad, ill-defined group that the term borderline personality derived as a finer delineation of a group of adolescents who were not primarily psychotic or neurotic in any classic sense of the term. The borderline is considered to be a form of character disorder, which may for practical purposes be considered as synonymous with the older term personality disorder, and, in fact, most severe disturbances of adolescence can be placed within this broad category.

The general term, 'reaction to adolescence,' is a common diagnostic label found in use which is meant to describe a nonpathological disturbance of adolescence resulting from difficulty in adjusting to the stress inherent in adolescence itself. While the concept is sound it has been used as a veritable dumping ground, along with that of 'antisocial behavior' to describe a vast array of character disorder problems stemming from a degree of rejection. I am not sure that the cure will not be as bad as the bite since the diagnostic label of borderline personality may be applied indiscriminately.

The term schizophrenia has lost popularity when applied to adolescents because of inappropriate use to the point of meaninglessness. It should be reserved, in my opinion, for a small group with persistent psychotic behavior involving major distortions of perception and reality. In contrast, the distortions of reality involving severe-rejection and ambivalent-rejection adolescents are not as total and do not have the persistent delusional basis. Nor does the schizophrenic adolescent have the need to act out on a consistent basis. It is true, however, that schizophrenic tendencies are found throughout the acceptance-rejection continuum with the bulk being within the borderline, ambivalent-rejection area. This in and of itself does not justify the schizophrenic label. Most severe emotional disturbances of adolescents are noted by the fact that they are poorly resolved, such that they must keep struggling and acting out against themselves, their family, and the society as a whole.

In this book I will attempt to construct a very general model of severe disturbances of adolescence that has a practical value. It should, at best, be regarded as nothing more than a road map through the maze of behaviors, symptoms, and inconsistencies of adolescence in general, and the borderline condition, specifically. In so doing I have chosen to use the term 'borderline personality' as a key concept. It is a term that has come into vogue somewhat recently (see the Diagnostic and Statistical Manual III of the American Psychiatric Association), although the term has been around for some time. I personally find the term somewhat objectionable semantically, but it does have the advantage of being based on sound developmental theory with a strong empirical basis (Mahler, 1975), and upon solid footing in terms of treatment approaches (Masterson, 1976; Giovacchini, 1978). It therefore need not rest merely upon symptomology classification and it certainly lends itself to an understandable model of development and family patterns. But perhaps even more important, I believe that the borderline phenomena is at the core of a broad spectrum of parenting problems.

The term 'borderline' does not refer to one's intelligence; it refers to what was thought to be the borderline between psychoses and neuroses—in other words, to a third entity. The term takes on more meaning when we realize that a borderline individual is oftentimes defined by periodically behaving in a psychotic manner but not remaining in that state. In fact, there is some difference of opinion as to whether these individuals enter a true psychotic state at all.

In 1968 Grinker, Werble, and Drye made a study of patients admitted to a psychiatric inpatient service. These patients were not schizophrenic and had no persistent impairment of reality testing, yet they were admitted for a variety of behaviors, such as suicidal ideation, impulse ridden behavior, phobias, compulsions, alcohol and drug abuse, and temporary confusional states. For the first time a wide variety of clinical behaviors were linked to a specific diagnostic entity not clearly psychotic or psychoneurotic in nature. This group of seemingly unrelated symptoms and behaviors was termed the borderline personality disorder.

The borderline can be described as having an ego defect

characterized by nonspecificity, poor reality perception, poor frustration tolerance, and poor impulse control. The individual in effect must resort to primitive defenses, such as splitting, primitive ideation, projective identification, denial, omnipotence, and devaluation (Kernberg, 1978, 1976). While a growing concensus has adopted the concept of the borderline as a structural disorder due to developmental arrest, disagreement persists regarding the developmental stage at which this has occurred. The position taken by Masterson (1972) following the developmental guidelines of Mahler (1975) is perhaps the most representative. He states that the borderline problem begins sometime during the separation-individuation phase of development (18 to 36 months) as the child begins a natural separation process from the mother on the way to becoming a separate ego identity. The mother, who may well be borderline herself, gives very ambivalent messages to the child. She encourages and rewards in the child the key defense mechanisms of denial of the reality of separation, which in turn allows the persistence of the wish for reunion with her, which later emerges as a defense against the abandonment depression.

The onset of adolescence is a critical period because it is thought by some to be (Blos, 1967, 1979) a second separation-individuation period comparable in some respects to the first 3 years of life. At the very least this early adolescent period coincides with the onset of overt acting out and no doubt greatly exacerbates the borderline development. Blos (1962) sees the adolescent developmental tasks as necessitating the achievement of independence from the parents and the rechanneling of libidinal energy from the parents to self, to homosexual objects, back to self, and finally to a nonincestuous heterosexual object choice. Such a hierarchy of tasks requires increasingly higher concepts of a self-object representation, an ability to sublimate, and an increasing mastery of the separation-individuation process.

Giovacchini (1978) makes the point that the term 'borderline' is a particularly apt description in two senses of the word: 1) The borderline regress rather easily to a psychotic or near psychotic state, but have the capacity to recapture quickly their former equilibrium, minimal as it may be; 2) Borderline adjustments are made to the external world. The adolescent character structure is fluid and transitional with feelings of helplessness and vulnerability. He sees the existential crisis of adolescence as little more than an exaggeration of the natural borderline qualities of the adolescent character structure. From this point of view (a view with which Masterson and others would disagree) the borderline condition is a part of adolescence in their search for identity. Erikson (1968), I believe, has referred to a similar phenomena when he talks about a search for integration and identity that he places as the cornerstone of adolescent development.

The borderline adolescent can be placed on a broad continuum of severe disorders. In this context, then, I am referring to a continuum of characteristics that imply degrees of separation-individuation difficulties in adolescence. I have been intrigued by the number of adolescents who have borderline features without being clearly identified as such on the basis of having clear-cut intrapsychic structure.

A more stringent diagnostic view is offered by Gunderson and Singer (1975) who suggested six criteria for borderline diagnosis: 1) the presence of intense affect, usually depressive or hostile; 2) a history of impulsive behavior; 3) social adaptiveness; 4) a brief psychotic experience; 5) bizarre, dereistic, illogical, or primitive responses on unstructured psychological tests; and 6) relationships that vacillate between transient superficiality and intense dependency. Other criteria, such as lack of empathy for others and self-glorifying fantasies, have been suggested by other authors (Anderson, 1978). The borderline condition essentially involves the inability of the adolescent to separate properly from the mother figure because of fears of being abandoned or rejected for what would be regarded as normal individuation. The threat results in fear, anxiety, and depression, which is defended against by acting out.

In many cases the fear of rejection and abandonment by the parents is quite obvious and the clinician need not look very far to find the problem. But with some adolescents the fear of abandonment and the rejection is denied. The process is more evident in the interactions and relationships that they have with others, where objects are put in positions of the rejecting parent.

We are presented with a broad continuum of adolescent behaviors that relate to various perceptions of acceptance and rejection by parental figures. The borderline adolescent's perception of the family situation is highly ambivalent—that is, an I-love-you, I-love-you-not situation. Most important, this ambivalent acceptance and rejection never clearly gets stated by either the parent or the adolescent. There is a covert agreement in the family never to state things as they really are such that messages are simultaneously overt and covert. Many hours can be wasted in family therapy where the therapist thinks that issues are being clarified and communication developed. The adolescent believes that the therapist does not understand the covert messages or, in other words, is unable to step through the looking glass to understand the ambivalent situation. The self-destructiveness is sometimes an angry retaliatory act to demonstrate that all is not going well.

I would suggest that a majority of the severe problems encountered by those who work with adolescents involves borderline dynamics to some extent. The borderline adolescents will often come to the attention of authorities because of their run from home, getting themselves into some life-endangering situation, returning home, and repeating the cycle. They will almost never stay in foster homes or group homes for any extended period of time. At the first opportunity they will return home regardless of how obviously destructive the family may seem to the observer. As a matter of fact, as we shall see, the more destructive the home situation, the more likely it is that the adolescent will return home.

The population of adolescents with severe behavior problems would include the diagnosis of borderline personality between 25 and 75 percent of the cases, depending upon the criteria one chose. Where one wants to draw the line and label the adolescent as borderline becomes a matter of personal conviction. But it is precisely because the borderline dynamic is so pervasive that it makes a useful model with which to explore the entire area of severe disturbances in adolescence.

One thing that becomes rather striking in working with adolescents who have severe problems is that everything that goes on in their life is in some way a reaction to their parents—or what they perceive to be the rejection. This may not be surprising yet we often try to treat adolescents as though this were not the case.

We treat them as we would an adult who had solved their identity crisis or at least effected a satisfactory separation. When it comes to the borderline cases in adolescence there is a magical attraction the family seems to have over them. The best made plans have gone down the drain with one phone call from the parent.

It became clear that the adolescent with severe problems followed patterns of behavior related to the degree of acceptance and rejection they perceived from the parents. This factor has a profound effect upon the personality, motivation, goals, and clinical symptoms of the adolescent. One can imagine moving the pendulum of rejection and producing different symptoms and behavior in the adolescent. Acceptance and rejection is clearly on a continuum and is effected by several factors, but there does appear to be four distinct categories along the way.

Borderline adolescents are tied to their family by an umbilical cord that can be hidden, stretched indefinitely but not prematurely broken. It is elastic such that the more the adolescents distance themselves from the family the more force there is pulling them back. The return route may be most circuitous and misleading to the observer but it is certain. The breaking of this elasticized cord is the natural process of separation from the parents and the development of a mature ego identity. In other words, it is what the borderline adolescents cannot accomplish and their parents will not allow them to do. In fact the adolescent is the only one who can finally break this tie, but only when he has accomplished certain necessary developmental and psychological tasks. We can help them accomplish this during the course of psychotherapy but we cannot force it to happen.

Most adolescents with severe emotional disturbances can, I believe, be understood if we view them in terms of four factors: early development; family pattern; perception of acceptance and rejection; and resolution. One cannot understand adolescent behavior by knowing any single factor. No one family pattern will always produce a pattern of behavior, although certain patterns will have a higher probability. It is helpful to think of each adolescent as a unique combination of each of the four factors. However, it is holographic in the sense that one factor possesses something of the final outcome. For example, a certain disturbance of early development will most likely occur in a given family pattern, which in turn will give a high probability of a degree of acceptance and rejection. And lastly, the behavior will reflect all of these. I have found that it is these probabilities that account for clinical cases that seem to defy all ordinary explanations. For example, the highly pathological adolescent who appears to come from a psychologically satisfactory family but who, upon examination, is found to have had an aberrant period of early development during some critical phase. Under the right set of circumstances this factor alone lead to an unsatisfactory outcome.

FOUR FACTORS IN PERSPECTIVE

Developmental Factors

The first factor is that of the developmental history of the adolescent with a particular emphasis given to the first few years of life as being the most critical. Much has been said about the importance of early development yet despite vast amounts of data there has been surprisingly little speculation about what types of early development factors are related to what sorts of adolescent behavior. The reasons are probably numerous but among them is a low correlation between early development factors and later behavior because of the multiplicity of intervening factors. In terms of more subjective clinical investigation, little effort has been put into weighing factors in accord with some theoretical model. By taking into account the four factors, early development itself becomes clearer in the role it plays in later life.

I have had an opportunity to study a residential adolescent population in a longitudinal study (Nielsen, Latham, and Engle, 1979). Clearly the age at which psychological trauma, disruption, or separation from parents occurs has some bearing upon later behavior, the probable course of development, and the stress the adolescent must resolve. In and of itself, however, some of the findings are confusing. For example, approximately 80 percent of the adolescents classified as severely disturbed come from homes where the parents were separated for a significant length of time before the child was 6 years of age. Yet the more borderline tend to come from homes where no such separation occurred. Clearly other factors must be taken into account in our analysis.

I have divided development into 7 stages each with a different significance as far as adolescent behavior is concerned. Imagine these 7 stages as a series of building blocks that form a pyramid; thus one can imagine that developmental insults at different stages will effect the total outcome of the structure in different ways. For example, a maternal separation during the latter part of the first year of life can have subtle yet profound effects on outcome even though later development is adequate. This is in keeping with Erikson's (1968) view that the development of trust is the essential psychological factors at this stage of life. Those with this building block missing have had a distinctive clinical character and behavior pattern even though later development can vary considerably.

Family Pattern

The family pattern tends to fall into four categories just as does the acceptance and rejection perceived by the adolescent. However, they must be kept separate because what the family is and what the adolescent perceives it to be are not necessarily the same.

How rejection is transmitted will vary: It may be pathological, nonnurturing, culturally based, or simply a disintegrated family due to separation. Total rejection is biased toward early severe abuse, neglect, psychological trauma in the first year, and multiple separations. In such a case we can say that not only are the early foundation building blocks missing but many of the later pieces are also not available.

Severe rejection, as opposed to a total rejection family situation, is often the most pathological in many respects and also may have the greatest hold over the adolescent. This sometimes causes difficulties for the clinician because it is not seen as logical. It may be viewed as a situation where reinforcement from the family is so intermittent that the response from the adolescent is extremely strong. This is consistent with a variety of research findings including Harlow's work with primates (Harlow, 1963) and Skinner's research on the effects of intermittent reinforcement (Skinner, 1957, 1961).

The third group, that of ambivalent rejection, can be described as the most borderline of the family patterns. Contrary to what is suggested in the literature (Bradley, 1979) this borderline family pattern does not have a high rate of early separation relative to the two previous groups. You are more likely to find a physically intact family partly, I suspect, because it uses the threat of separation as a pathological control mechanism over the child. The elasticity of the umbilical cord is obvious here as it is in the severe rejection family. The definition of the borderline problem as being a difficulty of separation and individuation reaches its zenith in this situation. The overall pattern and characteristics in this family are quite distinctive, as we shall see in the considerable space that is devoted to it in this book.

And finally the fourth family pattern that will be discussed is the low-rejection group. This is one of the most variable groups because it can include a delinquent pattern, simple inappropriate parenting patterns, and symbiotic borderline conditions. Ordinarily the more severe disturbances of adolescence do not come from this group because of the high degree of acceptance from at least one parent. The adolescents tend to be more amenable to treatment providing the delinquent and symbiotic borderline patterns are not too strong. In both of these instances treatment is made more difficult because these patterns represent strong resolutions to the stress and they may not be receptive to therapeutic solutions. There are also exceptions when you combine this pattern with a severe rejection influence from the family. Such a combination, as we shall see, plays a role in some of the more violent problems.

The Adolescent's Perception of Acceptance and Rejection

Perception is often neglected when working with adolescents because it may be very distorted from the objective facts of the family pattern and the observer's perception. I would suggest that it is not possible to deal therapeutically with severely disturbed adolescents unless one understands their perception. To the extent that it is modified in accord with the reality of the situation you have some index of progress in treatment.

The adolescent's perception of the degree of acceptance and rejection from parents is a barometer of psychological impairment. For example, we can say that the more unpredictable the messages of acceptance and rejection the greater is the stress that the adolescent experiences and thus the greater is the disturbance. Maximum unpredictableness would come from the most highly ambivalent or the more borderline family situation. One thing that this model suggests is that severe rejection does not produce the stress that ambivalence can produce.

The adolescent's perception can be placed in four categories comparable to those used to categorize the four family patterns. However, I would urge the reader to be cautious about two things: First, we are talking only about the adolescent's perception of the situation, which may not correspond to the facts the observer perceives; and, second, we are talking about the perception of two parents, even though one or both may have been physically absent for some period of time.

We will be discussing the adolescent who perceives total rejection from the family. The precise clinical picture will depend upon the other factors involved, but in general this produces moderate consistent depression. There are no double messages or contradictions present in the perception and high stress does not ordinarily result, but there is persistent acting out as a defense against the depression. It is also used as a way of calling attention to themselves, avoiding isolation, and being alone. These adolescents will often view agencies as their only real contacts or as a pseudofamily if you will. And of course the way you maintain attention from social agencies as an adolescent is to act out and defy finding a solution. There is often periodic fantasy about being rescued by the lost parent. This adolescent can ordinarily be seen as being on the extreme end of the rejection continuum with some borderline characteristics in some cases but it does not represent the primary clinical picture.

There is a large group of adolescents with severe behavior problems who come from family situations that are severely rejecting. Often the mother is more pathological compared to the parents in the other groups. However, the family is not totally disintegrated and there is a strong hold on the adolescent. The parents are happy to let agencies and therapists have their child for as long as the agencies want because they know that the child will return home. Some of the most pathological adolescents come from this type of situation where the threat of total rejection produces some bizarre behavior.

The third group we will be discussing are the more borderline who perceive the ambivalent messages from the parents. I would suggest that here there may be the least amount of distortion between what the adolescent perceives as ambivalent acceptance-rejection and what in fact actually exists. There is very high stress although it may be intermittent in its intensity.

The fourth group of adolescents is a broad collection of cases where the individual perceives either a high degree of acceptance—or low rejection as I have termed it—from both parents or total acceptance from one parent and rejection from the other. Two key factors are indulgence as a parenting pattern or symbiosis between the adolescent and the mother. Symbiotic relationships are also indulgent but, in addition, they have the borderline aspect to the development. The symbiotic adolescent never separated from the parent until adolescence, unlike the ambivalent rejection borderline situation, where separation was attempted during the early development phase. The adolescents in this fourth group are distinctive in part because they appear to be much more psychologically intact. When thwarted they will often resort to aggressive behavior that is not often seen in the ambivalent-rejection adolescent. Delinquent behavior is also more common in this group because of the indulgent parenting pattern. In essence what all of these adolescents have in common is that they cannot understand the word "no" either because of the indulgence of the parent or because the borderline will interpret this as a withdrawal of the libidinal supplies and a sign of separation.

Behavior: Resolved and Unresolved

The first three factors we have discussed result in some type of behavior pattern as a method of dealing with the stress created or simply as a learned behavior pattern. We can ordinarily do nothing about the first two factors in an adolescent's life (early development and family pattern) but we can do something about perception and behavior. When we try to treat behavior that may be serving purposes, such as defending against depression and rejection, we do not have adequate consequences to modify the behavior. It is for this reason that both factors should be taken into account in a treatment program.

The adolescents' behavior should be viewed in terms of type and degree of resolution they exhibit. In other words, we should ask what purpose the behavior serves. The behavior may be part of an overall coping strategy and thus the adolescent is not very amenable to your input as a therapist when you try to provide alternative resolutions to the stress. The unresolved borderline adolescents are also making a plea for help by the destructiveness of their behavior and are open to treatment. Delinquent behavior is often used by the adolescent with some borderline tendencies as a coping mechanism, which is why it is so difficult to modify or treat.

I am broadly defining the borderline personality adolescent as one who is caught in an ambivalent acceptance-rejection pattern with the parent. I hope to illustrate that these two variables are of critical importance in understanding adolescents with severe behavior disturbances, and, that the borderline characteristics in general decrease proportionately to the degree that either the acceptance or rejection message becomes predominant. This is not to say that adolescents with clearer messages from the parent do not have severe problems, but they tend to be less borderline in nature.

We will be largely discussing adolescents with acting out disturbances such as drug and alcohol abuse, running from home, suicidal and self-destructive behavior, severe aggression and homicidal behavior. In most cases such acting out can be seen as a defense against depression. This is not to suggest that every adolescent who does this type of behavior has borderline characteristics but if the behavior persists such a diagnosis is possible. If such a behavior pattern is being used as a defense against depression it will tend to become a vicious cycle that will lead to more outrageous, self-destructive behavior without control.

On a practical level we will be discussing adolescents who

simply cannot become adolescents in the sense that it represents a transition to independent functioning. By the nature of the borderline problem the adolescents will try to skip from pubescence to adult status literally overnight. Adult status is seen as a means of achieving independence and escape from the psychic pain accompanying adolescence.

Chapter 3

THE TWO-FACTOR MODEL

Acceptance and Rejection

The adolescents' perception of the acceptance and rejection coming from their parents provides us with a pivotal axis around which one can understand both intrapsychic phenomena and acting-out. While the acceptance and rejection factor must be viewed on a continuum from total acceptance to total rejection, there are certain highly probable combinations of these two factors that account for most of the clinical behavior that we term severe disturbances of adolescence.

Acceptance and rejection as perceived by the adolescent is made more difficult by two additional factors. First of all, very few severely disturbed adolescents will readily tell anyone what they in fact perceive. What they say about their family is quite often very different from what they actually feel. When they do tell you accurately they will more than likely give you an incorrect resolution. By this I mean that if the adolescent admits they perceive severe rejection they will invariably tell you that they have resolved it by in turn rejecting their parents. If such were the case it is unlikely that they would be sitting in front of you.

A second difficulty with the acceptance and rejection assessment has to do with the therapist or counselor who is dealing with the adolescent. Many of us do not like dealing with the subject. If we have resolved our own feelings stemming from our childhood we tend to buy into the adolescent's statements of resolution; we approach it pragmatically and want to dismiss the effect of the parents. Another possibility is that the therapist may have much unresolved issues of parental rejection and separation and is unable to deal with the adolescent about the topic and again will buy into the premature resolution. You will find out much later that the issue has only been set aside because you have given messages that it should not be discussed.

How do we know that rejection is an important issue with severely disturbed adolescents? We are often fearful of directly asking the adolescent about his feelings of rejection or acceptance; and when we do we are willing to accept statements of resolution and move on to another subject. The validity of the acceptance-rejection hypothesis is based on the fact that direct confrontation in a therapeutic setting will penetrate defenses and a poorly formed resolution, and unleash depression. The front of anger will turn to a deep depression to the extent that the adolescent is dealing with unresolved rejection issues. To the extent that your probing is turned back with apparent resolution you are either dealing with perceived low rejection, appropriately resolved rejection, or a pathological resolution that you cannot penetrate.

The confrontational approach (Masterson, 1976, 1978b) for psychotherapy with the borderline adolescent is appropriate for most severely disturbed adolescents involving rejection issues. Once the subject of perceived rejection has been broached and the defenses and malformed resolutions penetrated, the therapist will experience an almost immediate therapeutic alliance with the adolescent. From their point of view it is simply a matter of being able to trust you, at least to the extent that you understand the rejection feelings that they have been working hard to conceal. Not having to do this with you may be in and of itself a relief.

There does not appear to be a direct correspondence between the adolescent's statements about rejection and what the observer sees as actually being the case. The adolescents who protest the loudest that they are rejected by their parents are those who seem to have the most accepting families, while the family that is rejecting and abusing may get defended. In the more borderline cases the confusing ambivalence of acceptance and rejection reverses itself frequently. And perhaps most puzzling of all are those instances of rageful aggression toward family members where the acceptance is so high it is symbiotic.

When one begins to study severe disturbances in adolescents one finds that the separation-individuation problem with the mother is like a thread running throughout the array of problems. Not that all problems are borderline but most of them have developmental components in common that form a mosaic with the same theme throughout the adolescent's life.

The rather global terms of rejection and acceptance must be used without a specific behavioral definition. We must define them in terms of what the adolescent perceives. It is not just a problem of working with complex data but a limiting factor of our own two-dimensional perception. For example, there is nothing logical about the push and pull phenomena during the separation-individuation stage of development. It is not logical that the higher levels of acceptance produce rejection from the adolescent and that potential violence can come from symbiotic attachments. Such phenomena can be understood only in the context of the catalytic reactions produced by the variable mixture of acceptance and rejection.

Rejection stands in opposition to acceptance, with warmth and a feeling of being cared about at one end of the continuum and the absence of warmth and caring at the other. All of us can be placed somewhere upon this continuum because of our early experiences and parenting patterns which, by and large, are carried into adolescence little changed. Our behavior as such is largely a result of how we learned to cope with and resolve whatever level of stress resulted from our perception. It is assumed that some optimal development or combination of acceptance and rejection will depend in part on what one might be looking for in an adult. Perhaps we should not be too quick to assume that unequivocal acceptance is always the desired outcome. Most of us might agree that we want our dentist to be conservative in manner, stable, and not particularly creative (at least not on you), while the great literature we enjoy might not come from the same background of acceptance-rejection at all. The issue is how we resolve a degree of stress that stems from where we are on the continuum.

Rohner (1975) in his review of rejection patterns in parents from a cross-cultural standpoint points out that:

> . . . the absence of warmth and affection is revealed around the world in two principle ways by open or disguised hostility or aggression toward the child, or by indifference, which is often expressed as neglect. Indifferent, neglecting parents on the other hand are not necessarily hostile towards their children. They may simply be unsympathetic, cold and distant; they are often physically and emotionally unavailable or inaccessible to their children's needs and wishes. They show a restricted concern for their child's welfare (p. 46).

Parental rejection is associated with a cluster of traits across cultures, such as aggression, dependency, low self-esteem, emotional instability, emotional unresponsiveness, and a negative world view.

The child who perceives rejection is apt to become resentful and angry at his parents as well as fearful of provoking more rejection, thereby producing either a defensive type of independence and withdrawal or sublimated acting-out, such as firesetting. The severely rejected child may initiate a process of counter-rejection and may further act in such a way as to provoke even more rejection, thereby creating a vicious cycle. By the time a severe-rejection child becomes an adolescent almost anything the parent does will be interpreted as rejection because the perception of the situation is so distorted.

REJECTION AND EARLY DEVELOPMENT

The age at which the rejection, separation from parents, or other psychological trauma occurs plays a significant role in the nature of the perceived rejection. As Yarrow (1964) points out the available studies on the effects of maternal separation and deprivation do not differentiate clearly between the effects of separation, per se, and the reinforcing conditions following separation. It is not possible to precisely predict problems in adolescence as a result of any particular early development events; in part because we cannot predict the resolution that the individual will develop to the stressful early conditions. I will say, though, that I have never dealt with a severely disturbed adolescent who did not have developmental factors suggesting a significant degree of psychological trauma.

Goldfarb (1945) compared children fostered at birth with those fostered at age 3, and reported that institutionalized children who were not placed in foster homes until they were 3 were, when tested in adolescence, restless, hyperactive, unable to concentrate, impudent, and destructive. Other studies (Pringle and Bossio, 1960) have consistently shown similar effects of early separation and institutional placement. The effect of maintaining ties with even one parent has also been shown to have positive results in adolescence.

The institutionalized child is rare now and would more than likely perceive total rejection and be forced into an early somewhat pathological resolution to that stress. Such children would not ordinarily be the high-stress, highly-ambivalent borderline individuals that constitute much of the severely disturbed adolescent population. Bowlby (1969, 1973, 1980) describes a series of reactions that are made by the child as a result of separation from the maternal (attachment) figure. The sequence involves fear, anger, attempts to regain the lost figure, depression, and finally rejection of that maternal figure if it does not return before the child has resolved the rejection. After this resolution the child will typically reject all close relationships. It is here that you find some of the stronger resolutions variously described as severely pathological.

THE DOUBLE BIND AND AMBIVALENT REJECTION

In the context of rejection and ambivalence I would like to mention the concept of the double bind (Berger, 1978). The essence of the double bind is that there is a primary negative injunction and a secondary injunction conflicting with the first at a more abstract level, and, like the first, enforced by punishments or signals which threaten the adolescent's survival. This has been used as the paradigm for the conflicting messages that a schizophrenic receives from his family. The theoretical similarity to the two-factor model of acceptance and rejection is obvious. I was amazed to reread the literature on the double bind phenomena. Even the descriptions of the schizophrenic family patterns are similar to the borderline family dynamics. It seems clear that much of the population the authors were calling schizophrenic 20 years ago we are now labeling as borderline.

So are they schizophrenic or borderline, you ask? I believe we now have a better understanding of the psychodynamics, family patterns, and certainly the developmental effects that were not available earlier. The difficulty with the double bind was that it could never be consistently demonstrated or reproduced experimentally for the same reason that a behavioral analysis is not adequate; namely, they were depending upon direct observation of the ambivalent behaviors. The researchers were operating without any real developmental guidelines as to the origin of the double binding process. This process originates during the separation-individuation phase of development and during adolescence it may not operate any longer on a verbal level. Merely the perception of meaning in the actions of the parents would be sufficient to perpetuate the process; and, of course, you cannot do a direct analysis of the adolescent's perception and implied meaning.

Schizophrenic features in terms of the two-factor model basically stem from the contradictory acceptance and rejection messages that are very close together and difficult to distinguish. It is often the case that the emphasis is placed upon the positive and accepting qualities of the messages rather than the negative or rejecting. It has been my experience that the borderline adolescents with a prevalence of schizophrenic features come from the more accepting homes where the rejection is largely through guilt induction rather than overt behavior. This makes it difficult for the adolescent to act out toward the parent as the borderline adolescent is more inclined to do. In this sense then the stress is even greater for the adolescent and they have fewer options thus forcing internalization.

If we view the borderline adolescent with schizophrenic tendencies in terms of our continuum of acceptance and rejection they resemble the low-rejection, symbiotic borderline individual. The question then is, why do they act very differently? Or more specifically, why does one direct the stress inward and the other outward? It is tempting to label the symbiotic borderline as the schizophrenic turned inside out. When we look at these two apparently contrasting adolescents there are some surprising similarities. The symbiotic borderline seems to internalize nothing and act out constantly as a bubbling caldron. Yet clinically it is very clear that guilt and responsibility for the parent are major factors in their acting out and in their desire to escape from the symbiotic tie with the mother. It is possible that the difference lies in the lack of a contradictory injunction against acting out for the borderline adolescent. I might also add that there are those who believe that the schizophrenic problem originates early during the symbiotic phase of development, which would be in keeping with the suggested similarity with the symbiotic borderline development.

THE TWO-FACTOR MODEL

Perhaps the easiest way to view the function of the two factors is to visualize them on a balance scale where one side is rejection and the other is acceptance. We can get some sense of the stress forces operating with different positions of the figure, which I believe in some sense depicts the state of affairs with the adolescent.

The typical family is not entirely accepting of their children to be sure, but the preponderance of their behavior and attitudes reflects the balance in the model resting on the acceptance side of the scale. Granted there are deviations from this position but they will tend to be brief, as suggested by the dotted line in the model, and of relatively low amplitude. The behavior of an adolescent from such a family pattern will reflect that general acceptance. The deviations in behavior will be of short duration mainly because the individual's self-concept reflects his perception of how his parents regard him as a person. On the other hand, if the balance is depressed on the side where rejection predominates, there will occur a permanent state of rejection that, too, is relatively stable, and, to some extent, a low stress situation. I have never encountered a situation of severe disturbance in adolescence without an obvious rejection factor being present. Outside of neurological damage as the causal factor I doubt very much if such cases exist.

And what happens when the scale is in some state of balance between the acceptance and rejection ends of the continuum? It is here in the conflict of perceived acceptance and rejection that we get into some of the more severe and destructive emotional disorders of adolescence. The clinical symptoms of the individual can vary widely but they all have one thing in common and that is a degree of stress created by the two factors involved in the psychological picture. How the adolescent happens to process or otherwise resolve that stress can of course create widely varied results. The point is that it requires considerable energy to maintain a precarious balance and to keep it from tipping into the total rejection or abandonment area. The greater the stress, the greater are the symptoms or acting-out behaviors. The girl who has been the victim of an incestuous relationship may be under such stress, and with few choices for acting out, that it shows up in poor school performance and general depression. The point is that incestuous behavior may be perceived as being highly accepting and rejecting at the same time resulting in very high stress.

Below I have presented what I regard as the premise of the two-factor model.

1. The two factors that account for the majority of severe emotional disturbances in adolescence are perceived rejection and acceptance from the parents.
2. The definition of these two factors is determined solely by the adolescent's perception.
3. Early parenting sets the stage for accepting or rejecting patterns that will typically remain unaltered throughout adolescence. The parenting pattern that one observes in the family of the adolescent will ordinarily be the same pattern that would have been found at earlier developmental periods.
4. Maximum stress results from the conflicting demands

associated with dual messages of acceptance and rejection.

5. Minimal stress is associated with either consistent acceptance or rejection perception.

6. The earlier in the developmental stage that severe rejection or psychological trauma occurs, the more vulnerable the adolescent will be to stress associated with the demands of adolescence itself.

7. The greater the extremes of acceptance and rejection messages perceived by the adolescent, the greater will be the stress produced. This variability may come from the difference between two parents or from variations in both parents.

8. The adolescent's self concept will reflect his perception of the degree of rejection from the parents.

When the scale is tipped in one direction, whether it be toward acceptance or rejection, the stress is relatively low because the conflictual situation is low. To the extent that there are frequent movements away from this position stress will be created and will have to be resolved.

As I have said, acceptance and rejection must be defined only from the standpoint of the adolescent's perception and not from the standpoint of the observer's opinion about that family. The latter point of view is reflected in the facts portrayed in the family pattern information and the difference between the two becomes some index of the adolescent's problem. By the same token the intent of the parent's communication to the adolescent must be kept separate from how the adolescent perceives those messages. Where the individual has suffered severe rejection and trauma he will continue to perceive messages from the parents as being rejecting regardless of their content.

There are three components that describe the balance scale: Stress, Variability, and degree of Acceptance and Rejection. Stress has two primary origins: the variability of the movement between acceptance and rejection, and the position of the balance away from a static or at rest position. Given this paradigm, even relatively small but steady positioning away from a static position could generate persistent stress. The position of greatest stress is that state of near balance that occurs from the highly conflictual borderline condition. The stress occurs because of the tremendous variability of the situation between complete acceptance to complete rejection. In addition, the frequency of the movement is greater than in any other type of situation. Both amplitude and frequency, then, produce stress.

It is impossible for the adolescent to feel both accepted and rejected simultaneously and there is a need for one to predominate. The borderline adolescent responds to this by equally variable behavior corresponding to their alternately feeling loved and not loved. The high variability pattern may also be viewed as being stress-producing because it is unpredictable. Anytime we cannot predict our environment we will feel a degree of discomfort and stress as the result. The double bind situation essentially says that the adolescent should act and not act at the same time; obviously a conflictual situation where insulating oneself against the environment through a delusional system may be the only protection. The borderline adolescent perceives messages of acceptance only contingent upon regression and independent behavior would be met with a loss of that acceptance.

Variability at the two ends of the continuum may have different outcomes even though both represent a degree of stress. Variability in a Severe Rejection adolescent will often result in rageful acting out that will occur on a cycle roughly the same as the variability of the perceived messages from the parent. Typically a severely rejected adolescent does not act out against the parent for fear of total rejection but will vent the aggression indirectly. The situation can be viewed as one of the parent (usually the mother) dangling the carrot of acceptance in front of the adolescent. Since rejection is only indirectly related to stress, it is the variability here that does much of the damage.

Variability under conditions of very high acceptance would quite likely produce little acting out. If it is relatively minimal and not too frequent the periodic threat of rejection probably corresponds to a normal family situation, and may play a significant role in controlling behavior. Typically under conditions of perceived acceptance, while maintaining consistent and reasonable limits, the adolescent will act in such a way as to justify that acceptance. In other words, they will respond well to brief rejection as a form of management.

Chapter 4

FOUR ACCEPTANCE-REJECTION PATTERNS

Clinical and Family Characteristics

In assessing the adolescent's perception of rejection by the parents I have primarily used clinical information from therapeutic contacts. I have found that adolescents who trust me will respond quite validly with a sense of relief that someone is asking them directly the questions that get at the core of their depression and acting out. I carefully preface questions with statements around the importance of knowing the information. I would not suggest that a direct approach be used outside of a clinical or counseling setting because the individual's first response to any questioning about rejection will often be anger. Rejection is almost always a hidden, unspoken issue between the adolescent and the adults working with them. Some of the comments I got were very revealing. Several of the adolescents said that while the question made them angry, it was honest. Everything else was cloaked in a certain amount of indirectness in attempts to get at how they perceived their family and themselves.

One question that the reader may have has to do with the differences between the perceived rejection coming from the two parents. More often than not the level of rejection and acceptance between the two parents will be perceived as approximately the same. However, when there is a great deal of perceived difference it can cause considerable stress for the adolescent in much the same way as ambivalent messages of rejection and acceptance can for the borderline. As we shall see, a difference in the perceived rejection between the two parents is related to the occurrence of severe aggression.

REJECTION

Rejection can be seen as the loss, abandonment, or distancing of the parent from the adolescent. The adolescent perceives this as "I am worthless, therefore my parents choose not to care for me." It is only much later in a true state of resolution of the stress that they may be able to say that the problem lies with their parents more than with them. The adolescent believes that "My parents would care for me, if I were not worthless." Rejection is never discussed openly by the adolescents unless they are in a therapeutic situation. It is always couched in other language such as "I hate my parents," or "I am worthless." Paradoxically there must be a relatively high level of acceptance before they are likely to talk openly about being rejected by their parents.

There are often clinical differences depending upon just how the rejection occurred, aside from the level of rejection itself. Rejection through actual abandonment seems to result in pervasive depression and flat affect—and, above all, extremely low self-esteem. When part of the rejection comes about through a loss resulting from death there appears to be a particularly rageful acting out that occurs with little warning and just as quickly subsides. Much of their rejection then centers around the inability to mourn the loss in any satisfactory way. With most feelings of rejection by the adolescents they believe at some level that they are responsible for causing that rejection.

In this next section we will be discussing the clinical and family patterns related to four acceptance-rejection categories. They are: Total Rejection; Severe Rejection; Ambivalent Rejection; and, Low Rejection. The assignment of adolescents to these patterns was done on the basis of their perception of the family and on no other characteristics. The family pattern characteristics are presented along with clinical and descriptive information about the adolescent's belonging to these patterns. (See Appendix)

I. TOTAL REJECTION PATTERN

As far as the adolescents' perception is concerned I suspect there may be no such thing as "total rejection." I say this because their behavior in some fashion is directed at reclaiming their lost family regardless of what their verbal behavior would have us believe. From a clinical standpoint, it is a mistake to accept verbal statements about resolution of rejection as though the family were no longer an issue for the adolescent. When we talk about clinical symptoms related to the adolescent from the Total Rejection situation, we are talking to some extent about the lack of parenting or socialization generally; that is, if the parents were not available certain things may not have been acquired by the adolescent. However, keep in mind that total rejection can occur much later in the individual's development and produce an altered clinical picture which includes only some of the behaviors associated with Total Rejection.

THE TWO-FACTOR MODEL AND TOTAL REJECTION

In Figure 4–1 below I have depicted the Total Rejection adolescent pattern in terms of the two factors of acceptance and rejection. It can be seen that the position of rejection is near total with little variability, as suggested by the dotted line, and with relatively little stress produced from the situation. The adolescent's behavior in a sense mirrors this situation by being relatively steady with persistent depression and with brief nonviolent outbursts of anger.

The Total Rejection pattern is relatively uncomplicated when compared to the more accepting patterns as it lacks a double-bind quality of more ambivalent patterns. The family may remain physically intact, although it is more likely that there have been early separations from parents through death and abandonment. The family has essentially been nonnurturing,

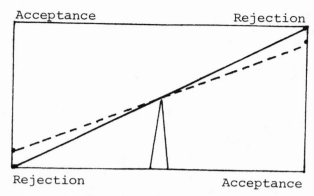

Acceptance   Rejection

Rejection   Acceptance

Figure 4–1   Two-Factor Model and Total Rejection

abusing, distancing, and, on the whole, shows few redeeming characteristics.

One of the most important elements of the Total Rejection situation is physical abuse. It is this element that seems to do more to reduce self-regard than anything else. There is a sense of resignation and despair and a failure of personality development generally. I have found it interesting that the adolescents from the Total Rejection family is rarely violent toward others to any severe degree, as is true of some of the other adolescent patterns. Yet they have frequently been the recipient of abuse themselves. They are often threatening and acting out but their rage is more symbolic and directed inward upon themselves, although it is short of the deliberate self-destruction and mutilation that one can find with the borderline. For the Total Rejection adolescent acting out is a way of defending against the undifferentiated depression; but perhaps even more than this, it represents a way of carrying out such ridiculous acts that it assures constant attention from authorities, which represent their family in a distorted sense.

The Total Rejection family is in some respects the least pathological of family patterns. This gets into problems of definition to be sure, but they are under relatively little stress because it is vented by means of immediate acting out such that there is no pattern of ambivalence. The messages, if nothing else, are quite clear to the adolescent. I believe it is this venting of frustration and anger with little ambivalence that prevents serious violence from occurring. When we get into split patterns including more acceptance we begin to see greater violence potential.

CLINICAL DESCRIPTION AND TOTAL REJECTION

The combination of less than adequate nurturing and the early loss of a parent through death seems to result in a combination of clinical manifestations that are quite unique. There is great distortion around the lost parent being the "good parent" who would have rescued them. This distortion can become part of a psychopathic type of resolution. In order for a violent psychopathic resolution to occur it seems that there must be the total rejection followed by a period of indulgence from parent substitutes of some kind. Otherwise the totally rejected adolescent does not possess the skills and motivation to resolve his problems beyond a most superficial basis and does not possess the ability to manipulate his environment the way a more highly resolved adolescent does. They see no reason to work on their problems, or face up to the issues, because they are waiting to be rescued by the lost parent. In the meantime, they can excuse their behavior because of the despair and hopelessness of the situation.

The Total Rejection adolescent is ordinarily easy to distinguish from others by physical appearance, and the fact that they set themselves apart from the peer group. For one thing the general level of behavior often resembles that of the five-year-old. They are quick to anger but just as quick to subside. The manner of dress is often with no regard to how they appear to others.

These adolescents are often notorious in terms of the amount of services that agencies have put into them. They have frustrated everyone's attempts to provide treatment and care. When you first approach the subject of family rejection they will become angry and if you persist they will admit that despite all the services that may have been provided them, no one has confronted them on their acting out against the rejection of their family. They will say something to the effect that they have very little intention of changing their pattern. They may recognize the rejection but no one else's right to tell them what to do even though they want your attention. They tend to superficially attach themselves to you and demand a high level of attention.

ATTACHMENT

If the adolescent has never been allowed to form an attachment during the first year of life because of separations from the maternal figure, a distinctive picture emerges with effects that are so profound all else becomes secondary. Later separations will only serve to confirm the already distorted perception and produce anger but no abandonment crisis (see case #2). The adolescent's perception is largely one of lack of trust and paranoia.

If separations from parents and the rejection occurs after attachment the picture is somewhat different. If the loss is of a permanent nature, during very early development, a severe abandonment crisis and depression will result. There may be a resolution that results in a psychopathic type of behavior pattern which will resolve the depression on a permanent basis. More often though this does not occur and the individual pursues life centered around acting out to avoid the abandonment depression and in a pseudo search for the lost parent.

STRESS AND REJECTION

The adolescent who perceives Total Rejection from the family is oddly enough under relatively little stress compared to other patterns in our two-factor model. Total Rejection produces a certain pragmatism toward life, as well as a rather obscure fantasy around their lost family ties. The adolescent will often confide to the therapist that they understand the difference between themselves and others, such as the Ambivalent Rejection, borderline adolescent. In turn, the borderline group looks upon the Total Rejection adolescent as a social misfit and a loser but yet sympathizes in some of their infantile needs.

The Total Rejection adolescent is ordinarily under no acute

stress because of the consistency of the rejection. Total rejection is difficult to perceive ambiguously. Because of abuse and a lack of nurturance, in most cases they have been forced to make pragmatic decisions about looking out for themselves in a way that forces a degree of reality never encountered in the borderline adolescents, who are ordinarily operating in an immediate relationship with their family. The totally rejected adolescent will develop distortions of reality mainly because it is more pleasant than the truth and because it serves as a rationalization for their anti-social behavior. However, it is rarely a true delusional system because it is easy to penetrate in a therapeutic setting.

THE BORDERLINE CONDITION AND TOTAL REJECTION

When considering whether the totally rejected adolescent is borderline one must first consider whether they have completed the very early attachment phase to the maternal figure. If one defines the borderline situation as revolving around the inadequate separation from the mother, then the necessity of the early attachment as a prior condition should be obvious. In this sense, the adolescent can be seen as being in an almost perpetual state of abandonment depression without the clinging and engulfing aspects found in the Ambivalent Rejection pattern. However, I am inclined to think that the acting out comes as much from the low self-regard, as well as calling attention to themselves, as it does from the need to defend against the depression as is characteristic of the borderline adolescent. We may say that the totally rejected adolescent has quite literally been abandoned and in that sense no longer fears it.

While the totally rejected adolescents will ordinarily have many of the infantile needs and other characteristics found in the borderline, they ordinarily do not have the intrapsychic structure. For example, their ego structure may be insufficiently formed, and very infantile, which in and of itself would qualify them as character disorder problems, but they do not ordinarily possess the split ego of the borderline adolescent. The difference shows up in the therapeutic situation. The therapist is not regarded as alternately good or bad, as with the borderline, but rather is always regarded as someone to get close to and trust only on a very tentative basis. I have never come away from a session with a totally rejected adolescent feeling that I was either a "great" therapist or a "terrible" therapist, which is probably a sure sign that the adolescent is not borderline.

RESOLUTION AND TOTAL REJECTION

The Total Rejection adolescents are rarely suicidal except as long-term patterns of self-destructive, risk-taking behavior, and as a means of calling attention to themselves. The adolescent is a "script follower;" a live-for-the-moment, hopeless, despairing, self-destructive ride to oblivion.

Delinquency can be considered as a solution (resolution) to a problem and not the problem itself—which of course is why it is so difficult to treat. Delinquent behavior is found in all four acceptance-rejection patterns, but is more prevalent among the Total Rejection and Low Rejection groups because both are more likely to choose delinquent behavior as a partial resolution to the stress. Here the similarity ends because the delinquent acts of the Low Rejection adolescents are more often than not goal-directed, while that of the Total Rejection adolescent fits the pattern of their overall self-destructive script. They will sometimes go to great lengths to make sure they get caught. They seem to have little or no regard for material possessions other than for immediate needs.

In summary, we can say that the Total Rejection adolescent often seems incapable of living an independent existence without calling attention to themselves by some outrageous behavior calculated to put themselves under institutional care. Despite protestations to the contrary, they have refused to accept total rejection and are acting out against it.

II. SEVERE REJECTION PATTERN

In this section we will be discussing the Severe Rejection group, which in our study of the effects of residential treatment

(Nielsen, et. al., 1979) represented approximately one-third of our population. This pattern was one of the most confusing because they represented early successes after treatment and later failures. We failed to understand the tenacity and character of the relationship with the mother. I generally consider the severely rejected adolescent to be quite borderline but with less ambivalence than found in the Ambivalent Rejection group. Also the parents are often much more pathological than the borderline parents.

THE TWO-FACTOR MODEL AND SEVERE REJECTION

The severe-rejection pattern is illustrated in Figure 4–2 below. It depicts the near totality of the rejection with the high amplitude and low frequency acceptance messages as perceived by the adolescent. These messages of acceptance become of critical importance and distinguish the situation from other rejection patterns because of the intermittent nature.

Severe Rejection adolescents have families who may seem innocuous by their absence but who are very powerful in terms of the behavior produced in the adolescent. They may have characteristics of the totally rejecting family but several things prevent the situation from being that straightforward. The relationship

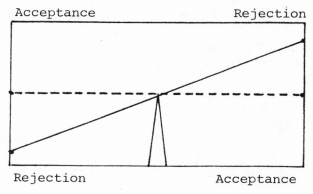

Figure 4–2   Two-Factor Model and Severe Rejection

with one parent is particularly pathological, which is the essence of the problem in this pattern. As a general rule, I would suggest that the more rejecting the mother, short of Total Rejection, the greater is her role in determining the adolescent's behavior. She has a strong need to maintain control in most cases, or at least she is able to do so inadvertently. When the adolescent is being treated in a residential program, for example, this tie is not apparent because there is no danger of the adolescent actually separating from her. It does become apparent as soon as the adolescent is returned to the community.

The Severe Rejection family is both abusive and rejecting but with certain redeeming characteristics which act like a carrot dangling in front of the adolescent. The mother tends to be more pathological than in any other group and the disturbance often runs to psychoses, as opposed to the borderline characteristics found in the Ambivalent Rejection group. She reminds me of a time bomb that goes off periodically with unleashed violence directed at the child. Between psychotic rages they may be calm and interested in the welfare of the adolescent. The relationship may be somewhat symbiotic and sensual with a fawning interest displayed by the mother. I see this as a pseudosymbiotic relationship to distinguish it from a true symbiosis. It is based on the adolescent's fear of provoking the mother and wanting to avoid total abandonment.

In our study most Severe Rejection males and one female were involved in fire-setting or sexual aggression. These behaviors are rarely found in other rejection patterns. The adolescents do not dare strike out directly at the family for fear of provoking total rejection and aggression. They have internalized the anger and frustration to a far greater degree than any other severely disturbed adolescent. The aggression then tends to be ventilated by directing it outside the immediate family in indirect ways that symbolizes the anger felt toward the mother. The sexual aggressions tend to be toward individuals who represent no real threat to the adolescents. They are ordinarily done in such a blatant fashion that getting caught is inevitable and seems to represent no threat or deterrent. In this sense they share the script following and attention-seeking of the Total Rejection Adolescent.

CLINICAL DESCRIPTIONS AND SEVERE REJECTION

One 16-year-old youth attempted to burn down his foster home of 7 years after his mother began to contact him again. During a family session with this writer, the subject of placement after treatment came up, to which his mother stated that it really did not matter where we placed him because there was always a way to get to him. She added that he would always be her son and she could get him to do whatever she wanted. It is unusual for a parent to be this open, but it illustrates what can happen in the Severe Rejection pattern. She possessed a severe affect disorder; she would smile when making negative statements and scowl when saying something positive to her son. Her three older sons had all been incarcerated in prison or a mental hospital for violent crimes and sexual assaults. After the meeting she and her son walked out to her car, where she reached in the glove compartment, pulled out a knife and laughingly handed it to him saying, "Here, see you in prison." This same adolescent insisted upon returning home after treatment. Placing him elsewhere would have been inviting disaster. He lived at home for over one year after leaving treatment despite periodic rages and attacks by his mother and other members of the family. Part of his treatment included making him aware of the dynamics of the family, his relationship with his mother, and the general ridiculousness of the situation. He took a rather benign, philosophical view of the situation which seemed to allow him some intellectual distance if nothing else. After he had been out several months he stopped by and left this message:

To Whom It May Concern:

One day when i was walking to the park i saw a bird and it flew over to me and started banging on my head and would not stop so i put it in a bird cage and after three days it died and i cried all day long.

Sincerely,

This particular case (#6) will be discussed in more detail. The rageful potential in this young man is difficult to comprehend.

In instances where the perceived Severe Rejection is of a relatively steady state and does not contain the violent pathological quality, the pattern of behavior in the adolescent is somewhat altered. Here the anger, both verbal and physical, is expressed more openly toward others but still not toward the family. The primary emotion of the adolescent is more likely to be anger, as opposed to paranoid fear found in those instances where the mother herself is severely pathological.

The Severe Rejection adolescent is the most difficult to treat of all the adolescent problems. Whenever we decided what was best for the individuals and sent them somewhere besides home, which was easy to do because neither the adolescent nor the family would protest, sooner or later there would be contact with the mother that would lead to bizarre acting out on the part of the adolescent. She might call at Christmas and the next day the youth would steal a car and drive to her. Or perhaps an adolescent would burn down the foster home on the assumption that there would be no place to go but home.

It seems to me that we are often willing to do what is "logical" for the adolescent, no matter what the outcome, secure in the knowledge that what we did was "right." We fail to understand the nature of the relationship with the family because it is so obviously rejecting. We want to sever the relationship when only the adolescents themselves can break that very elastic umbilical cord to the mother through a process of psychotherapy and experience. And unfortunately this Severe Rejection group represents the majority of adolescents placed outside the home. Granted most of them come from less pathological families than described here, but the relationship is not going to be broken by outside agencies nor easily modified through traditional family therapy.

The severely rejected adolescent tends to be highly manipulative and spends time in clandestine behaviors and activities. They like adult attention and will demand it in infantile, attention-getting ways, but they are the most fearful and cautious about verbalizing their feelings unlike the more borderline. They will deny there is a problem (they will project it onto someone else) and insist that they can take care of everything by themselves.

You have in effect a positive reinforcement schedule from the mother that is very powerful precisely because it is so intermittent. This can be compared with Ambivalent Rejection where the positive reinforcement comes about more frequently and is weaker in its effects upon the adolescent's behavior. The adolescent who perceives Severe Rejection from the family may be involved in delinquent behavior, but it can be traced directly to the family. In one case the mother said to the adolescent, "Go to the store and get some milk; you kids drank it all." The boy responded with, "We don't have any money," to which his mother replied, "That's your problem, not mine." He went to the store and robbed it of money and a gallon of milk which he brought home and gave to her.

I think the most frightening thing that can happen to a child or adolescent is to experience total abandonment. Without this, it is difficult to understand how the adolescent can hang on so tenaciously to the family. As a group, the Severe Rejection adolescent experiences more early physical separations from the parent than any but the Total Rejection group. Thus the threat of abandonment is very real.

VIOLENCE AND SEVERE REJECTION

It is characteristic of this group that they will accept no responsibility for their own behavior. They tend to be more paranoid acting than other adolescents and they have the psychological resources to plot and plan their behavior far more than the Total Rejection adolescents, which make them potentially more dangerous. It is possible to find homicidal acting out when several conditions are met. Essentially the primary condition seems to be that one parent presents abusive, violent, and Severe Rejection, while the other provides indulgent reinforcement of behavior. The adolescent must be severely curtailed in having a means of expression of the anger and frustration. Here the homicidal aggression will ordinarily be directed outside the family, unlike the homicidal rage of the Ambivalent Rejection borderline pattern.

The Severe Rejection adolescent is indeed caught on the

horns of a dilemma. They are drawn toward something that is destructive but so powerful that they cannot resist it. One 17-year-old girl is instructive in this respect. After leaving treatment she settled down in a foster home and appeared to be doing very well. She visited me much later and commented that although she looked good she was not good inside, and that she would never be satisfied until her parents accepted her. It was still all or nothing as far as she was concerned.

In general we can say that the Severe Rejection adolescents view human relationships as tenuous and dangerous; the underlying dynamics are fear, anger, and general mistrust. Dealing with the adolescents is like trying to fill a bucket with a hole in it. They will lead you to believe that they have resolved the problem and are rejecting their parents. They have a distorted perception of the world because of the fearful and pathological child-rearing practices of the parent. There is a preoccupation with morbid fantasy, death, destruction, the occult, demonology, and the illicit use of power. There is also an interest in artistic expression and occasionally with written expression, although the latter occurs more often with the borderline adolescents. The interest in artistic expression can be explained by the fact that out of necessity their feelings must be largely internalized and given no means of expression without the risk of total abandonment so that safer means must be found. There often seems to be a great sensitivity and creative urge so strong that it gives the adolescent a Jekyl and Hyde potential.

III. AMBIVALENT REJECTION PATTERN

Ambivalent Rejection corresponds to the optimum borderline personality pattern, which means that the parenting varies between pushing the adolescent toward separation and pulling them back in a clinging response. While this ambivalent response is found to some extent in all acceptance-rejection categories, it reaches its peak in the Ambivalent Rejection adolescents.

The adolescents perceive the parents as almost the "mirror image" of how they are, in fact, parented in an "I-love-you, I-hate-you" relationship. They are vocal about their family and their opinion may change daily. They also appear to be under greater stress than any of the other adolescent groups; yet their families are more accepting and caring than those of more rejecting patterns. One would logically expect that such strong negative feelings would be reserved for the more clearly rejecting parents but such is not the case.

In our study nearly all of the Ambivalent Rejection borderline adolescents returned home after treatment regardless of the plans made for them for alternative placements and treatments. They would run or put themselves in a position where responsible agencies and courts had no choice but to allow them to stay at home. This was similar to the Severe Rejection adolescents except that the more borderline group would return home sooner and choose running and self-destructive behavior in the process. However, they have generally done a very good job of extricating themselves from the home in time or have managed to maintain a stable existence within the family. They were able to do this with less trauma than the Severe Rejection adolescents, whose tie to the mother is even stronger and more pathological. The difference may be one of degree of abandonment fear. In either case the separation from the parent cannot be rushed arbitrarily it seems and will come about only as part of a therapeutic resolution to the problem.

From an intrapsychic point of view (Masterson, 1976) the borderline adolescents can be seen as being unable to internalize whole object representations. This includes the parent, especially the mother, and other adults with whom they are close. The adults are seen as either the good or bad parent who gives or withholds libidinal supplies. The adolescents cannot perceive others as the normal mixture of good and bad representations of some whole entity. This is an internal representation of their behavior and their parent's behavior toward them. It is either the loving responsible parents who appear more concerned about their child than families from other patterns or the withdrawing and punitive parents who are highly rejecting.

When someone is playing the role of the "good parent" and that part is being supplied to the adolescents, they will often appear to be psychologically intact. Or, to put it another way, when abandonment-depression has been defended against they possess appropriate emotions. The borderline has social skills and adaptability unlike the more rejected adolescents and usually demonstrate this by being popular with peers. The more rejected adolescents appear much more idiosyncratic and individualistic.

THE TWO-FACTOR MODEL AND AMBIVALENT REJECTION

This pattern refers to a unique and distinctive quality of Ambivalent Rejection as perceived by the adolescent. It is not accurate to say that Ambivalent Rejection means a particular level of rejection as can generally be said for the other groups in our model. The more borderline adolescent is in fact accepted and rejected to approximately the same degree and nearly simultaneously such that there is a double bind quality to the communication.

In Figure 4–3 the Ambivalent Rejection pattern can be seen. The key parts of the model are the dotted line which depicts extreme variance and the solid line illustrating the average level. Not only is the variance of high amplitude but it is also of high frequency compared to other patterns. It is by far the most variable pattern and as a result you have a group under high stress because it is not predictable. This stress results more from the ambivalence than from the particular position of acceptance and rejection. Messages that are clear and consistent are less

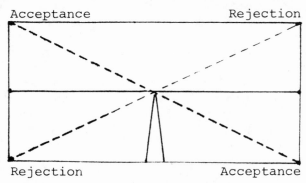

**Figure 4–3   Two-Factor Model and Ambivalent
Rejection**

stressful than mixed messages, regardless of whether they are rejecting or accepting. This high stress leads to periods of considerable emotional symptoms such as depression, hysterical behavior, or even schizophrenic reactions for brief periods.

AMBIVALENT-REJECTION CHARACTERISTICS

In order to fully understand ambivalent rejection one must step through the looking glass into the borderline world which the adolescents describe as being like a fairy tale where nothing seems quite real. They may express an interest in fairy tales, such as Cinderella or Alice in Wonderland and write their own personalized versions of these classics. For a more complete discussion of this topic the reader is referred to Masterson (1972).

The parents will not let the adolescents separate from them in any adequate fashion. Success and independence is essentially punished by the withdrawal of support (Masterson, 1976). The adolescents present a pattern of stress-produced behavior such as self-destruction, suicide attempts, severe rage reactions, hysterical behavior, and, to some extent, schizophrenic behavior. The acceptance-rejection pattern of the parents operates in unpredictable cycles, which is mirrored in the adolescents' switch from one behavior pattern to another.

In general, we can say that the Ambivalent Rejection adolescents are a mixture of infant and sophisticate often described as 3 going on 30. They have typically been everything but the chronological age they are. They may have been caring for younger siblings, caring for the mother, acting as her confidant, part-time housewife, and so on.

The borderline adolescents have difficulty in maintaining a mental image or representation of the object of the loved one. This may mean that they cannot adequately mourn a loss or grasp the fact that someone can leave them. Any temporary loss of the object can precipitate an abandonment crisis. I recall one adolescent (case #9) who slept with a picture of her mother under her pillow so that she could remember what she looked like despite the fact she saw her often. Separation may be akin to death and abandonment in the mind of the borderline adolescent. It is in the area of object relations where we find a difference between the Ambivalent Rejection individual and the other rejection patterns.

Practically speaking, object relations in the borderline adolescents refer to the fact that they almost never see anything in shades of grey if there is emotional content or threatened withdrawal· associated with it. This basically stems from viewing the mother as either the rewarding unit or withdrawing unit (Masterson, 1976) who distances herself from the child. This is why one of the diagnostic features in the borderline has to do with the extreme difficulty they have in dealing with close relationships of any kind. Even the therapist is not immune from being placed in the role of the rewarding or punishing figure.

AGGRESSION AND ACTING OUT

Aggression directed at members of the immediate family, such as the mother, sister, or grandmother does occur, but the borderline adolescent is not ordinarily seriously aggressive unless there is a symbiotic attachment which seems to act as a triggering device. But fantasies of homicidal rage against the withdrawing parent are common. Aggression toward others is associated with increased acceptance, while rejection, per se, is more associated with self-loathing and self-destruction; a mirror of how they have been treated.

The Ambivalent Rejection adolescents may act out by a combination of substance abuse and sexual promiscuity to the point where it is self-destructive. Regardless of the behavior, the adolescents act as though they are omnipotent and basically indestructible. During these acting-out phases the adolescents defend against abandonment depression such that they do not appear to be depressed. It is only when they come down from this destructive high, as they inevitably must, or they have miscalculated their omnipotence and the dangers involved in their behavior, that the depression and stress returns. This then prompts another round of depression relieving acting out. The primary function of psychotherapy with the borderline adolescents is to confront the destructiveness of their behavior and the basic motivation behind it. It is this quality of "being alright" when acting out that may differentiate the Ambivalent Rejection borderline from the more severe rejection adolescents.

IV. Low Rejection Pattern

The final pattern from the two-factor model involves the Low Rejection group of severely disturbed adolescents. This group consists of subgroups even more than the other patterns. The Low Rejection group has in common the adolescent who perceives at least one parent as being supportive and accepting. Because of this, the rejection that does occur, and the circumstances under which it occurs, can have a great impact.

The Two-Factor Model and Low Rejection

The Low Rejection pattern is depicted in Figure 4–4. The solid line is only slightly moved from the position of acceptance and the variability is usually low compared to the more borderline situation. It is easy to imagine that it is essentially a stressful position because it just falls short of being complete or satisfactory. It is not unlike a train running on tracks that are just slightly out of alignment; the friction and heat generated is considerable

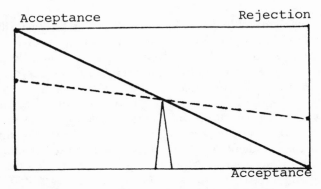

Acceptance   Rejection

Acceptance

Figure 4–4   Two-Factor Model and Low Rejection

without the train ever being derailed. It may be said that the more rejected adolescents are running off the tracks for periods of time, or running through the field as the Total Rejection adolescents. The nearer one is to the goal object (acceptance) the greater is the potential for creating frustration and aggression as a result of not being able to obtain it. It is just such frustration and aggression that describes what the Low Rejection adolescents have in common despite dissimilar clinical behaviors.

This pattern is distinctive because they appear as any other adolescents of their age. One might expect to hear such comments as, "She acts like a spoiled brat" or "He's just used to threatening until he gets his own way." The point is that they may appear quite psychologically intact until presented with some obstacle to their goal at which point they resort to infantile, regressive, or coercive methods to obtain it. We are talking about something more than just a "spoiled-brat syndrome." Although they may be all of that, they are also psychologically fragile because their self-worth disintegrates under frustration. It is a case of more than the simple possession of something they want; it is something they must have. The adolescents cannot operate as individuated beings if immediate gratification is not forthcoming as though they have never learned any alternate means of handling frustrating situations.

CHARACTERISTICS OF LOW REJECTION

Adolescents in the Low Rejection group can be borderline in the sense of having intrapsychic structure similar to that of the Ambivalent Rejection adolescents, although not ordinarily to that extent and with a more symbiotic relationship to the mother. However, the adolescents need not be borderline to perceive the Low Rejection and may simply be a product of an indulgent parenting pattern without the symbiotic relationship. Certainly the individual's relationship with the mother tends to be important whether it is symbiotic or not. It is more likely to be a clinging, symbiotic one as opposed to a withdrawing or withholding relationship. The rejection in this pattern is more likely to stem from the father or from the mother going through a period of withdrawal—perhaps as a result of her own depression—during some period in the child's early development.

The Low Rejection borderline problem is one of failure to leave the symbiotic union with the mother, as opposed to the Ambivalent Rejection adolescents who are at the later separation-individuation stage of development. The picture here is diagnostically somewhat clouded because it can be close to the sociopathic, and in some cases, the later psychopathic response. Why is it that the symbiotic borderline adolescent, who is at the earlier symbiotic stage of development, looks more psychologically intact in many respects than the borderline adolescent at the later separation stage? One might logically think that the earlier developmental disturbance would lead to greater problems than the later disruption. However, the two-factor model would suggest that what we mean by psychological intactness is in fact the lack of stress because the adolescent perceives less ambivalence.

Regardless of whether there is a highly symbiotic tie to the mother, the Low Rejection adolescents have generally been allowed to coerce their immediate environment into meeting their demands. A characteristic of this group is that their problems, as they perceive them, have more to do with the restrictions that others put on their behavior than with internal stress. Problems with the parents are not perceived as rejection. The parents decided to act like parents when the child became an adolescent and placed limits on them for the first time. The adolescents have particular difficulty because they have never had to learn to inhibit impulses to any great extent and more aggressive goal-directed behavior as long as they maintained the symbiotic relationship. The Low Rejection adolescents account for the majority of aggressive behavior although they are psychologically intact enough to avoid fruitless acting out against strong authority, unlike more rejected individuals. It is not intrapsychic stress that directs and motivates their behavior as much as it is striking out at thwarting objects.

The Low Rejection adolescents appear to have a good prognosis providing they can stay out of correctional facilities because of their aggressive and delinquent behavior. Another factor that tends to get the symbiotic adolescents into difficulty is a desire for risk-taking and creating new "highs" for themselves.

They are very much the impulse-dominated pleasure seekers who cannot predict their own behavior from one day to the next. This is particularly true where there is a strong symbiotic tie to the mother that they are trying to break. It is this type of borderline adolescent that I have found the most difficult to predict the risk factor in their behavior, regardless of how well I thought psychotherapy was going.

DELINQUENT BEHAVIOR AND LOW REJECTION

I want to mention briefly how I see delinquency fitting into the Low Rejection pattern. It is here that I would place the goal-directed or sociopathic delinquents, as opposed to the attention-getting problems of the more rejected or borderline adolescents. Here you find what I call the indulgent, delinquent-producing parent. Such a family provides a role model for antisocial acts and the mother reinforces, excuses, or allows herself to be coerced into reinforcing the delinquent behavior. She may well verbalize ethical standards of conduct but fail to reinforce them by allowing the adolescent to return to a protective relationship as a way of avoiding the consequences of their behavior.

ACTING OUT

This pattern appears to be more psychologically intact partly because of the resolution, as opposed to nonresolution of the more rejected adolescents. The Low Rejection adolescents are short-term goal-directed and able to avoid internal stress to some extent by obtaining goals and thus avoiding the frustration. Their resolution may be the constant satisfying of immediate goals. They present more of a shell around themselves and have less need for the self-destructive acting out of the borderline adolescents. The Low Rejection adolescents can in some cases be seen as sociopathic, delinquent, and even psychopathic. All of these clinical manifestations in one sense represent a maximum resolution. They may be comfortable as long as immediate goals are met and they can avoid frustration and act out.

The highest rate of intact families occurs in the Low Rejection group which allows for a unique stress pattern to be created. When you have one parent who is highly accepting, indulgent, or symbiotic it leaves room for creating stress when the other parent is much more rejecting. This is the family pattern that has shown up in cases of violent acting out in our population. This situation is a combination of the Severe Rejection and Low Rejection patterns combined in one family situation. Often the mothers partially infantilize and protect the adolescents, while the fathers are much like the mothers described in the Severe Rejection pattern; they are highly pathological of a paranoid type and unpredictably violent. One father would throw money on the floor in front of his son and dare him to pick it up. He would force the child to challenge him for it and take a beating in the process. A key element here is that the father's behavior is unpredictable, violent, and abusive, but not contingent on the adolescent's dependence and independence as in the more borderline situations. Before the adolescent is capable of carrying out acts of violence against a person, you must have the indulgent factor. This combination of Severe and Low Rejection is ordinarily not very self-destructive (except as acts of violence ultimately end up as self-destructive). It is not that depression is not a part of the clinical picture—indeed, there are those who would argue that it is a basic clinical symptom in delinquency—but rather that there is a learned behavior for ventilation of the anger.

SYMBIOTIC TIE TO THE MOTHER

The symbiotic tie to the mother plays a role in many borderline adolescent situations (Mahler, 1975, 1979a, 1979b; Kaplan, 1978; Volkan, 1979), and also plays a prominent role in family violence and violence directed outside the immediate family under certain circumstances. How does one recognize the symbiotic relationship? This is often made easy by the adolescent and the mother because of their physical behavior toward each other. They will often touch or caress or otherwise move into close proximity so you can usually get a good idea which way the symbiotic tie is going. It may be from the mother to the adolescent, from the adolescent to the mother, or a mutual symbiotic relationship from which neither appears to want to separate.

Violence can be induced because of the parent threatening to break the symbiotic tie. It appears to be the mother's striving for independence that can trigger violence directed within the family. On the other hand, aggression directed outside the family more often seems to stem from the mother striving to maintain the symbiotic tie and violence from the adolescent directed at thwarting objects that stand between them and independence.

The symbiotic borderline adolescent has been taught to feel responsible and to parent the parent. The threat of abandonment comes about through fear of the destruction of the parent if the adolescent does not care for them. The world is seen as hostile and frightening (frequently the father, or men in general, are seen in that light by both child and mother); therefore mother must be protected. It is up to the child to ward off disaster by being symbiotic and protecting. Whenever the child self-commits, or tries to separate from the parent, there is both guilt induction and some effect that threatens devastation of the parent. This guarantees, at least for a while, that the child will remain close to the parent. When they do "slingshot out" of the symbiotic relationship during adolescence, as a reaction to the intensity of the guilt-induction and the subtle coercion not to separate, they may become self-destructive because of the guilt. This self-destruction, unlike that found in other rejection patterns, comes about through the situations that the adolescents place themselves in rather than a direct attack upon themselves. They feel somewhat worthless because they are abandoning the parent, but the overall self-concept is higher than in other rejection cases. They will put themselves in a position where they receive love and where they are dependent, parented, and also punished. They get furious at the parent for being so infantile and want them to grow up without acting like a parent (meaning not to tell them what to do). At the same time, however, the child's acceptance and love has been contingent on parenting the parent, and if the parent does grow up they will have no source of love and acceptance.

Perhaps we can summarize by saying that the symbiotic borderline adolescents have learned that by parenting the parent and maintaining the symbiotic tie with the mother, they have found the key to continual acceptance; but, of course, it is at the cost of their own separation and commitment to self. As a result, they are more "intact" in one sense because they have been able to avoid the separation stresses of the Ambivalent Rejection group. The ultimate guilt comes about when the adolescents do separate and the parent gives them messages that they will self-destruct because of it. Tremendous motivation is then created for the adolescent which in some sense is far more powerful than that experienced by the less symbiotic borderline. It is here under such powerful drives that the capacity for aggression reaches its peak.*

*I would like to express my appreciation to Dr. Michael Ebner and Dr. James Masterson for their assistance in helping me formulate ideas around the symbiotic process.

Chapter 5

BORDERLINE FAMILY DYNAMICS AND CHARACTERISTICS

We have little difficulty recognizing the abusing or delinquent family, but few understand the borderline family structure. The problem is not confined to one generation but carries with it the seed from one generation to another; for the extended family is very much a part of the overall borderline dynamics.

We are primarily discussing the Ambivalent Rejection pattern because this implies that the essence of the family dynamics involves an almost equal distribution of conflicting positive and negative messages perceived by the adolescent. Borderline characteristics do occur throughout the acceptance-rejection continuum so that we will be giving some emphasis to the Low Rejection and Severe Rejection categories.

The study of the borderline family is probably the most direct route to understanding other types of family situations. Kernberg (1978) points out that:

> A normal or neurotic—in contrast to borderline and narcissistic—patient may also present violent conflicts with his parents and a tendency to criticize and devalue them bitterly, but this is usually mitigated by the capacity to value other

aspects of his parents and he would have other relationships that would not be affected by this self-affirmative and devaluation trend. (p. 353).

It is this splitting of goodness and badness that identifies the borderline adolescent's relationship with his parents. It is this intense aspect—or maximum stress as identified by the two-factor model—that distinguishes the borderline family from other patterns.

Fromm-Reichman (1940) introduced the concept of the schizophrenogenic mother which tended to represent the child as the helpless victim of the pathological mother. Historically it contrasted with the prevailing psychoanalytic view, which gave the mother an easier time of it from the standpoint of the child's pathology being bound up with stages of psychosexual development as much as with family pathology. Other authors extended this line of thinking (Bateson, Haley, Jackson, and Weakland, 1965) as the double-bind concept. As Shapiro (1978) points out these approaches presented the first empirical data on family situations, but they also presented certain other problems. To quote the author: "These difficulties derived from the static, nondynamic quality of the descriptions which tempted the reader to make value judgments about the parents in these interchanges." One implication was that these children should be rescued as a course of treatment from the bad mother; a process that was reversed by Bowlby's (1969, 1973) work on the effects of separation from the mother. It would seem that one who wished to make a decision based on such information would be in somewhat of a bind themselves.

Other authors (Lidz, Cornelison, Fleck, and Terry, 1957; Wynne, Rycoff, Day, and Hirsch, 1958) began to describe families in a broader psychodynamic view but still with fixed patterns, little emphasis upon mutual family defenses, and group dynamics of the family as a pathological but stable unit. Still other authors (Johnson, 1949; Johnson and Szurek, 1952; Szurek, 1942) concentrated on the same approach but with anti-social delinquent behaviors. Their view can be summarized as unconscious conflicts within the parents which lead unwittingly to their sanctioning of antisocial behavior in the adolescent. This approach also lead to the view that the child was merely the passive recipient of pressure from the parent and not an active participant of processing information, perceiving and generally making life difficult for their parents with their behavior.

It is useful to review here the double-bind concept because it is in some respects a good historical description of ambivalence in the borderline family. According to the double-bind theory (Bateson, Haley, Jackson, and Weakland, 1956), there must be a primary negative injunction, and a secondary one conflicting with the first at a more abstract level; and like the first, enforced by punishment or signals which threaten the individual's survival. It may have either of two forms: 1) Do not do so and so, or I will punish you, or 2) If you do not do so and so, I will punish you. Punishment may be either the withdrawal of love or the expression of hate or anger, or even more devastating, the kind of abandonment that might result from the parents displaying what to the child appears as extreme helplessness. The secondary injunction is commonly communicated to the child by nonverbal means, such as posture, gestures, tone of voice that may reveal a message to the child. This secondary message may negate any portion of the primary message.

In addition to the two primary messages contradicting or negating one another there is also thought to be separate tertiary negative injunctions which act to prohibit the victim from escaping from the situation. Implicit in the entire situation is abandonment if the child leaves the family. Furthermore, it is suggested that this complete set of injunctions, messages, and prohibitions is no longer necessary after it has been employed for many years in the family. The adolescent has learned to perceive the world in terms of this double bind. Almost any part of the sequence may be sufficient to precipitate rage or panic reactions. The pattern of conflicting injunctions may even be taken over by hallucinatory voices.

The double-bind process essentially says that the adolescent must discriminate between two or more messages from the parents where one invalidates the other. By comparison the ambivalence of the borderline perception may simply be seen as broader, somewhat less stressful, and of a more nonverbal nature. It tends to allow the borderline more opportunities for acting out that the schizophrenic does not have. In either case, though, clarification of the messages is not allowed.

The normal individual will respond to the double bind type of situation by taking a metaphorical statement literally when there is no way out of a situation that is contradictory. Bateson cites an example of an employee who went home during office hours and another employee called up and said, "Well, how did you get there?" The man replied, "By automobile." He responded literally because he was faced with a message which asked him what he was doing at home when he should have been at work, but which denied that the question was even being asked by the way it was phrased. The use of the metaphor in therapy has more recently been explored by Gordon (1978).

Masterson was referring to the metaphorical character of fairy tales when he discussed the similarities of such stories with the borderline family situation (1972). Cinderella, for example, represents an adolescent living in a borderline, rejecting family, who was rescued by the prince before she had to resort to acting out. Understanding the illogical nature of the conflicting metaphorical world of the borderline adolescent does a lot for gaining the trust of the adolescent.

The conflictual nature of the family situation demands that the child not correctly interpret the mother's behavior unless he wants to threaten his relationship with her. Thus he must perceptually distort the environment and the meaning assigned to the relationships. An overtly loving statement from the mother, such as "Go to bed, you're very tired," and, "I want you to get your sleep," may deny feelings that could be translated as "Get out of my sight because I'm sick of you." If the child admits to the interpretation he must admit to his mother's rejection. Although the schizophrenic family has been called highly rejecting, in my opinion it is only in the sense that it creates very high stress but not in the perception of the adolescent. In fact, such a family is more likely to be perceived as generally accepting; so much so that the adolescent is willing to internalize responsibility for the family system. By comparison, the more borderline adolescent will perceive greater rejection and act out because of it.

A description originally written for schizophrenic families (Lidz, Fleck, and Cornelison, 1960) would now more appropriately describe borderline family characteristics.

1. A failure in development of a nuclear family in the sense that one or both parents remain primarily attached to one of his or her own parents.

2. Family schisms or splits due to parental strife and/or lack of role reciprocity.

3. Family skews present, i.e., one dyadic relationship in the family dominates family life at the expense of the needs of other family members.

4. Blurring of generating boundaries or lines in the family, e.g.,

    (a) when one parent in a skewed family competes with the children;

    (b) when one parent establishes a special bond with one child, giving factual basis to the claim of the schizophrenic that she/he is more important to the parent than is the other parent; and

    (c) when persistent eroticization of a parent/child relationship exists.

5. Perversion of the entire family atmosphere with irrational, most often paranoid ideation.

6. Persistence of conscious incestuous thoughts and behaviors.

7. Isolation of the family socioculturally.

8. Failure to educate the children toward and to help them achieve separation or emancipation from the family.

9. The parents' uncertainty about or blurring of their own sex roles, leading to difficulty in a child's achieving his/her own sexual identity and maturity.

10. The parents' presentation of themselves as persons to be identified with in a form that is not reconcilable with what is necessary for a child to appropriately develop his own personality.

11. The siblings of the same sex as the labeled patient were more disturbed than the siblings of the opposite sex.

BORDERLINE FAMILY CHARACTERISTICS

Understanding the characteristics of the borderline family is of more than academic interest to those who work with the adolescent. It is a question of being trusted as a therapist, having credibility, and the adolescent's belief that we are capable of stepping through the looking glass and perceiving his world. If we know some of the particular family characteristics in a case we can guess that a lot more are there and what they might be. Having this kind of "knowing" ability can make a very constructive and useful confrontation tool with both the adolescent and the family.

In one recent study (Gunderson, Kerr, and Englund, 1980) they were able to discriminate the families of the borderline adolescents from two other psychiatric groups. One of their findings was that denial of the psychopathology of the acting-out behavior of the adolescent combined with a lack of involvment with the children identified this family situation. Their marriages relative to the other groups were marked by the absence of overt hostility and conflict. "Their attachment to each other seemed to be at the expense of their children, in that they failed to act as regulators and monitors of their children's behavior, as sources of gratification and support, or even as clear role models." They suggest that the pathology of the adolescent was a response to this vacuum.

Zinner and Shapiro (1957, 1978) described two basic groups of borderline families based upon Kernberg's (1967) definition of the borderline adolescent. First there was the chaotic defensive kind of family interaction which would arise when issues relating to the separation and autonomy of the adolescent were discussed. These families would complain when their children were too independent and spent more time with their friends than they did with their family. A second group complained that their children were too dependent upon them and not sufficiently involved with the outside world. These two groups illustrate the two sides of the coin, so to speak, in the independence-dependence struggle. I would question whether they are not merely the same families observed at different points in the cycle of ambivalence.

CHARACTERISTICS OF THE MOTHER

In any discussion of the origin of borderline problems the mother comes off badly in the sense of being the one who rejects or will not let go of her child. The therapist who deals with the family soon realizes that the mother is not the villain that theory would portray her to be; more than likely she has never gotten through her own adolescence in any satisfactory manner. In fact, in the more symbiotic cases, it is the mother's threatened separation and independence that may trigger aggressive behavior in the adolescent (see case #12).

One of the differences I have observed between the mothers of the borderline and schizophrenic adolescents is that the latter comes across as more demanding, aggressive, and generally in a less sympathetic manner. On the other hand, the borderline mother comes across as wanting a dependent relationship with an authority figure and as being much more passive and depressed. They will often have a very immature affect and relate to their children as a sister or a peer. They often seem incapable of relating to their children in terms of their problems except in a most superficial manner.

I never cease to be amazed that the mother's history and development is almost always identical in most respects to that of her daughter's. Yet oddly enough when this is mentioned it comes as a surprise to both of them and offers some insight. This is one of the advantages of knowing the characteristics of the borderline family because bringing out this information usually makes a positive impression and increases cooperation. It is apparent that the mother has no real concept of normal adolescence and really does not comprehend the destructive nature of the adolescent's behavior. She too has probably skipped from the first signs of adolescence to acting as though she were an adult. This is exactly what she is now telling her daughter not to do, but it is not based on any understanding of the dynamics behind it.

The borderline mother is typically very young and had the first child—usually the borderline adolescent—while still a teenager. In many respects she acts like someone in their late teens who is narcissistic and emotionally immature. They are trying to decide what they want to do with their life; whether to go back to school, get a job, start a career, and so forth. This sudden growth of course may be very threatening to the adolescent.

CHARACTERISTICS OF THE BORDERLINE FATHER

I have never encountered a borderline adolescent who had an adequate father from the standpoint of the needs or expectations of the normal paternal role. However, the characteristics of the father are generally broader and less well defined than that of the mother. One way to look at this might be to say that it is certain characteristics of the mother that leads the child toward borderline development, while it is more likely to be the absence of certain roles and functions (such as pulling the child from the mother during the separation stage) that is the problem with the father. The more seriously disturbed borderline adolescents appear to come from homes where the father is present and reinforces the pathological relationship between the mother and child. The father may compete actively with the mother for the child's attention or the parents may have a close relationship and the child is left out.

One of the most destructive characteristics that can occur in the family when the father is present has to do with the threat of violence that he may represent. The mother may be truly intimidated, but even if she is not she may use that threat as a means of controlling the child, and to assure that he remains in a dependent relationship with her. The two of them may conspire against the father as the "bad" and threatening parent.

Another situation involves the stepfather who may not have a chance to provide adequate parental input even if he has the characteristics to do so. In the case of the symbiotic relationship between the mother and child, the mother will see to it that the father is out of the picture as far as influencing the child. Inevitably the adolescent will end up with a very distorted view of the stepfather and will see him as a distant figure who only enforces rules.

Loewald (1951) suggested that the father plays a very positive role in terms of the child's "ego-ideal" and as a force to pull the child away from the mother during the separation-individuation phase of development. Anderson (1978) also suggested that the task of separation might be impossible without the father having some input into that developmental stage.

Cooper and Ekstein (1978) have emphasized the role of the father in the development of the borderline female. There is role confusion and no clear image of what the father should be, which means that they cannot have an understanding of their own identity. The father may variously be seen as seducer, protector, oppressor, and as someone to be both desired and avoided.

The role of the father seems to be a critical one in the sexual identity of the adolescent girl. He sets the expectations and attitudes about feminine behavior in some respects even more than the mother. The daughter uses the father as the first male figure by which she develops attitudes toward her sexuality. The borderline family is similar in many respects to the incestuous family (Meiselman, 1979), but even when it is not overt it is still a sensual and eroticizing environment for the child. Sexual identity confusion, as well as sexual acting out, almost always goes along with borderline problems.

CHARACTERISTICS OF THE BORDERLINE ADOLESCENT

I have found that there is about a four to one ratio favoring females over males in the Ambivalent-Rejection pattern. Other authors (Masterson, 1980; Scarf, 1980; Kimsey, 1977) have also reported some sex differential, although the whole issue is obviously clouded by problems of definition. The explanation might be in the fact that the Severe-Rejection group has a four to one ratio in favor of males over females; in other words, the males who have borderline characteristics are more likely to perceive greater rejection and less ambivalence from the parent. This also suggests that the male is less likely to be involved in a highly symbiotic relationship with the mother, although this certainly does occur. Mahler (1979b) has suggested that there is a differential responding of the mother toward the male child as early as the second year of life, which suggests greater withdrawal and less ambivalence in her behavior. I have also noted that those females in the Severe-Rejection pattern have more masculine characteristics, are generally more assertive, and tend to be more delinquent. Conversely, those males in the Ambivalent-Rejection group have more feminine characteristics than do the males in any other group.

Adolescents in the Ambivalent-Rejection group are often blond (more than would be explained by chance alone) and have developed secondary sexual characteristics relatively early compared to those in other groups. As a matter of fact, their physical appearance often tends to be rather striking. I know of no other researcher who has written on this subject nor of any other data that would support these suggestions. I am reminded that many years ago, before much information was available about the borderline condition, it was sometimes referred to as the "Marilyn Monroe syndrome."

SIBLINGS OF THE BORDERLINE

There are few patterns concerning the siblings of the borderline adolescent. The problem can occur in any ordinal position in the family, but appears to be most common with the oldest child, and secondarily with the youngest. It is more likely to affect one sex only within a particular family. It is also true that the problem may to some extent be transferred to another child when the borderline adolescent leaves the immediate family. The reason for this is that one of the siblings must act as a scapegoat for a pathological family structure.

THE ELASTIC UMBILICAL CORD

Probably the most important feature of the borderline family is what I refer to as the invisible "elastic umbilical cord" that holds the pathological, dysfunctional family together and keeps the borderline adolescent within the family structure. It is, of course, critical that the therapist understand that the adolescents do not have the power to sever this cord despite all of their good intentions. This umbilical cord is invisible to the observer unless they fully comprehend the psychodynamics of the borderline family structure.

Each family member has an immature ego structure that

requires a degree of sustenance from some other member. It is the borderline adolescent who typically acts as the venting device for this interdependent system and thus is the one who acts out. It can also be viewed more specifically in terms of the relationship with the mother because no adolescent can separate easily from a rejecting or ambivalent relationship with the mother.

DEPERSONIFICATION

One of the most psychologically damaging characteristics of the borderline parent is that they tend to treat the child as a "nonperson." This goes beyond the reluctance or inability to talk about feeling expression; it goes to the heart of what the adolescents most complain about in their family; the feeling that nobody understands. The complaint that is so often heard is, "They will buy me anything but they won't talk to me."

In one 16-year-old girl (case #9) we find a good example of what is meant by depersonification. She had recently made a serious suicidal gesture which required some medication. Her mother volunteered, without knowing any of the details of the incident or the medical complications, that she was sure her daughter could get along without medication. She then changed the subject and asked the doctor if he knew where she could get some DMSO for her ailing horse that was really worrying her.

Depersonification can be either the highly valued "object" in a symbiotic relationship or the worthless possession in a more rejecting situation. In the symbiotic relationship the adolescents may receive much affection and material things, but it still leaves them so dissatisfied that they act as though they were rejected. Depersonification can be seen from the beginning as the mother views the infant as a doll or object to be fondled. Later the child is treated like an object to be shown off to others.

A characteristic related to depersonification is the family's oftentimes inordinate interest in pets and animals. Obviously this does not occur in every borderline family but with high enough frequency to be of interest. Pets can play an important role, I believe, because of the complex needs for closeness without risks and feeling expression being involved. They can be owned and must be dependent without risk of distancing.

SOCIO-CULTURAL ISOLATION

The borderline family tends to be isolated as a family unit with relatively few outside activities or friends beyond the extended family. They may often live in some relatively isolated place.

MULTIGENERATIONAL FACTORS

The multigenerational nature of the borderline family is one of the most interesting and perplexing aspects of the phenomena. Because it is so prevalent it often goes unnoticed by those who deal with the adolescent. I would go so far as to say if a grandparent is significantly involved in the history of the adolescent's problems, one should suspect a borderline situation. If the essence of the borderline problem is a failure to separate then it is logical that we should be dealing with a multigenerational problem on the mother's side of the family. In cases where the parents are both borderline we find the involvement of both sets of grandparents.

In keeping with the looking glass perspective, the involvement of the grandparents is subtle. When the adolescent's problems are presented to the therapist the grandparents are never mentioned by either the adolescent or the parent. If questioned, the parents may say something to the effect that they have settled that problem and that finally they have been able to get away from their parents.

How well hidden some of the multigenerational problems are is well illustrated by a case (case #9) where both parents spoke very negatively of the maternal grandmother; they stated they did not allow the children to visit her and she was not welcome in their home. The girl herself said her grandmother was a "bitch" but that she gave her everything she wanted. Whenever she ran she usually went to the grandmother's home, sooner or later, where she would negotiate her way back to her parents. It was quite by accident that I learned that her father and grandmother shared a joint checking account and that she controlled the family economically. When I asked the father about this he said he saw nothing strange about it.

The situation between the girl and her grandmother, and her parents was more complicated than even the economic control would suggest. For example, there was rather an intricate pattern involving distancing and engulfment of the adolescent that seemed to operate in a dynamic sense to maintain the equilibrium of the entire family network. If she ran from her grandmother to her parents' home her grandmother was excluded. If she stayed with the grandmother her parents excluded both of them. If she ran from both parents and grandmother, grandmother was welcome and she was excluded.

The borderline adolescent may act out a homicidal rage toward the grandmother, suggesting the dynamic role that the grandmother can play in the situation. She will invariably take the borderline adolescent in because it is a way of assuring that the parents cannot actually distance themselves entirely from them— the adolescent becomes a sort of psychological hostage in the separation game. One way to keep the adolescents, of course, is to indulge them with money and material things. The grandparent is likely to place limits on the child's behavior only when the parent criticizes the grandparent. At this point, the grandparent says that is enough and the adolescent, who has little frustration tolerance because of the indulgence, reacts aggressively.

From the adolescents' point of view, the grandparent serves as a drop-in center whenever they do not have any other place to go. However, they have learned that the price they pay is that the grandparent is even less likely than their parents to understand and talk to them about what is going on, and they will have to listen to a lecture about the inadequacies of their parents.

The three-generation cycle operates in such a way that the third generation seems to be more severe because the adolescent is caught between two opposite forces. It often seems to be the case that if the grandparent's primary mode of dealing with the mother was that of rejection or threat of abandonment, then the mother's method of dealing with the borderline child is more symbiotic. Maximum stress is caused by having two borderline parents available, and thus it seems that the stress can be even greater when the grandparent is involved.

THE ROLE OF AGGRESSION

There is no simple formula for understanding aggression in the borderline family. The adolescents can come from families where aggression varies tremendously but regardless of whether it expresses itself through violence, the family is seriously curtailed in the expression of emotion. They cannot talk about feelings as a form of anger release or blend and integrate emotions (Plutchik, 1980).

The father, since he usually is the most violence-prone (mother may vicariously take her feelings out through father's acting out) may become a feared object; loving and playful one minute and violent and rejecting the next. Mother says in effect, "You had better stick with me kid because you can't trust your father." On occasions I have recorded visits that families had with the adolescents in treatment (they knew they were being taped) where the conversation would take on a theme of sex and violence. Certainly cultural and socioeconomic levels play a role in determining how the violence is expressed in the family. If it is not acceptable in any blatant form you will find it in more subtle forms.

Aggression in the family will usually come in the form of rageful bursts that are soon forgotten. I once went to a home to visit an adolescent (case #6). As we all sat in the living room I noticed that the kitchen in the background was partially destroyed. When I asked what had happened the mother and children laughed and described a sequence where father had become angry over something that the children had done (which seemed rather minor at the time) and proceeded to dismantle the kitchen. They showed me how the trail of destruction lead to the garage and made it clear that it was rather routine (although infrequent). Father for his part was rather embarrassed but offered no argument. The impression that he gave was of a quiet, though somewhat inept father, who was genuinely interested in helping his daughter. She portrayed him as someone who was terrifying.

THE ADOLESCENT AS FAMILY SCAPEGOAT

The adolescent represents a vital cog in the dysfunctional dynamics of the borderline family. There is a genuine sense of discomfort and anxiety at the thought of the adolescent being absent from the family in some independent fashion even though a sibling may take his place as the scapegoat. I suspect the reason for the scapegoating has to do with the inability to express feelings and stress in any other form but projecting it onto the adolescent who in turn acts it out.

SEXUAL ABUSE

Some of the descriptive material on the sexually abusing family sounds much like aspects of the borderline family (Meiselman, 1979). One important feature is the general immaturity of the parents and the role of the mother in contributing to the incestuous situation. I would estimate that actual sexual abuse occurs in perhaps as high as 35 percent of the borderline families.

Borderline parents tend to be erotic and sensual in the way in which they relate to the children. They can take many forms, such as the rigid proscription against sexual behavior or the deliberate eroticizing relationship between parent and child. The adolescents may be frequently told that they will become "tramps" or "whores" or that they should feel guilty about their sexual acting out.

The borderline may fantasize sexual relationships with the parent to such a degree that they cannot separate fact from fantasy. The eroticizing is so stimulating and guilt-inducing that the boundaries of reality may have been blurred (see case #9). In a clinical sense the therapist must deal with the erotic nature of the parenting and the fantasy as though it were reality.

More often than not the borderline adolescents are in a responsible position caring for younger children. They may have combined the erotic element of their own parenting with that of sex play with younger siblings which may tend to further confuse the situation. Most physical contact with the children involves an erotic, or aggressive component. In other words, physical contact of a loving nature is often not simple and straightforward.

THREAT OF ABANDONMENT AS PARENTAL STYLE

All parents at some time have said, if only jokingly, that their kids were driving them crazy and they were leaving home. With the borderline family it has been carried to an extreme. In one case I estimated that the mother got into the car and ran away from home at least once a week throughout the child's early development. Father would leave less often but might be gone for several days, while mother would return in 30 minutes. This is why you must look beyond the actual physical separations from parents during the early development years. Such physical separations are important when they do occur largely because they make the threat of abandonment even more threatening.

IMPLICATIONS FOR FAMILY INTERVENTION

Most family therapy techniques are based on the assumption that there is faulty communication in the system; in the borderline family this is a gross understatement. However, discussing the communication process gets redirected by the parents to the adolescents' acting out. This creates more problems because the borderline will be convinced that the therapist does not understand what really goes on in the family resulting in even more acting out or self-destructive behavior.

The borderline parent does not have the empathy to understand every range of emotion and feeling in the communication process. I am not saying it is impossible; just something that may not happen through the usual therapy approach. The borderline family is so pathological that it must hang on to the role and double-bind communication it has in order to avoid disaster. Each member plays a discrete and critical role in the system, as faulty as it may appear to the therapist. It cannot be modified unless the psychological need each member has for keeping it that way is explored.

I have found that some constructive changes can come about if the therapist who is seeing the adolescent starts with an informational approach to the family with little expectation of making significant changes. This should be clearly communicated to the parents, which will often put them in a more open and less defensive position. This in itself can result in some constructive improvements. The adolescents' acting out can be put in perspective within this system.

Shapiro (1978a) suggests a similar process for working with the families of the borderline adolescents. He terms it group interpretation aimed at helping family members take responsibility for those projections on one another, which means that the therapist assists the parents to put their own problems into perspective (Berkowitz, Shapiro, Zinner, and Shapiro, 1974). I refer to much the same thing as an informational approach to the borderline family in which some of the dynamics and development (including the multigenerational nature of the problem) are explained and discussed. I find much the same reaction from the parents as I do from the adolescents when I make clear some of the internal structure of the family. They tend to be cooperative and willing to drop some of the defensiveness to professionals, which they have developed over the years. The result is often some actual improvement in the situation from the adolescents' standpoint.

THE ADOLESCENTS' ACTING OUT AND THE PARENTS

It is easy to lose perspective and credibility when it comes to the relationship between acting out and the parents. By the time the adolescents are seriously into methods of dealing with depression they are also making life very difficult for the parents who are putting up with a lot of abuse because of it. The therapist should not confuse the fact that the parents were largely responsible for the problem in the first place with the fact that they are justified in wanting to place limits on the behavior now. The therapist should communicate to both the adolescents and the parents that the acting out serves only to cover up the real problem and is potentially destructive. At this point, the parents do not have the power to stop it, but the therapist can help them, not only to understand what is going on, but to give the adolescent reasonable expectations that are consistent. This type of straightforward communication to both the adolescents and the parents will give the therapist the necessary degree of authority and credibility with all parties in the battle between the adolescent's behavior and the parent's right to expect something better.

Chapter 6

PERSPECTIVE ON BORDERLINE DEVELOPMENT

In this chapter we will be emphasizing the borderline characteristics in developmental perspective. While there are probably numerous developmental patterns that could conceivably lead to a failure to separate properly from the mother and to the array of borderline characteristics, there is an optimum pattern. A borderline problem can occur from mother's absence, separation, symbiotic ties, and so forth (Masterson, 1980), but the behavior pattern of the adolescent will also vary, as will their perception of rejection and acceptance. Here I will discuss the situation that seems to produce the maximum amount of stress, ambivalence, and the greatest number of borderline characteristics in the adolescent.

EARLY DEVELOPMENT

The mother of the borderline child is often young and has never properly separated from her own mother. She is in a constant struggle prompting moves, love affairs, and acting out. The father is usually also young and quite often can be described as borderline himself; he is in the same dependent relationship with parents or in-laws. He, too, is likely to act out this immaturity and dependency through various ways acceptable to his particular socioeconomic and cultural background. He may be a workaholic, alcoholic, womanizer, or just passively withdrawn from the family, but in any case there is usually a tacit agreement to let the mother deal with the children. Father periodically acts out his own anger, which is then used as a means of control over the child.

The mother views the child as an object and responds to him as though he were a doll during infancy, although there are moments of rejection stemming from the child's intrusions and demands. Basically the level of care and nurturance provided during the first year is adequate and sometimes rather engulfing. This symbiosis may be to the total exclusion of the father which places the child as a pawn between the two parents. Even by the end of the first year the child may be mirroring the mother's behavior by alternately clinging and distancing.

Mahler (Mahler, 1979a & b) and her associates have studied the early relationship between the mother and child with observational studies. One of her descriptions is presented below as an example of early borderline development.

> From his sixth or seventh month until the last quarter of his second year, Sy's life was a saga of daytime attempts to extricate himself from his mother's suffocating envelopment and intrusiveness. During the night, on the other hand, he behaved or was seduced into behaving as the "child-lover at the breast." At seven to nine months, when normally the specific bond with the mother is at its peak and stranger anxiety appears, Sy strained away from his mother's body when she held him. (p. 198)

The tendency of the parent to be seductive or erotic with the child, which is suggested by a symbiotic relationship, seems to be related to precocious sexual behavior during pubescence (see case #14). Sy at 11 years was described by one of his teachers as a "fresh, sexually precocious child who bragged and engaged in disruptive, exhibitionistic, clowning and crudely inappropriate sex talk."

The role of the father is illustrated by the description of Sy's father as taking over the role of the over-stimulating mother once the child had reached two years of age.

> He at once threatens and cajoles, manhandles and caresses, slams about and seduces Sy. When the father's rage reaches a peak, he switches to seductive kissing and tickling. The whole thing is sadistic, sexualized, and hysterical. (p. 200)

The age of two seems to be a critical time for physical separations from the father. The role of the father should be a moderating influence between that of the child and the mother; not the overstimulation which perpetuates the erotic, dependent situation that may exist with the mother. In Sy's case, for example, one can well imagine the father criticizing (rejecting) him for moving away from the mother's engulfment and then in turn criticizing him for having a sensual, symbiotic relationship with the mother ("grow up and be a man, don't be a sissy").

The borderline development has its inception during the separation-individuation phase, as put forth in Mahler's (1975) stages. This means that it would occur somewhere between 18 and 36 months; the later it occurs the more psychological intactness or ego development the child would have. Arrest during the earlier symbiotic phase of development would have potentially more serious consequences based upon the failure to ever strive for separation-individuation until reaching adolescence (see case #12 and #14).

The child vascillates between distancing himself from the mother and clinging to her for support and libidinal supplies, and for relief from the threatening anxiety of the world about him. Her withholding is a very powerful weapon. The separation-individuation stages requires that she be able to tolerate the distancing, as well as the unpredictable negative behavior of the child, who just a few short months before had been so totally dependent. As the mother is confronted with her own poorly resolved feelings of rejection and abandonment from her mother she resists such behavior from her own child. She of course does this under the guise of parenting such that the observer might not notice anything wrong, as she alternately engulfs and distances herself much as the child himself is doing. The child quickly learns the price to be paid for separation. It should be kept in mind that the behavior of the parent represents unconscious drives and not deliberate creation of problems for the child. As far as they are concerned the child deserves to be punished for misbehaving just as they were punished when they were children. The difference between the borderline pattern and other rejection patterns lies, in part, in the high degree of stress created by the ambivalence. At least the more rejected child receives a more predictable message. Ekstein and Wallerstein (1954; Ekstein, 1966) describe the emotional delay that occurs in the borderline as being like a thermostat that has gone haywire. The emotions are governed by an unpredictable controlling device for regulation; mood swings become erratic and unpredictable, out of control, and frightening as they sense their own erratic behavior and their inability to control it.

By the time the borderline child reaches the beginning of the latency age, the severe ego defect or split ego has been created. They have poor reality perception and must distort what they do perceive, poor frustration tolerance and impulse control. In terms of split-ego function and object relations there will be splitting, primitive ideation, projection, denial and omnipotence. There is the splitting into good and bad objects, as in the good and bad mother, a lack of integrated self-concept, a dependence upon external objects, contradcitory ego states and behavior. Also the failure to develop an integrated object representation limits the development of the capacity for empathy for others.

LATENCY

One of the ways in which the borderline pattern can sometimes be identified from other severe disturbances of adolescence is through the analysis of the latency age period. This age span covers approximately the ages 6 to 10 and can be viewed as a period of low stress between two high stress separation-individuation periods. It follows the psychologically tumultuous early development that placed great demands on the child in his drive for independence of ego functioning. By the beginning of latency, then, the basic psychological structure is complete and the normal child can enjoy latency as the period of childhood with relatively low demands. During the latency the borderline child is often described as a 'model child' by the parents. This is not the case on close examination, but what the parents are noting is that there are few demands for separation during this period and the child can exist within the conflictual situation of the family. While there may be some acting out, it is likely that he will remain in a largely dependent relationship with the mother and not risk withdrawal of libidinal supplies. The child may be described by the mother as, "She was such a little pixie—always cheerful and happy;" or "She was always mother's little helper, I don't know what I would have done without her, the way she took care of her brothers and sisters."

Behavior is controlled during latency through the implicit threat of abandonment. If actual separations have occurred they only serve to make the threat even more real. This dependent role is really a double bind situation for the child because he is being told to be adult-like and assume some of the responsibilities of the mother, while at the same time being highly dependent. The mother may be exchanging roles with the child by confiding in her as a sister, as though the child were the mother, or as a confidant in alliance against the father. Thus the child may fantasize incestuous relationships because of the general eroticizing and role confusion.

PREADOLESCENCE

During preadolescence we are frequently distracted by the beginning of the acting out. Suddenly the model child of latency has blossomed into a major behavior problem. We can be mislead into thinking the acting out always existed but if it did a diagnosis other than borderline might be considered.

Blos (1979) refers to early adolescence as a second stage of separation with its demands for emancipation, independence, and, at the same time, security. Not surprisingly then nearly all physical separations from parents in a severely disturbed population of adolescents have occurred during either the first 6 years

(most of them during the first 3 years) or during early adolescence. The most difficult and resistant cases have had physical
separations from parents during both periods of development.
But as previously pointed out, borderline problems strictly speaking do not originate during the latter period. The difference
might be thought of as a failure to deal effectively with the
ambivalence of emancipation problems as opposed to the much
more severe failure to separate and individuate into whole object
relations.

During latency the borderline live in their fantasy world of
imaginary escape to a less conflictual and more accepting world.
The first signs of sexual development are taken as signals that
they no longer have to tolerate the stress of the family and can live
as adults. The more symbiotic adolescent will be the most intent
on finding another place to live as opposed to just being on the
run. The child who was so close to mother takes off as if fired
from a slingshot. The "freedom" he wants often turns out to be
another dependent relationship with an older person.

One 12-year-old girl, who had a very symbiotic relationship,
described her mother as not really being her mother but a friend
and a sister. She would wistfully say that she wished her mother
was older and would grow up. Descriptions of her runs from
home would lead one to believe that she was out of control and
highly self-destructive. Her motivation was more than merely
escape from the family and finding new highs and excitement;
she needed to find people who would listen to her. Life was
simple without conflictual messages. While most young adolescents are resolved in their behavior because they have not had the
experiences to disprove their resolution of escape and independence, the more rejected adolescents will be less determined.
They are more likely to be involved in alcohol and drugs as a form
of self-destruction, as opposed to seeking new "highs" to relieve
the feelings of abandonment depression. Their runs from home
will be less planned and shorter in duration than the symbiotic
borderline. These runs of the abandonment depression borderline take on a Narcisses and Goldman (Hesse, 1968) trek with no
beginning and no end in search of nothing in particular. It is the
journey itself that is important because it relieves depression. I
have asked several such adolescents whether they would rather

travel the highways in their own car with money or the way they had been—hitch-hiking without money. They looked at me as though I really did not understand or I would not have asked such a stupid question—their way, of course, or it just wouldn't be the same.

The highly dependent child that was controlled either through the threat of abandonment or through the symbiotic union with the mother now has other means of dealing with the family situation because of their new found independence (adolescence). The mother in effect kept telling the child to "grow up" and be responsible during latency, while demanding dependence. The mother now is frightened by the independence of the adolescent bringing to the surface her own fears that have not been resolved. She will assume the worst and set limits on the adolescent's behavior for the first time. I have frequently heard girls complain that their parents did not care how late they stayed out until they reached adolescence. The adolescent says in effect "you didn't tell me what to do before so you have no right to tell me what to do now." One girl complained how illogical the rules were; her parents never acted angry after she had been gone for two days on a drunken, sexual binge, but they became angry and called her a tramp for talking to a boy on the telephone and asking him to the house.

ADOLESCENCE

Almost every borderline individual as he enters adolescence can be considered strong in his resolve to escape the stress through leaving the family. From a treatment standpoint he is most difficult to deal with at this stage precisely because he is convinced that he has the solution. Reality usually catches up to these adolescents as they find that separation is not that easy after a succession of runs. Their resolution results in greater need to escape from the abandonment depression through drugs and alcohol, as well as self-destructive behavior. Suicide attempts are largely a form of 'Russian Roulette' for depression relief and attention-getting; this behavior can become frequent, along with psychotic episodes under the influence of drugs, alcohol and acute stress, as separation fails.

The more highly resolved symbiotic borderline adolescents may in fact escape by finding someone to take care of them in a dependent situation much like their own family, but without the conflicting demands. The phone calls to mother will in all likelihood never cease and they will continue to regard her with mixed feelings. The symbiotic borderline, with the best chance of separating, often run afoul of the law because of their desperate attempt to escape and their somewhat sociopathic, omnipotent attitude.

BORDERLINE DEVELOPMENT AND INTERNALIZATION OF STRESS

The difficulty with viewing clinical symptoms exclusively is that borderline development can lead to an array of symptomatic behavior that can make differential diagnosis impossible. As Kernberg (1978) points out that one must look carefully at acting out in the adolescent, since behavior can have many possible meanings and significance. Acting out is a normal part of adolescence and any given behavior may be directed at normal rebellion, a result of peer group influence, or as a means of dealing with depression and family problems. It is not possible to treat the borderline adolescent only by treating the behavior; you must take into account their perception of acceptance and rejection, which in turn results in the behavior that reflects their resolution. Developing a therapeutic alliance that will offer support and confrontation is necessary before the adolescent will give up the acting out that serves an important defensive role in relieving abandonment depression.

The problem with the psychodynamic or intrapsychic approach to the borderline is that it is difficult to comprehend without considerable training and experience. And the fact is that the vast numbers of severely disturbed adolescents will always be dealt with exclusively by mental health professionals without this theoretical background. I would hope that an understanding of the two-factor model, as well as the other factors, would assist in understanding the intrapsychic structure.

AMBIVALENCE

The bordernline adolescent perceives ambivalent rejection from the parents—particularly the mother—which is split between the good feelings of acceptance (for regressive behavior) and the bad feelings of rejection (for independent behavior). The mother responds to the child in an ambivalent fashion during the separation-individuation stage and the child in turn responds with ambivalent clinging and distancing. This ambivalence is carried throughout adolescence both in terms of actual behavior and in terms of the ego structure being split into good (rewarding) and bad (withdrawing) parts as part of the primary defensive structure. The adolescent's perception of the parents is ambivalent in the sense that the "I-love-them, I-hate-them; they-love-me, they-hate-me" cycle changes almost daily in some cases.

The ambivalence and splitting phenomena occurs less dramatically at both the behavioral and intrapsychic levels in the Severe Rejection adolescent; the fear, paranoia, and perceptual view of rejection is much more consistent. This is usually reflected in the decreased ambivalent behavior, and in less defensive splitting of the ego structure. However, this does not necessarily mean that the ego is less pathological but only that it has less of a rewarding part so to speak.

INTRAPSYCHIC DEVELOPMENT

Two of the most influential proponents of the intrapsychic approach to treatment of the borderline adolescent have been Masterson (Masterson, 1972, 1976, 1978a, 1980; Masterson and Rinsley, 1975) and Kernberg (Kernberg, 1967, 1971, 1979). Much of the developmental basis for the theoretical work has come from the research of Mahler (1975, 1979b) and her empirical approach to mother and child relations during the first years of development. The authors disagree about the developmental stages at which the borderline problems emerge but agree on the primary causal factors.

The intrapsychic theory focuses on the differentiation of the self from external objects. This differentiation is for the most part developmentally complete at the end of the separation-individuation phase around 3 years of age (the age of 3 to 5 serves as a consolidation of the separation). It is this stage that is in theory disrupted in the borderline development so much so that the adolescent has a very poor differentiation between self and objects and a very inadequate identity.

The ego, or sense of self, develops through the slow, progressive differentiation of the self from the external objects and through defense mechanisms used to protect the ego (Jacobsen, 1964; Kernberg, 1971). There are four stages to this development (Mahler, 1975) which will be discussed in the next chapter: They are the Autistic, Symbiotic, Separation-Individuation, and On-the-way-to-Object-Constancy, as the final stage to the integrated ego state. A developmental failure along this continuum will result in an arrest of the differentiation of both the self and object representation (Masterson, 1978b).

Masterson (1978a) suggests that if the arrest occurred in the symbiotic phase, the self and object representation might be fused, such that the individual's ego defenses would be those of the psychotic: splitting, projection, very poor ego boundaries and reality testing and often delusions and hallucinations. The symbiotic borderline (Kernberg would call them narcissistic) in a sense never gets out of this stage of clinging to the mother and into separation, such that when separation occurs later the ego is not intact without the symbiotic closeness. If the arrest occurred in the separation-individuation phase, the self and object representations would be separate but split into a good and bad object and self-representations; this then is the borderline condition.

If the developmental arrest occurred during the 'On-the-way-to-Object-Constancy' the self and object representations would be separate and whole rather than split. In other words, both good and bad would be combined into one perception as opposed to the borderline structure where there are two parts that are either all good or all bad. At this later stage the ego defenses would be more mature than the usual borderline defense, such that repression would be the primary mechanism instead of splitting and projection. Likewise denial and acting out would be replaced by reaction formation and sublimation as defensive measures against stress.

INTERNALIZATION OF THE GOOD AND BAD MOTHER IMAGE

The borderline mother experiences satisfaction with caring for the infant at the autistic and symbiotic phase of development because it fulfills her own needs. There is a oneness between infant and mother. The developmental crisis begins when the child starts to behave in an ambivalent way toward her because of the unfolding drive for separation. The separation-individuation stage overlaps with the symbiotic stage, such that the child's behavior is ambivalent; needs for clinging and being dependent exist simultaneously with the drive for pushing away and distancing from her. The crisis really begins during the rapprochement subphase (Lax, Bach, and Burland, 1980) of separation-individuation when the mother responds with her own ambivalent behavior. The child needs her libidinal supplies in order to develop and grow psychologically, but is cut off if he does begin the separation process. Thus this becomes a repetitive cycle which generates anger that does not have an adequate means of being discharged (Masterson, 1976). The borderline adolescent then is unable to internalize anger and dissipate it through normal means; they must act it out or discharge it through self-destruction.

Thus there are two images of the mother internalized by the child; the good mother who rewards dependency and the bad mother who withdraws upon separation. The two images are represented by a withdrawing part consisting of aggressive energy and a rewarding part composed of libidinal or positive energy. These two parts remain separated from each other through the splitting defense; each part of the ego remains isolated. An extreme example of this might be a case of multiple personality, which represents this good and bad side (or multiple variations of them) as total personalities. The borderline adolescents will frequently have partially developed personalities that represent the same function. They may be more metaphorical representations, such as "eyes that watch me" or "voices that tell me to cut on myself," and so forth. They are not psychotic in the sense of hallucinations, but are representations of the stress of split-object relations.

When the child separates from the mother, fear results from

the withdrawal of libidinal supplies or acceptance. The mother reinforces those aspects of the child's behavior that allows him to cling to her, which then reduces his fear of the withdrawal of libidinal supplies. This sets the stage for the use of the key defense of denial of the reality of separation and perpetuates the wish for reunion with her (Masterson, 1976). While this temporarily relieves the feeling of depression and abandonment, the clinging and dependency may set up the feeling of engulfment—or the return to the symbiotic state—which forces a distancing reaction. When this happens other defense mechanisms, such as running away and self-destruction must be used to stem the feeling of depression.

The child's ego fails to develop, such that he must rely on the more primitive pleasure principle (Masterson, 1976, 1978a). To operate on the mature reality principle level would mean that he would have to accept the reality of separation. The ego of the adolescent borderline is split into the pathological pleasure ego and the reality ego; the former pursuing relief from the feelings of abandonment and the latter utilizing the reality principle. Here again we see the splitting of the adolescent's perception of the external world and the internal world—in other words, a disturbance in self representation and object relations. Anyone familiar with borderline adolescents knows that they can readily switch between the pathological pleasure principle and being the rational observer of their own behavior.

In essence then the borderline adolescents continue to feel comfortable as long as they are regressing or acting out under the control of the pathological ego. This scenario is played out in all avenues of their life; through the significant adults they come in contact with and in all close relationships. They are never more comfortable than when they are acting out in some self-destructive behavior that defends against depression.

The split-object relations can then be viewed as having two parts which originate in the relations with the mother. The withdrawing or aggressive part is attacking, critical, hostile, and withdrawing of libidinal supplies and approval in the face of assertiveness and separation. When this is predominant the borderline adolescents perceive themselves as being worthless, inadequate, helpless, guilty, and very empty—a veritable nonentity. This prompts feelings of anger, of being thwarted, all of which defend against abandonment depression. The rewarding or libidinal part offers approval, support, and acceptance for regressive and dependent behavior. When this is predominant the adolescent perceives himself as being the good, passive, and compliant child, which prompts feelings of warmth and gratification of the wish for reunion.

The splitting keeps the rewarding and withdrawing parts quite separate. This presents little problem to the adolescents in that they are able to generate little or no insight around the meaning of their own behavior and life is viewed as one large contradiction, in any case. If the withdrawing, rejecting part is in operation then as far as the borderline adolescent is concerned the parents are always rejecting. And, of course, when the accepting, rewarding part is present the parents are viewed as always being accepting. Many a mental health worker has been surprised at the sudden and dramatic shift in the adolescent's perception of the acceptance and rejection coming from the parents; no sooner were plans developed for an out-of-home placement when the adolescent decides they are going home. This same ambivalent relationship is transferred to the therapist; he is either perceived as the good parent or as the withdrawing, rejecting parent who receives rageful disdain.

Masterson (1978a) suggests that an alliance is formed between the child's rewarding part and the pathological pleasure ego; the primary purpose of which is to promote good feeling and to defend against abandonment associated with the withdrawing part. This alliance serves the purpose of promoting and channeling the discharge of aggression through regressive acting out. This is directed toward the withdrawing part by means of symptoms, inhibitions of perceptions associated with separation, and self-destructive acts. Actual physical separations from the parents are not necessary for the borderline development, but when they do occur they may solidify the pathology by activating the withdrawing part of the maternal image. Later when the adolescent experiences loss of loved objects this internal process may be quickly activated.

The rewarding part, which is pathological, becomes the borderline adolescent's primary defense against the feeling of abandonment and depression associated with the withdrawing part. They are faced with two alternatives: to feel bad and abandoned with the withdrawing part, or to feel good with the rewarding part at the cost of denial of reality and self-destructive behavior. Thus, whenever the withdrawing part is triggered an entire sequence of events may be set off that can be interpreted only in the context of the splitting defense and object relations.

NARCISSISTIC AND SYMBIOTIC BORDERLINE STRUCTURE

For the most part the terms narcissistic, as defined by Kernberg (1975), and symbiotic borderline, as I have used the term, may be used interchangeably. We are talking about the one component of the Low Rejection group where the symbiotic attachment has been strong and not merely the indulgent type of parenting. On the surface they appear more psychologically intact, which is quite misleading. The symbiotic borderline or narcissistic individual is emotionally at the symbiotic stage, as opposed to the later separation-individuation stage. One of the reasons for the strength or drive surrounding the running from home has to do with the symbiotic borderline's attempt to get into that separation stage. This was illustrated by a 15-year-old girl who was being treated in a residential program. She talked constantly about how much her mother rejected her and how she in turn hated her mother. When mother came to visit the girl tearfully climbed on to her lap and curled into the fetal position. Following this they went out together and had dinner, after which the girl ran from her mother and was picked up on an assault charge several months later.

Not all adolescents with borderline personality present a narcissistic structure. Kernberg states, "While all patients with narcissistic personality present an underlying borderline personality organizaton they do function much better than the usual borderline case" (Kernberg, 1978). According to Kernberg only the more severe narcissistic personalities present overtly borderline features such as a lack of impulse control, lack of anxiety tolerance, and a lack of the ability to sublimate desires and impulses. He defines narcissism as "character pathology characterized by pathological self-love and pathological internal relations with significant others centering around the presence of a pathological grandiose self." (Kernberg, 1978, p. 311). Their predominant defense operation consists of grandiosity, omnipotent control and devaluation. They have difficulty committing themselves to long-term goals or to any in depth human relationships. There is usually a disturbance in object relations which will determine how much underlying borderline pathology exists.

Kernberg (1978) also points out the paradox that the more apparently intact the narcissistic or symbiotic borderline adolescent appears to be, the more severe the narcissistic problem may be in terms of basic character structure. He suggests that part of the explanation lies in the fact that the narcissistic character structure is usually reinforced by some adaptive narcissistic features within the family structure, which may lead to the apparent "intactness" within that family structure. The Low Rejection adolescent is under minimal stress because of the lack of ambivalence within the family, and because his immmediate needs are met with less frustration. In keeping with this Low Rejection pattern, Kernberg (1978) also emphasizes the importance of the antisocial behavior of the narcissistic adolescent. He feels that its existence is a very negative prognostic sign for treatment, which is in keeping with the delinquent character of the Low Rejection pattern.

The symbiotic borderline and the narcissistic problem stem from the symbiotic period of development, at least in the more severe cases. The problem is that the child never emotionally left the symbiotic stage. Physical separations or lack of mothering during this stage would result in pathology during adolescence of severe proportions without the symbiotic attachment. The symbiotic borderline is still an extension of the mother's ego much more than any other type of borderline problem. The adolescent acts like the omnipotent infant struggling to free himself but yet needing the nurturance of the mother to survive. They are at once both highly vulnerable, as well as very strong and omnipotent, depending upon the closeness of the libidinal supplies. Not only does the adolescent act in an egocentric fashion related to the omnipotence and special status feelings, but he has failed to develop empathy for others which developmentally occurs during the separation-individuation process. If you combine this with using a delinquent style as a partial resolution and the panic reaction that may occur from the engulfment and striving for separation, you have the potential for very aggressive behavior.

I have observed two basic types of symbiotic styles from among the more severely disturbed adolescent population: There is the adolescent who has maintained close symbiotic ties with the mother, with no moves toward separation until early adolescence; A second type appears more fragile and disturbed because the withdrawing parents part is well exercised and very real as a threat. They had tried to move into the separation-individuation stage but had not been successful because they had been overwhelmed by the withdrawing part. Their perception of the parent is much more ambivalent but the symbiotic tie is very clear. In both types of symbiotic borderline there may have been a loss of the father during the period when the child would normally be consolidating the separation-individuation stage of development, which serves to reinforce the symbiotic tie with the mother.

Chapter 7

EARLY DEVELOPMENT AND SEVERE DISTURBANCES IN ADOLESCENCE

In this chapter we will explore some of the possible relationships between early development and severe disturbances of adolescence. This must of necessity be viewed as an insufficient job of covering a multitude of complex factors that are poorly understood at best. With my apology dutifully stated we will delve into the fascinating task of teasing out inferences from clinical data.

The information in this chapter is based largely on the sample of 150 severely disturbed adolescents in our study population. In addition to the clinical information and follow-up information after treatment, a study of the families was made including as much early development information as possible on each adolescent (Nielsen, Latham, Engle, 1979). I have tried to combine this with available literature on early development and arrived at some general statements clinicians can use as working hypotheses in the treatment of severely disturbed adolescents. The reader should understand that while many of the relationships between the early years and adolescent problems do seem clear, one cannot know from our study the number of adolescents with similar backgrounds who do not suffer from severe disturbances. Thus one should be cautious about taking a causal view. I doubt that there are psychological factors during early development that must inevitably lead to negative effects during adolescence. On the other hand, this scientific caution must be balanced against the fact that you do not find severely disturbed adolescents with satisfactory early development.

The assumption that the early years have a profound and lasting effect on the status of the adult is found throughout the literature (Thomas and Chess, 1980; Murphy and Moriarty, 1976). The importance of the preschool years as the formative basis of the adult is inculcated in the history of western thinking (Clarke and Clarke, 1976). It was Freud's view (1949) that the neuroses were entirely formed before the age of 6 even though their effects may not show up until many years later. This is the one area where psychoanalytic and learning theories agree, since both are based on a deterministic view of behavior. The intellectual impact of both these theoretical points of view has been profound yet surprisingly little has been done beyond the analyst's couch to trace the later impact of the early years (Levy, 1941).

The study by John Bowlby (1951) for the World Health Organization has had a great impact on our notion that early development leaves an indelible mark on our psychological well-being. In a more recent work Bowlby (1969, 1973, 1980) has elaborated a theory through studies of the effects of attachment and separation and concluded that the loss of the mother figure can generate psychopathology in adult life. The impact of this rather simple notion has been quite profound on all levels of treatment of children. It has paralleled the broader theoretical notions of Erikson (1950) and his emphasis upon the development of trust as the building block of later psychological development.

Every trend seems to have its countertrends and the field of early development is no exception. More recent authors have challenged the notion that maternal deprivation and early trauma is instrumental in leading to psychological problems in adults (Rutter, 1972; Thomas and Chess, 1977; Kagen, 1978). These studies have shown that there is no simple and direct correlation between the quality of early development and later status as an adult. There does not seem to be any highly significant pattern that emerges from correlational type follow-up studies. Thomas and Chess (1980) have also pointed out that our psychodynamic developmental concepts have made it possible to relate later behavior with early development even when the two, on the face of it, appear to be dissimilar. Such continuity over time can be guaranteed by simply interpreting behavior that is opposite as a reaction against earlier influences. Since clinical analysis of an adolescent or adult is always retrospective this is a valid consideration.

Rutter (1972) reviewed the literature and concluded that there were considerable individual differences in response to any early environmental or maternal deprivation. Other studies have also shown that predicting later behavior from any particular set of early development factors is a risky business. MacFarlane (1964) found that many of the most competent and apparently psychologically healthy adults had backgrounds that were very negative and troubled. Based on the analysis of the Fels Longitudinal Study data, Kagen (1976) concluded that there was little correlation between the mother's treatment of the child during the first 3 years and the psychological status during adolescence or adulthood. Vaillant (1977) concluded from the Harvard Grant Study that successful adult status could not be predicted from an unhappy childhood. It is clear that a simple linear prediction from early childhood to adolescence is questionable. Thomas and Chess (1980) state the matter succinctly:

> It should be no surprise that the research data from many sources converge to discredit the concept that the child's early life fixes decisively the course of his subsequent psychological development. Interactionists' theory postulates that behavioral characteristics can change at any age period, and even change qualitatively, if a significant change in organism or environment alters the dynamics of the developmental process. The unique capacity of the human brain for learning and for plasticity in developmental pathways would be wasted if the individual's potential for mastery and adaptation were frozen, or even severely limited, by his early life experiences (p. 107).

Our inability to make accurate predictions about later personality in no way negates the importance of those years of early development. To say that we could predict accurately would be to say that the other factors in our holographic model were of no importance in determining the outcome.

HOLOGRAPHIC CONSIDERATION

The holographic concept means that each of several factors in determining the outcome of the individual carries with it, in some small way, a prediction of final outcome and the probability that certain things will be true about those other factors. This is particularly true, I suspect, of the early development factor. For example, certain negative factors in early development will most likely be true in situations where the family pattern is disrupted and rejecting, which will lead the adolescent to perceive Severe Rejection; where a certain early resolution of the stress will be forced. This means that you cannot predict the status of an individual as an adolescent until you know all four factors and not just early development. It also explains why prediction from any one of these factors alone must be low in correlational value.

EARLY DEVELOPMENTAL FACTORS

Early physical separation from a parent occurs in the majority (80%) of adolescents experiencing severe emotional problems. When actual separations have not occurred one should be suspicious of the threat of abandonment and a lack of libidinal supplies as being a factor in a borderline situation. As Bowlby (1973) has suggested, the psychoanalytic school has paid scant attention to the separation-anxiety phenomena. The fact that a child becomes upset when the attachment figure leaves has never been accepted at face value by psychological theorists (Fairbairn, 1954).

Bowlby's theory is that separation from the attachment figure (the mother) is in and of itself threatening and anxiety-producing. When the child is separated from the attachment figure unwillingly he shows signs of distress and the behavior follows a typical pattern. First, there is a protest of a vigorous sort and the child tries to recover the lost figure. This turns into despair and withdrawal, but he remains vigilant for the mother's return and seemingly preoccupied with her absence. Later still, he seems to lose interest in the mother and to become emotionally detached from her. If the period of separation is not too long this attachment is easily renewed. After he is reunited with the attachment figure he exhibits intense anxiety at any real or imagined threat of losing her again. From this point on the threat of separation or abandonment becomes of critical importance in the child's development.

The psychological effects of prolonged separation from attachment figures, fear of abandonment, and feelings of rejection are deep and play a role in our later behavior. Perhaps they are feelings that those of us who have not experienced cannot fully comprehend. The contemporary writer, William Saroyan (1976), wrote about his own early childhood separation and the later effects this had on him. His father died when he was 3 and his mother left him at an orphanage at the age of 5 because she could not care for him any longer. He describes the experience as follows:

> . . . soon after Takoohi Saroyan had taken me to that place and then in accordance with staff instructions had taken me to a small room in which to negotiate the separation. I began to cry and she said, "No, you are a man now, and men do not cry." So I stopped crying . . . (p. 22–23)

Saroyan describes the rage he felt after the separation and sums it up when writing about his role as a father. He considers the relationship between his early experiences and his own later behavior as he describes coming across a tape recording made many years earlier when he was with his young children.

> I was abashed by the monster I had clearly been . . . I sounded insensitive to them, and yet, this is the terrible and puzzling thing, I had been full of nothing but profound love, easy intelligence, abundant comedy, enormous health—and yet, unmistakably a monster. (p. 199)

I believe these excerpts describe the feelings that can be associated with early traumatic separation and how the effects can be carried with us, perhaps latent, and passed on to the next generation. But let us consider that in any longitudinal study of the effects of early development, William Saroyan would be considered as one who suffered no ill effects.

For me the pursuit of clinically useful information about early development has been reminiscent of a fascinating Sherlock Holmes mystery. In sifting through data and comparing them to later behavior patterns of adolescents I know from psychotherapy and family sessions, one begins to get a picture of what can happen. As long as you keep in mind that early development is not strictly causal and that there are three other critical factors in the holographic model, it is possible to appreciate the impact it can make. Clearly its effects are not random, but fall into predictable clinical patterns and later effects on the psychological status of the adolescent.

When I refer to physical separations I ordinarily mean prolonged separations from one or both parents. Bowlby and others have put the total emphasis on the separation from the mother and not from the father, which I do not believe is clinically justifiable. The absence of the father is interpreted by the child as a threat of abandonment of the mother and thus increases behavioral disturbances and the child's sensitivity to separation. In many cases there is a change in the mother's parenting behavior after the separation from the father, which combines with the child's heightened sensitivity to change in the immediate environment.

In our sample of severely disturbed adolescents there were no apparent separations from either parent in approximately 20 percent of the cases before the age of 6. As might be expected the cases without the separations tended to be the more accepting and more borderline family situations. It was clear that fear of abandonment and loss was a real factor for the adolescent. What we could not measure in the borderline cases was the frequency of brief separations preceded by arguments, fights, threats to abandon and then short separations. The child would have heightened anxiety and fear of loss, but never be allowed any resolution of the separation because of its brevity.

I have been fascinated by the data from the first year of life.

This of course is a risky proposition because of all the later compounding factors that have occurred in the life of the severely disturbed adolescent. However, I have been struck by the uniqueness of those adolescents who have had significant psychological trauma during this period. I am reminded of descriptions of infants who have been institutionalized (Provence and Lipton, 1962). In many instances it seems that psychological disruption during the latter part of the first year left such a profound impact on the individual that even relatively positive factors in other areas could not alter the damage. There is no other single impact on the individual that seems to carry this kind of broad effect.

Provence and Lipton (1962) noted that toward the end of the first year the institutional infants would no longer seek out adults for play or even to meet their basic needs. There did not seem to be any anticipation that their needs were going to be met. Even where some attachment to an adult did exist there was still considerable tenuousness and minimum emotional investment in the presence or absence of that adult. In a follow-up of institutional infants placed in foster homes between 18 and 24 months of age, they reported obvious improvements; however, they were impressed with impairments of certain aspects of development, such as modes of thought, learning, and emotional development. Their relationship with adults remained tenuous with impoverished emotional behavior that was described as bland. Even after months in the foster home, utilization of the mother as a source of comfort, as a relief from tension, or as a source of help in problem-solving remained quite impaired. Goldfarb (1945) also noted the superficiality of relationships in adolescents who had inadequate parental care or institutionalization during the early years.

It is the quality of the maternal care and the age at which separation from the parent occurs (or other psychological trauma) that determines in large part the later effect. It is probably correct to speak of an optimum level of stimulation that must be maintained within certain limits for each child. It is up to the mother to become so symbiotic with the infant that she is aware of the subtle cues as to the need and discomfort of the infant; too much stimulation can certainly have negative effects, forcing the infant to withdraw from the stimulating object. This can be termed as communicative matching between mother and infant (Mahler, 1975).

Wallerstein and Kelly (1980), in their follow-up of children separated by divorce, concluded that the impact seemed to show up as a generalized depression. "Hardly a child of divorce we came to know did not cling to the fantasy of a magical reconsiliation between his parents." After 5 years, 34 percent of the children and adolescents appeared to be doing especially well psychologically. These children were noted by their sense of self-sufficiency and the fact that they still had frequent contact and support from both parents. Twenty-nine percent of the children were in the middle range of psychological health. While functioning normally in most areas, there was a definite lack of self-esteem and anger present. Another one-third of the youngsters were intensely unhappy and having moderate to severe depression in their lives. One predictor of a successful outcome was having a father who was still very involved and the availability of frequent and flexible visiting rights. The father who had abandoned his family always left behind children who were very depressed and who had very low self-esteem. The authors conclude, "the father's presence kept the child from a worrisome concern with abandonment and total rejection and from the nagging self-doubts that follow such worry." Age was not reported as being a significant factor in the follow-up, although nearly all of their samples were in latency age period at the time of the separation. This is interesting in light of the fact that separations at that stage rarely occur among severely disturbed adolescents. I would conclude from this that their results might have been much more negative had the parental separations occurred earlier, at more critical stages.

Because of limitations of space and scope of this chapter I am giving scant attention to predisposition, or as some authors (Thomas and Chess, 1980) have termed it, "termperament of the child." It has been suggested that the child is born with certain characteristics or predispositions toward behaving in certain ways and to respond to environmental and parenting input in unique fashion. In our study of severely disturbed adolescents a factor that I term "sensitivity of the organism" seemed to be significant. There appeared to be higher frequency of such things as soft neurological signs, birth difficulties, anoxia at birth, learning disabilities, asthma, allergies and so on. Although this is certainly not indicative of any causative interpretation, I prefer to view severely disturbed adolescents as being more likely to be sensitive to environmental impact.

Toward a Framework of Early Development

The work of Margaret Mahler (1975, 1979b) offers us a developmental model that combines observational, empirical and theoretical data that can assist us in clinical tasks. In this section I have briefly outlined the first three years of development according to this model.

The Normal Autistic Phase

The newborn is wrapped in a cocoon as a closed psychological system that need not depend on the immediate environment for needs other than physical. The infant remains somewhat protected from extreme stimulation or the lack of it and is brought out of this phase by what Ribble (1943) has called "mothering." It seems that the infant can remain, in many respects, at this autistic phase through a lack of proper nurturing and stimulation.

The Beginning Symbiotic Phase

The beginning of personality development may be said to start with the symbiotic phase. It is also the beginning of what Bowlby calls the attachment stage. The symbiotic phase is, in many respects, the most critical of all early development because of effects from over-stimulation and not allowing separation to begin.

The infant moves from homeostasis to the differentiation between good quality feelings and unpleasantness in relation to his environment and, in particular, to the mother. From the second month on there is a dim awareness of the need-satisfying mother and thus the beginning of the phase of symbiosis. It is this phase where it may be said that the infant and the mother act as one omnipotent system. The autistic shell has cracked and the phase of complete attachment has begun. This symbiotic stage is a critical building block or foundation for all later development. The infant remains in a hypersensitive state (Benjamin, 1961) to environmental input or the converse, the lack of stimulation. Either extreme will force the infant into some early coping response (resolution) that may have profound later consequences.

The essential feature of this stage is an omnipotent fusion with the representation of the mother as one entity with the infant. According to Mahler this is the state to which the ego regresses in cases of the most severe disturbances of individuation and psychotic disorganization. During the second and third month of life, the need for total sensory contact with the attachment figure is of primary importance to development and setting the stage for differentiation from the mother, which comes at the later separation-individuation stage of development.

Homeostasis is a key factor in understanding the process that goes on between the infant and the attachment figure. There are several conflicting patterns going on at the same time and the balance between them must be maintained by the attachment figure receiving and interpreting behavioral cues from the infant. The infant struggles for attachment and symbiosis with the mother, while internalizing psychological features of the mother (good and bad), and being conditioned to respond to her as a source of need fulfillment. The mother must select when to respond, when to allow the symbiotic behavior and need fulfillment, and when to demand separation of the infant.

The First Subphase: Differentiation and Development of Body Image

At about 4 or 5 months of age, the peak of symbiosis with the mother, the first stage of separation-individuation begins. During the symbiotic months the infant has familiarized himself with the mothering half of his symbiotic self. From about 7 or 8 months there is a visual pattern of checking back with the mother, which is a sign of differentiation. There are many reasons why the onset may be delayed and the infant stays in the symbiotic relationship with the mother for a longer than usual period. The symbiotic borderline has never left this period of development in a sense. Mahler cites an example of a young girl whose mother responded to her mechanically by rocking her without apparent interest. At an age when other children take an even more active interest in their mothers, she turned auto-erotically back to her own body. She indulged in rocking rather than distancing or approach behavior. In another case an infant with a very depressed mother was simply slow in developing because of the lack of interaction and stimulation. In the case of the mother who was unpredictable in her responses to her infant, there was an early adaptive ability or a forced resolution in that he developed greater distance and autonomy.

By the end of the first year separation-individuation has two intertwined developmental tracks that may proceed at different rates. One is individuation, the evolution of the intrapsychic autonomy, perception, memory, cognition and reality testing; the other is the development of separation that runs along the track of differentiation, distancing, boundary formation and disengagement from the mother. All of these structural processes will eventually culminate the internalized self-images, as distinct from internalized representations of other objects. In a real sense then the child's self-image and separation should be well underway at this point and have layed the framework for all future development. Disturbances in the symbiotic relationship phase can be seen as setting the stage for disturbed separation either because the symbiotic attachment is maintained or because a premature distancing and coping resolution was forced upon the child.

The Second Subphase: Practicing

The stage in Mahler's scheme of development that completes the first year is the practicing subphase which continues well into the second year of life. It can be divided into the early crawling period and the upright walking period of the second year. There are three developments that contribute to this period: rapid body differentiation from the mother; an established specific bond with her; and growth and functioning of the autonomous ego apparatus in close proximity to the mother.

The infant separates from the mother at a distance that

allows for moving, exploring at some physical distance from her while feeling comfortable. During this early practicing subphase, following the initial push and pull away from mother into the outside world, most children seem to go through a brief period of separation anxiety. At the end of the first year the exploration of the world begins in earnest. The child must have total trust in the mother, that she will be there when needed.

During this period there is a longing for closeness with the mother when separation anxiety has been aroused through the practicing process. Mahler has noted that this longing for a state of well-being and unity with the mother was lacking in children whose symbiotic relationship had been unduly prolonged or had otherwise been disturbed. It seemed diminished and irregular in children in whom the symbiotic relationship was marred by the unpredictability and impulsivity of a partly engulfing and partly rejecting mother.

The Third Subphase: Rapprochement

In this final stage of the "hatching process" the child reaches the first level of identity—that of being a separate individual (Lax, Bach & Burland, 1980). There is a need for optimum emotional availability during this period because he is aware of his mother's presence or absence. The need for closeness has been held somewhat in abeyance during the practicing period and now reverses itself. The mother must accept the child's ambivalence toward her and the role of the father takes on an increased importance in moderating the relationship between child and mother and directing the child toward the reality of the outer world.

The refueling type of bodily approach that has characterized the practicing period is replaced during the period of 15 to 24 months by the deliberate search for, or avoidance of, intimate bodily contact. There is much darting away and warding off of engulfment during this time. The fear of losing the love object (mother) should be in evidence instead of the fear of object loss. The child fights giving up the omnipotence and the separation through fights with the mother, which leadstotherapprochement crisis.

The Rapprochement Crisis: 20 to 24 Months

During the rapprochement crisis there is a renewed concern for the whereabouts of the mother amidst a newfound independence and individuation. Most children with appropriate earlier development have a sense of object permanence and can realize that mother could be elsewhere and still return. It is significant that this stage produces a widening range of emotional behavior and what might be regarded as the beginning of empathy; a characteristic that is usually diminished in the borderline adolescent.

By 21 months of age, rapprochement problems have diminished and there is an optimal distance established from mother. While the fear of object loss and abandonment is partly relieved at this stage, it is also complicated by internalization of parental demands, which may be considered as the beginning of the superego development. Under normal circumstances, the child becomes very sensitive to approval and disapproval of the parents and fearful of losing the object's love.

The Fourth Subphase: Consolidation of Individuality and Emotional Object Constancy

This phase covers the entire third year of life, where the previous two years are consolidated and the result will be a stabilized sense of self. The development of emotional object constancy is a complex process involving all aspects of psychological development. The essential prior determinants are trust and confidence through the regularly occurring relief of need-tension provided by the need-satisfaction from the mother. According to Mahler this satisfying of need states is gradually attributed to the whole object (mother) and is then transferred by means of internalization to the intrapsychic representation of the mother. It is only during this third year after object constancy is well on its way that the mother can be substituted for during her absence by the presence of a reliable internal image. Mahler feels that the presence of intense libidinal and aggressive ties to the object may make for more rapid and less fixed attainment of a permanent representation of a permanent object. The process of emotional object constancy is still so fluid in the 3 year-old that it is reversible.

The well-adjusted child in the third year of life can sustain most separations from the mother with a simple explanation of her whereabouts. They will have a sound and satisfying inner image of her and an intrapsychic representation which is positive and invested with confidence. This permits autonomous ego-functioning despite some slight distress and longing for the mother. Even this cannot be maintained, though, if some shock or separation trauma occurs at this age.

During this stage in the borderline child we are already seeing splitting into "good" and "bad" external objects. They show little capacity for self-regulation and self-esteem which stems from their perception of themselves as a separate, positive object. They will act out aggressively toward the mother in order to get her to act as an external ego, as was the case during symbiosis. The moderating function of the child's own ego has not been allowed to develop because of engulfment, or by distancing of the mother from the infant.

Toward a Clinical Interpretation: Seven Phases of Development

In this section I will be discussing the development of the severely disturbed adolescent in terms of 7 phases. I find it useful as a clinician to review the adolescent's development and general history in terms of specific age periods, which helps focus on the needs of the individual during that developmental period, and the external factors that were taking place. My comments represent the accumulation of clinical data from the large number of cases I have studied. Trying to relate the effects of factors during early development to later pathology in adolescence is a risky business, at best, but one where some conclusions are warranted and the rewards are rich for the therapist.

I. Birth to Six Months

The most obvious problem during this beginning phase after birth has to do with a lack of nurturing and care from the mother.

Physical separations from the mother may in and of themselves be of minimal importance for later development, provided the attachment or symbiotic phase is not delayed beyond this period and that there is reasonable substitute care. In our study sample approximately 29 percent had separations from a parent during this stage, but only a few were from the primary attachment figure. Separations at this stage seemed to signal that things were going to get worse, with more separations to follow that would have a profound effect. Problems at this stage can be divided into two basic types: those that prevent the attachment or symbiotic process from beginning, and those that stem from a general lack of proper care and nurturance.

II. Six to Twelve Months

This is the first stage where a separation from the parent, per se, has a definite effect. Separations during the latter part of the first year seem to have the potential for creating long-term profound problems for the adolescent, more than any other single period of development. Erikson (1950, 1974) suggested that by the end of the first year the child has developed the capacity to trust others; the most basic and profoundly reaching of human abilities. It would seem that it is just this ability which is absent in those adolescents who have suffered an extended separation or disruption from the mother figure at this time (see cases #2 and #4). For the most part, this group can be said to be failures in treatment and are usually classified as Severe or Total Rejection cases. It seems quite likely that the parent would be inclined to respond to this child with rather cold indifference commensurate with what they might well receive from the child who has experienced this failure of development.

Separations or other severe psychological disruption of development at Phase II may force a premature and very pathological resolution in the child. Bowlby refers to this when he talks about the child going through a series of stages when reacting to the loss of the maternal figure: fear, anger, striving to retrieve the lost object, and then despair and resignation. It is the resignation that forces a coping mechanism that in a sense rules out depending on adult figures for libidinal supplies and warmth. Such adolescents may well be disguised because of adequate later development, but they also have a flaw in their relationships with others. Their perception of the world is predominated by fear, paranoia and a lack of relationships on a trusting basis.

These adolescents are ordinarily not borderline because it was the symbiotic phase that was disrupted not the separation-individuation phase. Depression comes about largely as a result of having resources cut off and because they are thwarted in some way not out of abandonment-fear. When confronted with their behavior and the destructive quality, they may project it back to the therapist as anger.

The majority of the cases I have dealt with at this stage have involved adolescents having committed some sexual offense. The degree of fear and general ineptness was so great that the attack usually occurred against children or older individuals who offered little threat of retaliation. To some degree we are talking about the same adolescents that were discussed under the Severe Rejection group, where the association between sexual aggression and rejection from the mother was made. The firesetting group with the same rejection pattern are less likely to have the Phase II developmental disruption.

III. Twelve to Twenty-Four Months

The child goes from close physical proximity and attachment to being ambulatory and well into the separation-individuation phase of development. The foundation of all later emotional development has been established. Physical separations that occur between the ages of 12 and 18 months, may be of minimal significance for later development, providing they are not of long duration. This is based on the fact that they do not occur with great frequency among severely disturbed adolescents. This corresponds to Mahler's developmental scheme as being a period between two critical stages.

The period of time between 18 and 24 months is more critical in that a high proportion of the more severely disturbed adolescents have had parenting disruptions and separations occurring during this period. I am talking about separations from either parent because the role of the father has taken on greater importance for the child in terms of aiding in the separation process from the mother. The loss of the father figure at this point can have profound effects because it emphasizes fear of abandonment and loss of the maternal figure. The depression appears to be much deeper and more persistent than the more cyclical borderline qualities of later developmental disruption.

IV. Twenty-Four to Thirty-Six Months

Physical separations from parents are quite common at this stage because of the stresses created by the demands of parenting. The father becomes critical because he must act as a support system and moderator for both mother and child, as well as assisting in the separation process from the mother. The father leaving the family is in some respects as potentially damaging to the child as the loss of the mother at earlier stages. The child is old enough to realize the loss and it tends to reinforce any abandonment fear that the mother could just as readily disappear. Thus the loss of the father tends to increase symbiotic clinging. The mother may react negatively to the separation from the father by reacting ambivalently toward the child. As a general rule, anytime there is a physical separation from either parent during the developmental stage, between 2 and 3 years, I would suspect that borderline characteristics are involved.

Most children can survive separation at this age providing previous developmental periods have been satisfactory and the remaining parent performs in a satisfactory manner. When the adolescent presents severe disturbances and has a separation at this age it suggests that the physical separation was compounded by failure of adequate separation-individuation development.

V. Three to Five Years

By the age of 3 the separation process—in the sense of ego identity as a separate and independent being—should have been formed. By the age of 5 that development should have been consolidated so that the basic personality is complete. It is rare to find a severely disturbed adolescent who has not had some major psychological trauma, abuse or separation before that age. If there is not a problem of separation prior to this phase, later physical separations may have little effect. It would more than likely be classified as psychoneurotic centering around a failure to deal with developmental fears and anxieties.

Masterson* is of the opinion that separations from the mother that occur after the age of 3 can seriously affect the borderline problem to such an extent that abandonment depression may not be treatable. As such, the separations that occur even after 5 years of age will have a negative impact far beyond what they might otherwise have. Separations prior to the age of 3 will increase the likelihood of severe character disorders that will force some early and undesirable resolution.

Problems originating at this stage will result in a degree of internalization of fear and anxiety that could otherwise be coped with effectively. The child should have normal object relations, unlike the borderline, and would comprehend the loss of the parent. They may be angry, fearful, anxious and depressed, but it tends to be something that can be resolved without serious pathology.

VI. Six to Eleven Years

This is a period of consolidation called the latency period— in preparation for the demands of approaching adolescence and a respite from earlier stressful development. It is truly the period of childhood and creative play symbolic of later adult demands. In severely disturbed adolescents it is not common to find separation from parents during this period of time. When they do occur they are of little significance relative to other developmental periods.

As we have previously discussed, the borderline individual ordinarily does not exhibit overt behavior problems during the latency period. There is no separation stress during this period, unlike the preceding and following stages. The borderline child does manage to get attention from the parent by being dependent and responsible within the family. This is not the case with the more rejected child who may behave in a manner to attract

*   Personal Communication with Dr. James Masterson.

attention and to punish the parent indirectly by such acts as firesetting. Problems during this stage are usually school related, peer related or acts of retaliation to severe rejection.

VII. Eleven to Thirteen Years

The final period of development before adolescence is roughly between 11 and 13 when rapid growth and a renewed motivation for separation and independence begins. This period of development is comparable in some of its demands to stages 3 and 4 because they have to do with problems of emancipation from the parental figures. In this sense, then, both the first year of life and the latency period can be seen as preparation for stressful periods to follow. It is apparent that most severe problems of adolescence become critical or more overt in the beginning of stage 7. The demands for emancipation may either provoke a striving for immediate distancing or fearful clinging.

The importance of this stage is examplified by the typical individuals with borderline characteristics. They go through the latency period anxious but submissive for the most part waiting for the time when they "grow up" and can get out of the home. When they reach period 7, the first signs of sexual development, they may see nothing inconsistent about running from the family to live independently. The sexual development of the female at early adolescence is particularly disturbing to the parents who have not dealt with their own adolescence effectively. The child who was in effect told to get lost during latency is now finding all sorts of limits and rules laid down by the parents who are telling them they cannot now be trusted.

An adolescent with an otherwise satisfactory development can have serious ambivalence, some acting out, and problems of emancipation, resulting from this period of development. But the more borderline or severely disturbed adolescent must also have had physical separations or other parenting problems during the earlier years. Ordinarily problems that have their origin during the preadolescent stage tend to be of a transitory nature and are readily treated.

Chapter 8

RESOLUTION

Acting Out, Aggression, and the Defensive Structure of the Adolescent

In this chapter I will be discussing the adolescent's resolution to the problem which is the last factor in the holographic model. The model can be stated thus: A combination of developmental factors and parenting produce the adolescent's perception of acceptance and rejection, which in turn results in a degree of conflict and stress. It is this stress that must be dealt with through some defensive structure that constitutes the resolution. Thus resolution, the culmination of the three earlier influences, can refer to such diverse symptomology as aggression, defense mechanisms and any internalized or externalized method of defending against depression.

Why put such a diverse group of behaviors and symptoms under one category? Because it is just this diversity that comprises the adolescent's defense structure and will determine to what extent he is amenable to treatment. Psychotherapy then may be viewed as offering the adolescent a supportive relationship so that he can reconstruct his own resolution into a less destructive pattern or accept a resolution that the therapist offers. We can say that a highly resolved (or highly defended if you prefer) adolescent is not going to be receptive to therapeutic offerings. This is why we speak of confrontation as a form of therapy to penetrate the defenses masking the borderline adolescent's depression. If you can penetrate that defense you render the individual receptive to what you might offer.

Resolution refers in part to a wide variety of behavior that we may see directly yet we often do not interpret it in the context of the psychodynamics of the adolescent. We may attempt to modify the behavior by establishing consequences, but fail to take into account the role that the behavior might serve for the individual as a means of acting out the stress and as a defensive structure. If it is secondary to the primary defense mode the rearrangement of the environmental contingencies may indeed modify the behavior. However, if you are trying to shut off the primary means of expression, then you would probably achieve symptom substitution or produce an eventual explosion in some form of acting out. This model neither negates nor supports environmental management, but merely suggests that it must be put in perspective. Substance abuse, for example, might serve the purpose of acting out to defend against abandonment depression, in which case no amount of contingency management will be successful, or it might be a secondary hedonistically oriented behavior in which case it can more likely be modified.

I should briefly mention the term resolution in the context of psychiatric diagnostic labels. Most categories of diagnosis are based on a description of a number of symptoms that the individual is judged to possess. The borderline personality diagnosis is of course, an exception when the determination is based upon intrapsychic structure and not on clinical descriptive material. Basing a diagnosis strictly on behavior can lead to a very mistaken picture of what is going on with the adolescent. For example, what does delinquent behavior mean? Obviously it could serve a variety of purposes such as a means of acting out the stress of rejection or it could be the result of modeling within the family and the indulgent parenting pattern. Clearly a sociopathic label is inappropriate if the adolescent is primarily acting out against depression, but it might be appropriate under other circumstances.

In previous sections of this book we have discussed various

manifestations of this stress in terms of the borderline adolescent's defensive structure, such as projection, denial and distortions of perceptions. The borderline may be receptive to therapy because they must rely heavily on such defensive mechanisms as their primary form of resolution. As such they may not be terribly well defended and the depression can be reached by the therapist. In this chapter I will devote the discussion more to other types of acting out and stronger resolutions, such as severe aggression. But because aggression on the surface appears to be so different from other defensive measures, one should be cautious not to lose sight of the fact that they are all methods of defending against or ventilating stress and conflict. The fact that one type of defensive measure or stress reduction behavior will be chosen over another has to do with the nature of the other factors in the holographic model.

The idea of conceptualizing all forms of acting out and defensive behavior under the term "resolution" was slow in developing. It began from my trying to understand the differences between types of borderline adolescents. There was the Ambivalent Rejection adolescent that I began to refer to as being like "silly putty" because their defenses were relatively easy to penetrate and shape therapeutically. Their defense structure consisted of such things as drug abuse, sexual acting out or the distortion of reality.

There was yet another type of borderline adolescent that I began to think of in terms of an "eggshell" defense that was much firmer and more resolved. Yet they were vulnerable inside and the outer shell was seemingly brittle. This adolescent would reflect all but the most penetrating of confrontations and seemed capable of reforming the shell rather rapidly to protect the deep depression inside. The ventilation of the stress that occurred in such a case would be in the form of projection and anger toward others, as though to deflect the entire situaton away from themselves and their vulnerability. This projection would at times take the form of aggression and striking out at others, although not ordinarily of a severe nature.

Still a third form of resolution that I found puzzling was the more psychopathic adolescent. This individual was obviously so well defended that not even the depression was in evidence as it was in the borderline condition. It was as though the eggshell had become hardboiled or that the structure had been sealed off. In any case, if it could be said that abandonment depression existed it was certainly not in evidence. Confrontation would be met with indifference or projection back at the immediate environment. To further confuse the issue there was the fact that the behavior did not always correspond to the degree of resolution. The psychopathic adolescent, for example, depending on when in development the resolution was formed, seemed to be under little or no stress except as the immediate environment became frustrating. As such there might be little stress to be ventilated and little acting out. The fact that the individual was psychopathic might never show up unless a particular set of frustrating circumstances was created. I took to conceptualizing the psychopathic individual as possessing a strong shell-like resolution that would allow for easy passage out of the stress, to the extent that it existed, but no entry in by those attempting to confront.

In order to make a determination of the resolution of severely disturbed adolescents, we need to ask ourselves several questions with regard to their behavior and how they respond to a situation where they are confronted. First of all, we should ask what purpose their acting out serves given the probable degree of stress that has resulted from their particular history. Second, what is the nature and strength of their resolution that must both contain the stress and allow for ventilation when the pressure is excessive? A strong resolution that covers great depression may result in infrequent but violent explosions. This would account for the apparent paradox that it is the adolescents who appear to be the most "intact" (highly resolved) who commit the most serious aggressive acts. A weaker resolution that allows for frequent ventilation will be less likely to result in serious aggressive acting out.

Behavior that appears to be similar may be quite different from a clinical standpoint. Suicide attempts, for example, may represent a strong resolution or drive to solve the stress, preceded by a period of relative calm intellectual processing (this does not necessarily mean it is rational) before the act itself. Once the strong resolution has been made there is relatively little need to act out in some other manner. Such adolescents would present themselves as being depressed, but probably not to the extent that the highly conflictual adolescents are who cut on themselves at peak stress periods. The latter self-destructive act represents a breakdown of the defensive structure and a lack of a strong resolution to deal with the conflict.

The clinician should ask whether the adolescents believe they have the answer to the problem and if so what is the nature of that resolution. Are they acting out indiscriminately? Or is it more solidly formed and therefore more difficult to penetrate therapeutically? In other words, how much of a shell have they constructed around themselves? The therapist should keep in mind that when they do confront a poorly formed resolution the result will be depression. The highly resolved adolescents, on the other hand, may have such a firm shell around themselves that they bounce the confrontation back, projected as anger, as with the psychopathic adolescents.

The two-factor model of acceptance and rejection suggests that the ambivalent-borderline condition will produce great stress, forcing the adolescent to frequently act out in some way. At the same time, the nature of the conflicting ambivalent situation is such that forming a firm resolution is made difficult. Their energies are usually centered around intrapsychic factors in search of something beyond the temporary acting-out behavior they have relied upon. The more resolved, symbiotic, Low Rejection adolescents will appear to be under less stress until their resolution is threatened.

For the more unresolved borderline, running is a way of avoiding depression. It is the process of being on the move that is important rather than actually separating from the family. As one girl put it, "Even if I ran to the North Pole, the first thing I would do is look for a phone to call home." Running for the resolved borderline, on the other hand, is more likely to be an attempt to actually separate and become independent.

As long as there is a shell of defensive behavior they will be unable to accept a therapeutic resolution. This means that the 13-year-olds may have to spend time trying out their independence before they will be undefended enough to be open to treatment. It has been my experience that the 16-year-olds are easier to treat than the younger adolescent who has less experience.

ACTING OUT

Observers of adolescent behavior are in agreement regarding the predisposition toward impatience with restriction, independence of action, gregariousness, recklessness, irritability and more potentially serious forms of behavior (Dollard, Miller, Doob, Mowrer and Sears, 1939; Offer, 1979; Blos, 1979; Robins, 1966; Abt and Weissman, 1976). With the onset of adolescence there is increased sex hormone activity and striving for the achievement of separation and independence. These activities suffer from some interference from society, which can lead to frustration and aggression. One of the functions of society is not only to control the acting out but to offer substitute behaviors. To the extent that these are not readily available, the adolescent will select among alternatives. Severely disturbed adolescents are noted for having few normal adolescent activities in which they participate, such that they have developed few accepted ways of acting out.

Buhler (1933) demonstrated that in a group of girls ranging in ages from 9 to 17 the greatest percentage who expressed negative feelings toward their families occurred among 13-year-olds. The percentage of those having negative social relations with their family increased steadily from ages 9 to 13 and then decreased at the same rate to age 17. Ackerson (1931) looked at several thousand cases of delinquents and found that the peak age for those judged to have personality and conduct problems was 14 years. Interestingly enough, there were no more cases of 17-year-old youths reported than there were 5-year-old children. Likewise, the most frequent age for referral to a treatment program for adolescents is 14 years. Sollenberger (1938) observed the behavior of adolescent males between the ages of 13 and 16 over a period of 6 months and rated their aggression. He determined male hormone level as well and found that where the level was just beginning to increase, there was more aggression and less aggression furthest away from the time of this increase.

The onset of physiological changes in the adolescent may act as a catalytic agent for borderline problems, as well as for more normal levels of acting out. This sudden growth is a stage (Blos, 1979), where support of the parents is essential for proper separation. This is why the phenomena of borderline development becomes more overt with problems of normal adolescence.

Aggression

Aggression is a topic that is not well understood because of the multiplicity of factors involved (Feshbach, 1970). It has been held that aggression is more likely to occur in relation to a rejecting family, but the situation is far from being that simple. Lewis (1979) compared the neuropsychiatric, intellectual, and educational status of extremely violent and less violent incarcerated boys. The more violent adolescents were more likely to demonstrate psychotic symptomology, such as paranoid ideation and illogical associations, and to have minor neurological abnormalities. In addition, they were likely to have experienced and witnessed extreme physical abuse.

Aggression should be viewed in terms of resolution, stress and the history of having frustrations relieved and demands met. This latter factor can be called the indulgence pattern of our Low Rejection group. The closer one is to the goal (of having needs met), the greater is the drive to achieve it. This describes our Low Rejection adolescent who is either indulged and inappropriately reinforced or has the symbiotic pattern which produces the same result with a borderline intrapsychic structure. It is this Low Rejection group who has a much higher incidence of aggressive behavior compared to other adolescents. Aggression, then, appears to be more directly related to acceptance than to rejection.

The Frustration-Aggression Hypothesis (Dollard, et al, 1939) is one of the oldest and simplest explanations of aggression. This approach has much in common with the psychoanalytic view, while at the same time being a drive-reduction learning theory model. The Frustration-Aggression Hypothesis predicts that the natural result of frustration is aggression. Frustration of an ongoing activity produces an instigation whose goal response is injury to some person or object. Aggression may be one of a number of possible behaviors elicited by frustration, but the association between the two is learned very early. If the resolution is frustrated and the drive originating from the stress is high, aggression is likely to occur in the severely disturbed adolescent.

The Low Rejection adolescents may rarely have been frustrated for long and aggression, or the threat of it, produced results. They get themselves into difficulties because those outside their immediate family do not respond to their frustration. There is another group of a more severely aggressive nature that is a combination of the Low Rejection and the Severe Rejection category. Here you have the addition of the element of severe pathology and violent models that is ordinarily not part of Low Rejection or symbiosis. It has been shown (Bandura and Walters, 1959) that the punishing agent (usually the father) can serve as a model for the child, who may incorporate these aggressive behaviors.

Violence

Ordinarily violence among severely disturbed adolescents requires that there be a strong drive or resolution to overcome inhibitory factors, which are paradoxically often strongest in homicidal adolescents. The exception to this occurs with very psychopathic resolutions where only a minimal frustration of a goal object may be required in some cases.

Bender (1940) suggested that the most common factor in homicidal aggression was "the child's tendency to identify himself with aggressive parents and pattern after their behavior." In a study of 9 adolescents who had committed homicide at age 14 (King, 1975) it was noted that they had been subject to beatings as children, episodic desertions by the father, and possessed poor cognitive skills and language development. Easson (1961) reported that in 8 cases of murder by adolescents, one or both parents fostered or condoned murderous assault. In a study of adults who had committed murder (Tanay, 1969) it was noted that 35 out of 41 had been subject to severe corporal punishment as children. Of interest is the finding that only 15 percent of the homicides involved strangers and that 58 percent of the acts were committed within the family; a fact that seems to be related to the borderline condition. Russell (1965) studied 15 murders committed by adolescents and concluded that "all of the murders had their roots in the frustration attendant to the maternal deprivation with faulty human conditioning in the earliest periods of life."

The results of these studies are in basic agreement with my own findings from adolescents considered to be a danger to themselves or others. Of this population only about 25 percent had behavior that was severely aggressive toward others including homicide and attempted homicide. I am impressed with how nonviolent severely disturbed adolescents are in general. Fortunately aggression, such as homicide, occurs in an extremely small proportion of even the most psychologically damaged adolescents and is not a typical method of acting out. The borderline adolescents generally are very nonviolent toward others no matter how regressive their condition.

I have taken the cases of severe aggression and violence and reviewed them in terms of the two factors of acceptance and rejection and from the standpoint of the holographic model. The instances of severe aggression fall into broad categories, which I believe can account for much of the severe aggression in adolescence. The salient features of violence in this population seem to be: 1) A violent model within the family; 2) severe physical punishment during the early years; 3) disturbed parenting relationships with possible symbiotic attachment to the mother; 4) identification with the aggressive parent; 5) the condoning of violence as a method of feeling expression and venting of frustration; and 6) indulgence as a parenting pattern that essentially reinforces aggressive behavior.

One characteristic that is found in all severely aggressive adolescents is stress resulting from the discrepancy between acceptance and rejection. This shows up in terms of Severe Rejection along with a violent, pathological model and the Low Rejection indulgent parenting. There are no cases of severe aggression in my sample of adolescents that did not have both these factors operating in their developmental background.

Types of Violence

What I call a primary (early) psychopathic resolution constitutes one type of severely aggressive pattern. This resolution stems from early and probably repeated separation from the mother, much as Bowlby has theorized as the final stage of a reaction to permanent loss.* This is not to suggest that all adolescents who experience an early loss are psychopathic or will commit severely aggressive acts, but certainly it is one highly probable resolution. A key factor has to do with the later addition of even mildly indulgent parenting in such a case.

I will briefly present a case of a 14-year-old male who represents this pattern of severe aggression. Roger was convicted of murdering another teenager in a bizarre act carried out in a game-like manner. Roger had been in a residential treatment program during early adolescence and part of latency. He was intelligent and charming, a leader who could gain the attention of both his peers and staff to achieve his own ends. One thing that was always clear was his lack of stress under most circumstances including his many minor transgressions. When confronted by adults he would choose verbal persuasion; with peers he would resort to manipulation, threats or physical aggression.

For nearly a year after leaving treatment Roger maintained himself in an open residential setting. Finally, he was placed in a correctional facility for theft and menacing with a gun. I visited him while he was incarcerated and he seemed satisfied with himself and under no particular stress, although he complained about the restraints on his behavior.

His ultimate success was always questioned because of his early history. He had four early separations from his mother before the age of 4; the first critical one during the latter half of the first year. It was at this early stage that his firm resolution began to take form. After the four separations there was a period

---

*Personal communication with Dr. James Masterson.

during latency where parenting was adequate in most respects—from his father and from foster parents—but it was clearly indulgent and delinquent-producing. Here he developed a coercive style of getting what he wanted from adults.

Roger perceived total rejection from his mother, while the perception of his father included components of violence, neglect and indulgence. He had lived with his father about a month when the murder took place. Since the psychopathic resolution came very early in his development, it outweighed all other factors in its significance.

Having a psychopathic resolution to early repeated separation and rejection does not mean that the adolescent will be severely aggressive. It does mean that they will have little capacity for empathy, trust in others, and no real inhibitory factors to overcome in order to act out. This is in contrast to the intrafamily violence of the borderline adolescent, where intense psychological stress over an extended period of time is necessary before there is homicidal acting out. In the next two cases I will discuss, there are psychopathic elements to be sure, but there are also more complex borderline factors and somewhat more inhibitory strength to be taken into account.

It is common for the borderline adolescent to fantasize homicidal rage directed toward the withdrawing or withholding parent (especially toward the mother), but this is not often acted out. However, out of all forms of homicidal acts committed by adolescents this type is common. The borderline dynamics within the family can, under certain circumstances, result in violence directed within the family.

The recipient of the aggression is ordinarily the mother or a symbolic figure related to the mother as the withdrawing object, such as a sister or grandmother. We have discussed the multigenerational nature of the borderline condition, so the role of the grandmother is understood. As for the sister, the competition for the mother's attention is quite clear. It is also possible for a process of what I would call projective identification of self or family characteristics to take place. Here various attributes of the self or family members are projected onto other people who become the objects of the aggression. The stress then becomes ventilated through this projected focal point with a particular precision and rage, as we shall see in the case to be discussed. The relevance here is the fact that while the individual is not directly a member of the immediate family, the projection brings them psychologically within the family. This type of violence can then be distinguished from the merely psychopathic, antisocial violence that is almost always directed outside the immediate family. In the latter instance the recipient of the violence may be seen as an object that is thwarting goal-directed behavior of the adolescent.

Although in one sense the dynamics involved in the two types of violence (that directed within the family and that directed outside) are quite different, it is true that they are both means of ventilation of stress which becomes concentrated within a specific object. The within-family violence will invariably have borderline features in the development, even though the final resolution may be psychopathic.

Prior to the aggressive act in the within-family violence there is, in all cases I have dealt with, a specific series of events taking place over several months, which involves the increasing threat of separation from the mother. The borderline adolescent reacts to this by greater attempts to cope with the depression and fear of abandonment and loss through some form of acting out. When the resolution has become psychopathic, as in the case we will be discussing, the events threatening separation occur and the resolution prevents depression. The adolescent's psychological equilibrium is maintained by clinging to the mother. It is this symbiotic union and indulgence in that relationship that acts as the trigger for the homicidal act. As she threatens to disengage herself from the symbiotic attachment—or someone else threatens to cause the breaking of the symbiotic attachment—the adolescents may react with panic at the threat of loss of their primary defense mechanism, i.e., clinging.

The symbiotic adolescents with a psychopathic resolution will often have a great resolve to perform well even though their behavior does not meet their own expectations. They have more concern about personal behavior and ethics in general; so much so that there may be stress caused by the discrepancy with their own behavior. The paradox is similar to that found with the symbiotic tie to the mother whom they aggress against. The adolescent is strong in resolution, as well as fearful and very easily threatened. It is possible that the fragile ego structure can become so well defended that the borderline symbiotic development becomes a psychopathic response. The difference between this resolution and that described in Roger's case, has to do with the later age at which it develops. As such, there will be borderline features in the development and in the family structure. The violence, while carried out as part of the psychopathic resolution, is directed at the threatened withdrawal of the object.

Because of the strength of the resolution, whether psychopathic or merely symbiotic, the borderline who become severely aggressive appear to be more psychologically intact as long as the symbiotic union is not threatened. They verbalize a profound love and respect for the mother and are convinced that everything will be alright if they are allowed to go home. They may explain away their behavior as being due to drugs or alcohol; and indeed drugs do play a role in lowering inhibitions enough for them to commit the act if there is not a psychopathic resolution.

One need only observe the adolescents in the clinging relationship—in other words, when the resolution is operating—to see the inconsistencies present. They will typically act out in some subtle ways while verbalizing the opposite behavior expectations for themselves and others. For example, they might steal something from a peer out of petty jealousy or physically attack a friend suggesting that the symbiotic relationship is not sufficient to deal with the underlying depression and conflict. Also, the very nature of the symbiotic relationship means that the borderline adolescent must act in a regressive manner, i.e., 'acting bad is feeling good.'

Masterson (1976) suggests that if you confront the adolescent with a psychopathic resolution you cannot get at the depression, if indeed it can be said to exist at all, because it is so well defended. The aggressive borderline adolescent will have many of the characteristics of the psychopath (and will in some cases have a true psychopathic resolution, thus negating the diagnosis of borderline personality) because of the shell-like qualities of the resolution. A critical distinction lies in the firmness of that resolution and whether there is still abandonment depression.

The case I will present in brief is a very complex one that I use for illustrative purposes only because it contains so many of the factors we have been discussing. In two respects it is not entirely representative of the threat of withdrawal type of borderline aggression (see case #12 in the case study section for a more representative case that does not have a psychopathic resolution): first, the direction of the aggression was projected outside of the immediate family, while I believe in most cases the mother is the recipient; and, second, most symbiotic borderline adolescents have not developed such a solid psychopathic resolution as in our case example. Nonetheless, the case does illustrate the powerful combination effects of early separation, symbiosis, homicidal models and projective identification.

Mary, a 14-year-old, was charged with murdering two young children. There was disbelief in the community because she was known as a dependable baby-sitter who was very responsible and mature for her age. She professed not to like "blue jeans, drugs, or wild teenagers."

One look at Mary's developmental history and some of the intrapsychic structure is clear. She was abandoned by her mother sometime during the first year of life to the care of her grandparents. Her mother would periodically return and try to care for her but would soon leave again; a pattern that was to continue for 11 years. Her father never cared for her directly but visited regularly during her latency years. He, too, abandoned her approximately 6 months before the first homicide, after making numerous promises about caring for her.

Mary's relationship with her grandmother was symbiotic to the point where she could not be away from her even overnight. Shortly before the homicide she had gone on a camping trip with other girls and had become hysterical. Her relationship with her grandfather was nearly as close and he was the only one she could talk to with any feeling. When Mary was 11 years old, he shot and killed her mother while trying to shoot her mother's boyfriend. Shortly before this shooting Mary had tried living with her mother, next door to the grandmother, but did not like her mother's hippy lifestyle and her sexual activities. She apparently thought it somewhat justified when her grandfather shot her mother. Here you have the violent model, the grandfather (her natural father was also known to be unpredictably violent), eliminating someone who was bad in her judgment and the one who perpetually abandoned her. The grandfater returned home on a medical leave, but was returned to prison just prior to the first homicide at about the time her father left.

There are many borderline characteristics to the family. The paternal grandmother lived next door to Mary as did at least one of her aunts. Another of her aunts moved in with them a few months prior to the homicide, along with several children for which Mary was responsible. Only the grandfather protested that it was too much responsibility for a girl of her age, but the grandmother and aunt would have none of it. It was shortly after this that he was returned to prison.

Mary drowned a 4-year-old girl who lived next door in the same building as her aunt. She was close friends with the girl's mother and was in charge of caring for the children much of the time. At this time she also admitted that she had drowned a 3-year-old child of the aunt, who had moved in with them several months before, while baby-sitting him at the park.

Mary's motivation in the two murders involved several factors. First, she was angry that she had responsibility for caring for the children. Second, both children were behavior problems and she had branded them as "bad children" in her mind. She saw nothing inconsistent about getting rid of bad people just as her mother had been killed by her grandfather. Third, the murders followed separations during early adolescence, which had a definite impact on her. Both children were linked to the threat of losing her grandmother (as she had lost her mother, father and grandfather) both because of the time they took on her part and the attention that she felt they got from her grandmother. Mary stated that she was sure she was going to lose her grandmother and admitted that she was intensely jealous of the attention her grandmother gave to the children. I believe there was a good deal of projective identification of a number of 'bad' traits from herself and from her mother. Such splitting projections represent the borderline condition involved in the development. The sequence usually follows a form where the adolescent first sees the other person as being in need of help, nurturance or rescuing in some way (being rescued from the bad mother). This is clearly a projection of the self at this point. This then prompts the projection of withdrawal from the 'bad child,' who is demanding and unworthy of the attention and nurturance, just as it was withdrawn from Mary. The self projection continues in the form of projecting all of the person's bad traits or behaviors onto that person and the conclusion is that they are unappreciative of the attention and it must be withdrawn. Furthermore, because the flaw in the person is seen as inherent they must be eliminated. Beyond this they are also seen as someone who in the final analysis is deliberately trying to threaten or harm them by depriving them of their much deserved nurturance and attention. Thus the splitting between the 'bad' and 'good' object is complete and the aggression takes place relatively free of inhibitory factors. This projective sequence, though, must take place over a period of many months and culminates in what only appears to be an impulsive homicidal act.

The case of Mary illustrates a psychopathic resolution that can come from separation anxiety at critical periods in development and borderline conditions. It also shows the powerful impact of early separations followed by symbiotic and indulgent parenting patterns, as well as the effect of violent role models for ventilation of stress and rage reactions. Finally, Mary can be classified as both Low Rejection and Severe Rejection that taken together have caused stress by their very discrepant and unreasonable nature. There was really no way to ventilate the pressure from fear of loss and stress without risking the symbiotic relationship which was her lifeline to her grandmother. Because of her apparently strong and powerful resolution everyone took her for granted as being very intact and adultlike—the fact is, of course, that she was as totally dependent as a symbiotic infant.

Another variation of severe aggression and homicide in an adolescent with a borderline background is what I have termed "the threat of engulfment" or a reaction to thwarting of goal-directed behavior. It is distinctive because the aggression is directed outside the family, unlike the threat of abandonment aggression, without the need of either symbiosis or projective identification to provide the trigger or motivation for the behavior. To be the recipient of this type of aggression one must be perceived as a thwarting object, or perhaps as attempting to engulf them in a manner of the parent from which they had escaped seeking independence. The violence is not random or arbitrary and simply stems from a resolution that allows for easy aggression. The object must be perceived as a threatening object in the sense of the borderline condition. Such conditions produce a fear and panic reaction similar to the threat of abandonment except that the direction of the aggression is not within the family, simply because they can almost always run away from home to escape. A strong resolution is very important in this category and it usually takes the form of a desperate striving for independence. In our study sample, most mild and moderate aggression comes from this category, which is likely to be a Low Rejection pattern compared to Ambivalent Rejection that is more often associated with the threat of abandonment aggression (although by no means exclusively). A moderate resolution to separate will lead to mild aggression, while homicidal aggression usually demands that the resolution be both very strong (in the sense of drive or motivation) and psychopathic.

Typically the adolescent in this category has some history of delinquent acting out that is goal-oriented and anti-social. There is an indulgent pattern ín the family, a borderline relationship with the mother during the early separation-individuation years of development, a severely rejecting and perhaps pathological component and certainly violent and aggressive role models. These adolescents see themselves as being relatively stress free (and they are relative to the threat of abandonment individual) and as being dependent on no one. Their defense is the striving for total and premature individuation as opposed to a more clinging resolution.

Violence is learned from the family and is seen as a legitimate means of removing anyone that stands between them and independence. Needless to say, the threat from someone outside the family will be seen out of proportion to the reality of the situation. The unreasonable fear must come from the paranoia and threat associated with the Severe Rejection component of the family that also provides the violent model. The Low Rejection, indulgent pattern provides the frustration and in a sense the trigger to commit the act through having immediate needs met.

As a way of illustrating this category, I will present a third homicide committed by a 14-year-old. Martha shot and killed an older man who had been providing shelter when she was a run-away from home. Martha was in residential treatment for over one year after the murder where she rarely acted out and like most homicidal adolescents with borderline characteristics, she was often accused of acting like a staff member. She was critical of others and the way they acted, but saw no real restrictions on her own behavior.

Martha's history included early separation from her father, indulgence from her stepfather, separation-individuation problems from the mother, who she later came to see as severely rejecting, and ample violent models for acting out the stress. Martha was a Low Rejection adolescent with some symbiotic characteristics and Severe Rejection that became more prominent during latency. It was during this period that the psychopathic resolution was developed, in contrast to a somewhat earlier resolution in Mary, and the still earlier psychopathic resolution in the case of Roger.

I would like to present part of Martha's MMPI profile that was interpreted by computer so that there was no bias by knowing the act committed.

It appears that she may have been overly self-critical. She feels vulnerable and defenseless, which may reflect a readiness to accept professional assistance. This patient exhibits contradictions in her behavior and in her view of herself. The contradictions may appear behaviorally as an alternation of phases. For a period she may act with little control or forethought, violating social restrictions, and trampling on the feelings and wishes of others. Following such a period of acting out, however, she may show guilt, remorse, and deep regret over her actions, and for a while she may seem overly controlled and contrite. The activity swings may be associated with excessive drinking and socially unacceptable behavior. While her conscience pangs may be severe, even out of proportion to the actual behavior deviations, her controls do not appear to be effective in preventing further outbreaks. She is talkative and distractible and if faced with frustration she may become irritable, aggressive, or impulsive, often out of proportion to the reality of the situation.

On the other hand, the normal expression of this trait is enthusiasm, energy, and goal-directed activity. She shows undue sensitivity and suspicion of those around her. She may tend to mistrust the motivations of others leading to difficulties in her interpersonal relationships. She appears to be a conventional and perhaps somewhat constricted person. Although she may be considerate and sincere in her dealings with others, there seems to be a lack of warmth and spontaneity about her. This person feels unable to deal with the environmental pressures facing her or to utilize her skills or abilities to full advantage. At present, she feels unable to cope with life as she sees it. She may respond to these feelings of inadequacy with increased rigidity or withdraw, depending upon individual factors.

This illustrates a resolution struggling to rid itself of the borderline conflicts. It is not as well formed as either Roger's or Mary's psychopathic resolution since conflicts in those situations were better defended. It differs from Mary in that there is no clinging to the parent or parent substitute.

There are examples of severe aggression that would fall into this category of violence directed outside the family, which present a variation on the same theme. In these situations the Severe Rejection component is much greater; in other words, the paranoid fear, and violent model, along with inadequate means of expressing anger, tend to predominate over the resolution.

Each violent adolescent should be viewed in terms of a weighing of factors that make up a part of all severe aggression. The violent model, indulgent parenting, symbiosis, type and degree of resolution, and degree of severe pathological rejection can all be weighed. In some, resolutions to the early rejection and borderline conditions may be the predominant factor; in others, the severe pathological rejection and violent model may be the most important factor leading to the aggression. In still others, it is almost entirely the symbiotic resolution and clinging that triggers the aggression.

Chapter 9

SUPPORTIVE PSYCHOTHERAPY WITH THE BORDERLINE ADOLESCENT

The more the adolescents possess borderline characteristics the greater is their need for approval and support, yet they are skeptical that the therapist can understand the reality of their world. If you are in a position of having regular contact, it is difficult not to get drawn into a therapeutic situation with them; their need to be listened to and for honest human contact is so great.

It cannot be shown conclusively that one form of psychotherapy is more effective than another, but there are certain ingredients shared by all (Frank, 1974; Garfield and Bergin, 1978). To the extent that therapy is effective the therapist must have congruence with the client, empathy and, above all, the client's belief that the therapist has the power to help. Acting as a therapist for the borderline adolescents is like trying to mold a near liquid mass at times. You are dealing with an inadequately formed, highly changeable ego structure that is rarely the same on consecutive days. They will alternately engulf you, as the good parent, and distance from you, as the bad parent; if you are seen as an ego that they can attach to—in other words, one that does not distance from them.

The therapist must be a real person capable of displaying a full range of human emotion and not overly defensive in his own psychological makeup. Masterson (1976) states " . . . the therapist must maintain a positive attitude towards the patient's individuation. This entails a constant and consistent expectation that the patient will act in a realistic, healthy and mature fashion, combined with an attitude of curiosity, concern and investigation when he does not." (p. 91) The borderline adolescent must have a therapist who has, above all, worked through his own adolescence, so that there is no over identification with the adolescent (Lamb, 1976). There are potential negative effects of adhering rigidly to a therapeutic stance or model without having the flexibility to adapt to the needs of the adolescent. The traditional psychoanalytic stance of neutrality, inactivity and intellectualization is not appropriate for the borderline adolescent because it may not offer the needed confrontation and structure.

The therapist must keep in mind the libidinal unavailability of the mother and the ambivalence of the acceptance and rejection under which the adolescent has been operating. Life becomes a process of looking for new supplies of libidinal affection from husbands, lovers, children, wives and, finally, from the therapist. When someone is offering them this support under the guise of therapy the umbilical cord is attached from their ego to you, the therapist. It is the process of moderating this attachment that determines whether you, as the therapist, are an effective healer or only one more split object for the adolescent. If you try to deny this attachment once you have allowed it to exist (covertly or overtly) or try to alter it prematurely as part of a therapeutic distancing through transference interpretation, you may provoke rageful acting out.

The looking glass concept may be difficult to comprehend unless one was raised in a borderline family environment. To receive incompatible acceptance-rejection messages that both push and pull is inherently frightening and confusing. The borderline adolescents have learned to deal with this by defensive behaviors and manipulation of the environment. They know that the therapist, as an observer, may see only the acceptance side of their family. It is imperative that the therapist understand the total dynamics of what is going on in order to achieve even a beginning level of trust and influence over the acting out of the adolescents.

APPROACHES TO THERAPY

Understanding the world of the borderline adolescent will establish trust and a certain amount of initial credibility for a therapist, which will be solidified through a supportive, confrontational approach. But through what model of therapy can this best take place? Traditionally, our two choices are a directive or a nondirective approach; each with his own advocates and rationale. Both approaches, however, can present major pitfalls when dealing with the borderline (Masterson, 1976).

If the therapist takes a passive, nondirective role, the lack of interaction and direction from the therapist can be misinterpreted as some form of rejection or lack of concern. In addition, most severely disturbed adolescents do not have enough coping ability to put together for themselves what this approach implies; and since the therapist would not be in a position to adequately confront the various defenses, the result might be acting out to get the therapist's attention.

It is probably fair to say that the directive approach to therapy is closer to what is required for the borderline adolescent. However, there is a danger of the adolescent being all too willing, after a strong therapeutic alliance has been formed, to let the therapist take over management of his life. To some extent this may be necessary with very regressed or more psychopathic adolescents in that high structure is demanded. However, it also represents one of the deadliest traps for the therapist, who is not on sure ground as far as their own whole object relations are concerned. The borderline adolescents are so needful of libidinal supplies that they will make no effort to develop their own independence. The supplies and acceptance are associated with dependent behavior. They will cling, as they may have, to the parent and separation or distancing will be interpreted as rejection.

Perhaps the best rule of thumb is that directiveness in therapy should be largely confined to the confrontational aspects. Otherwise a more nondirective approach of encouraging independent, responsible, and appropriate behavior would be preferable. The adolescents will let you know when the passive stance has been carried too far by forcing you to confront them about some acting out or regressive behavior. If this is the case it should be identified as such to the adolescent, but it should also serve as a warning to the therapist.

CONFRONTATION

Confrontation does not imply a hostile or angry response from the therapist, but rather it is a direct statement identifying defensive language, or behavior that implies an understanding of the perceptual model. Confrontation will ordinarily be directed at some behavior that is used to defend against basic depression. The therapist should learn to recognize the various defenses employed by the borderline, such as projection, avoidance, denial, distortion, generalization and, most important, splitting into withdrawing and rewarding objects (Masterson, 1976).

A confrontation will ordinarily not consist of more than a line or a phrase from the therapist. If you require more than that it may be because you have missed the essential point of the distortion or meaning behind the behavior; in other words, you are either lecturing or on a therapeutic fishing expedition. What should have been a confrontation in uncovering depression will result in the use of other defenses, such as anger and projection. Furthermore, to the extent that you are inaccurate because you do not understand the essential dynamics of the behavior, you have invalidated your credibility to carry out further confrontation with the adolescent. Confrontation is a technique that will be required throughout the course of therapy because periodic regressions will demand it (Masterson, 1978b).

The borderline can be seen as establishing a sense of internal psychological equilibrium or homeostasis through their acting out. The risk is a small price to pay for relieving the feelings of despair and rejection. Once a trusting therapeutic alliance is formed and the therapist confronts the adolescent by pointing out the harm that the behavior can lead to, the adolescent can no longer act out without a degree of conflict. At this point there will

be anger directed at the therapist because they have been responsible for removing the easy defense. The adolescent must
now recognize the cost of "feeling good."

LISTENING

Being able to listen is an important quality in any therapeutic
situation, but it has particular relevance to the borderline adolescent. As adults we are not particularly prone to listen to
adolescents; we hear them and we lecture them, but seldom do we
listen to them. The parent of the borderline never listened because to do so might necessitate hearing expressions of feeling.
They speak as though they already know the thoughts and feelings of the adolescent. Having an adult actually listen without
constant interruptions or impatient smiles, which imply not really
comprehending, depersonifying, or lecturing, will be a new experience for the adolescent and a powerful tool for the therapist.
Listening implies being silent and being silent can be one of
the best confrontation methods. If the therapist has demonstrated the ability to understand by being able to go through the
looking glass into the borderline world, the adolescent will often
provide the confrontation once the therapist identifies the behavior. If therapy is effective it will often get to the point where
most confrontations are actually provided by the adolescents
themselves.

PROVIDING STRUCTURE THROUGH SUPPORTIVE THERAPY

Supportive therapy can be seen as a therapeutic relationship
whose objective is to assist the adolescent in coping with separation through a process of confrontation. Masterson (1976) defines supportive psychotherapy as that which enables " . . . the
patient to learn conscious control of the defense mechanisms of
his pathologic ego, and thereby to strip from the reality of his life
structure those defenses along with their destructive effects."
Supportive therapy implies that the abandonment depression
will not be totally worked through as it theoretically would in

psychoanalysis. Supportive therapy can be anything from a few months to several years in length. In addition to the confrontation of defenses and providing awareness of the dynamics, you are also providing a structure around which the adolescents can construct new resolutions to the problems they face. The more regressed the borderline the more formal the therapeutic structure must be. The structure implies something solid, identifiable and consistent in terms of limits and information to the adolescents. It is supportive without allowing the adolescents to be regressive in their demand for libidinal supplies. The structure is something that is predictable and therefore the opposite of the ambivalent rejection of the borderline family.

The adolescents should be provided with information around the dynamics of the effects of acceptance-rejection, the ambivalent messages, and the resulting defenses used to resolve the stress. It is through knowledge of the borderline condition that they will survive new life situations and relationships. At best, intermittent contacts with the family will occur in the future and they must develop a degree of understanding and conscious control over feelings and behavior associated with that. I find it helpful to think of the therapist as acting as a life preserver keeping the adolescents afloat until they are capable of surviving without destructiveness.

ACCEPTANCE-REJECTION: AMBIVALENCE

The ambivalence of parental rejection is always couched in defensive acting out and cannot be dealt with directly until therapeutic alliance has been formed. Almost all behavior of the borderline adolescents, in some manner, revolves around this issue. They almost never do anything just for themselves that is not related to defending against the depression in some way.

The ambivalence can be seen in all objects or human relationships being split into good and bad parts corresponding to the rewarding and withdrawing parts of the mother image. This split can be viewed both literally and metaphorically because it pervades all areas of the adolescent's existence. The mother is either rewarding regressive, self-destructive behavior by making libidinal supplies available or she is withdrawing and punishing behavior that suggests separation and independence. This is why acting out and self-destruction is associated with "feeling good." If this concept is not understood the paradox of the adolescents who have just been severely self-destructive but feel no depression afterward cannot be understood. Therapeutic progress means that the adolescents must sacrifice "feeling good" in the search for less destructive resolutions. The therapist must use the alliance to persuade them to give up the acting out as a resolution.

RESOLUTIONS AND BEHAVIOR

The adolescents should be faced with the consequences of their actions and not be rescued by the therapist; they should be confronted about the destructive quality of their behavior and the fact that it is used as a means of avoiding issues. They have learned to survive by becoming master manipulators and escape artists. They feel justified in their behavior as any prisoner of war would feel about putting something over on their captors. Very well intentioned people can end up excusing these actions out of a reaction to the self-destructive quality of the situation. The therapist should avoid playing this role and set clear expectations for the adolescents' behavior in a firm, consistent and positive manner.

One must perceive the destructive acting out and manipulation within the context of defensive behavior to avoid painful feelings. Abandonment depression has been variously described by borderline adolescents as being akin to falling into an abyss, a black hole in space or the worst nightmare you can imagine. If this is the general feeling they are trying to avoid by staying high, cutting on themselves or constantly staying on the move, then one can imagine the driving force behind the behavior and the reason why consequences may have little effect. The therapists must make it clear that while they disapprove of destructive behavior because it is harmful and prevents therapy, they still accept each of them as a person. This is difficult for the borderline adolescents to understand since their parents often depersonalize them and relate behavior with acceptance.

The therapist is under pressure to conform to the borderline dynamics. One of the results of effective therapeutic procedures is what Masterson (Masterson, 1978b) refers to as transference acting out. The adolescents will try to get you to conform to the parental model of providing sympathy, acceptance, and so forth when they display regressive behavior. To meet the behavior expectations you set for independence and responsibility also means separation from you as the therapist. This will periodically meet with regressive acting out to show you that they do not want to separate and that you are responsible for them. They will in effect demand that you disapprove of them personally for their behavior while at the same time providing them with a dependent relationship and libidinal supplies. It is easy to become angry because the acting out often comes just when you are congratulating yourself on the job you are doing. It is at this point that the therapist must understand the dynamics and not become a part of it in a way that is destructive to the adolescent.

KNOWING

An important part of supportive therapy includes the imparting of information about the borderline condition and family dynamics to the adolescents. This should be done discretely and gradually as the confrontation procedes and certain insights are acquired. It is not a lecture series on the borderline personality. As these therapeutic connections are made another piece of the puzzle falls into place for the adolescents. This means that you are the therapist and "know" certain things that they do not know about themselves, e.g., thoughts, feelings, perceptions, and conflictual states. You give information that implies that you are capable of stepping through the looking glass into their perceptual world in a way that their parents never could.

Knowing requires that the therapist have a thorough understanding of the borderline dynamics, such that they can apply it to each new case. When you are correct about most of the factors in a case but incorrect around some details, the adolescent will usually correct you with no loss of therapeutic credibility. Knowing then is like a picture puzzle where through your knowledge of the dynamics you have many of the larger pieces which will allow you to "know" some of the other pieces before they are given to you. This allows the therapist to do several things. First of all, you have a degree of trust because they are anxious for someone to interpret their confusing world. Second, you can confront them about their distortions and their interpretations of reality—the problem is that they perceive the entire world operating on borderline dynamics.

Success leads the therapist into a major problem of dealing with their own feelings of omnipotence. There are more pitfalls here than can be dealt with in this short chapter, but unless the problem is handled appropriately the balloon of omnipotence will be punctured every time an adolescent severely acts out in the transference.

TRANSFERENCE AND COUNTER TRANSFERENCE

The terms transference and counter transference refer to the nature of the relationship between the therapist and the adolescent (Searles, 1979). They are particularly relevant to the borderline because of the intensity of the relationship and the demands placed upon the therapist. Transference refers to the attitudes and attributes that the adolescent projects on the therapist—such as omnipotence, or the attitudes of the good or bad parent. If there is no transference there is no therapy so it should not be construed as negative.

Lamb (1976) suggests that the younger adolescent in particular may have a great need for a strong transference reaction even to the point of seeing the therapist, for a period of time, as a very omnipotent figure. In this way she suggests that the therapist can set limits on the acting out behavior of the younger adolescents because they see the therapist as someone who can actually curtail their behavior by strong suggestions and expectations.

I would urge a note of caution about the traditional view of interpreting transference to the patient. With the borderline adolescents this should not be done as quickly as with the psychoneurotic individual because premature destroying of omnipotence and transference feelings will be interpreted as rejection and distancing. You may be perceived as either with-drawing because they are worthless or because they show inde-pendent behavior as the parent did.

Counter transference refers to the therapist's transfer of unconscious attitudes, which he has to important people in his life, to the borderline adolescent. As Masterson (1976) points out this can be a particular problem with therapists who have border-line propensities themselves which may lead to their distancing (perhaps rationalized away by traditional interpretation of trans-ference feelings of the patient).

The pitfalls of counter transference are many. Because of the essential ambivalence and splitting you are involved in emo-tional ping pong that will put your own whole object relations to the test. Because of their tremendous need for libidinal supplies and affection, the borderline adolescents have a "radar" for sen-sing ego intactness of the therapist and exploiting any cracks.

The borderline adolescent will throw out material to distract the therapists from pursuing critical areas and involve them in counter transference problems. This point, I suspect, was made by Masterson* when he spoke of training psychiatric residents to be therapists for borderline adolescents. He stated, somewhat facetiously no doubt, that "if you can just get the therapist to deal with their counter transference problems the adolescents will teach them all they need to know about therapy." I would support this view because in my experience the borderline adolescents want effective treatment and will see that you stay on task as the therapist. A part of the transference problem is that the adoles-cent projects onto the therapist a degree of omnipotence and may escalate his behavior to test you. You must ask yourself how much of the adolescent's projection is not a part of your own counter transference. The adolescent will survive the shock of finding out that you are only human after all (providing the therapist can) and should not be rushed through it.

The therapist must be very clear about how they are using this temporary power therapeutically and not be deluded into believing it. As Giovacchini (1973) points out the therapist usually unconsciously accepts the assigned role projected onto him and it

*Personal communication with James Masterson, M.D.

is a potentially dangerous situation because the client inevitably becomes disappointed. However, as Lamb (1976) also points out ". . . the therapist should occasionally allow such a transference— when it is clearly in the interests of the patient and when it is clearly temporary—and not insist that the patient view the therapist more realistically until she is ready to do so." (p. 135) Sometimes the inexperienced therapists feel uncomfortable with the dependency and will try to distance themselves, destroying the therapeutic alliance.

COMMUNICATIVE MATCHING

Communicative matching implies that the adolescent can freely exchange thoughts and ideas with the therapist about a variety of age appropriate subjects (Masterson, 1976). It is a term taken from Mahler (1975) in her observations on the ideal relationship between mother and child. Therapy with the borderline adolescent should get to the point where some time is spent in freely discussing a variety of topics of interest to the client. While to some this may seem like irrelevant subject matter, it is essentially the normalization of interests for the borderline adolescent. Fraiberg (1955) in psychotherapy with adolescent girls preferred to talk about seemingly unimportant things, such as clothes and everyday happenings at school, while minimizing interpretations.

THE LANGUAGE OF THE BORDERLINE ADOLESCENT

We might well ask what is it during the course of a therapeutic session that makes it effective? We have discussed the importance of confronting the defenses of the borderline adolescent but not the content of that confrontation. This of course is difficult because there is no exact formula to follow and it requires a degree of skill and understanding of the borderline dynamics, as well as experience. It may be helpful to consider the work of Bandler and Grinder (1975). What they found was that effective therapists, regardless of the particular model of therapy, used a similar process of interpreting the client's language. The skilled therapist—often without realizing it—is able to analyze language in terms of structure, completeness, distortions, and probable meaning. This would be used, for example, in analyzing the borderline adolescents' stated reason for acting in a particularly destructive way. Accepting their statement as it stands would mean that you accepted their distortions of reality.

The basis of the two-factor model is the adolescents' perception of the world in which he lives. This is merely an extension of the parenting pattern compounded by other factors. One difference, then, between the adolescents who cope adequately with life and those who do not are the options they perceive to be available to them. The borderline adolescents will characteristically see themselves as having few options from which to choose. They see themselves as being boxed in on a downhill slide into oblivion. When you, as the therapist, suggest other resolutions their resistance will be high because you are not only challenging their defenses but their perceptual model of how the world works. Their model might hold the following things to be true: Expressing your feelings is dangerous; you cannot trust adults; I am too worthless to be loved for myself; getting close to others means rejection and so on. As Bandler and Grinder (1975) put it:

> The difficulty is not that they are making wrong choices, but that they do not have enough choices—they don't have a richly focused image of the world. The most pervasive paradox of the human condition which we see is that the processes which allow us to survive, grow, change and experience joy are the same processes which allow us to maintain an impoverished model of the world—our ability to manipulate symbols, that is, create models. The process which allows us to accomplish the most extraordinary and unique human activities are the same processes which block our further growth if we commit the error of mistaking the model for the reality. (p. 114)

There are several distortions of language that are used by the borderline adolescents that describe their perceptual world. These may be considered as both defensive behavior to avoid the basic rejection and as representations of the perceptual world.

Generalization in Language

Generalization is a process by which elements of the individual's perceptual model come to represent an entire category of behaviors or experience. Our ability to generalize is essential for coping with the world about us. If we are harmed in some way by a person, we learn and generalize that people can, under certain circumstances, be harmful. However, the rejected child may generalize that getting close to anyone is risky and should be avoided, making a later therapeutic alliance difficult unless the perceptual model is confronted. This generalization, however, will only be indirectly expressed in language because to say outright that all people are dangerous—or some such statement— would itself be risky, because it would expose the model to attack and be punished by further withdrawal of the parent.

If the adolescent is generalizing from a rule of his perceptual model then the confrontation of a particular incident is of little value unless the generalization is stated by the therapist. The generalization might, for example, involve something like running away or aggression as the only possible response to threatened withdrawal of the parent. The act would no doubt be presented to the therapist in terms of justifications and reasons for it happening, as though it were understood that there were lots of options.

Deletion in Language

Deletion is a process by which we selectively give attention to certain dimensions of our experience and exclude others by denying their occurrence. People have the ability to filter out certain sounds and concentrate on others depending on what they expect to hear. This same process allows the borderline adolescent to block messages that have occurred, such as acceptance that may threaten their existing model in such a way that they have learned to delete them.

If we did not delete messages that had no place in our model of how the world operates, we would cause ourselves great distress. In the case of the borderline adolescent who receives ambivalent communication from the parent, deletion of certain conflictual elements may be a matter of survival. This accounts for the fact that the adolescent is ordinarily not conscious of the ambivalence itself, but feels only alternate acceptance and rejection. I have many times had the experience of sitting through a family session with borderline adolescents who later denied that certain messages ever came from the parents. Even when confronted with the audio tape of the session they would act as though it was all new information to them.

Distortion in Language

Not all information can be deleted and some of it that does not fit our perceptual model must be distorted. As a matter of fact, distortion is probably the most common element in the language of the borderline adolescent. It serves many useful purposes, such as fantasy that allows us to prepare for experiences prior to their actual occurrence. Indeed all forms of creativity involve some form of distortion of reality.

The world of the borderline adolescent involves distortion as a way of making messages fit their perceptual world. The adolescent who listened to the taped session with the parents distorted the message that he had previously deleted in the actual session. Upon being confronted with the parents' communication on the tape he responded with something like, "They just said that because you were in the room," or "They just said that because they want me to come home and be a live-in baby-sitter again." From a therapeutic standpoint this throws the emphasis on the content of what the adolescent said rather than on the distortion itself.

Since the adolescents who have had a significant degree of rejection will have a commensurate low self-concept, they will project it as being how others view them and delete or distort communication that is positive. Their behavior then leads to rejection and provides a feedback loop to confirm the perceptual model. The therapist's job is to confront this model.

LEVELS OF LANGUAGE

The therapist's job can in part be described as one of reestablishing the relationship between the adolescent's actual experience and the language, by challenging the idea that the linguistic model is really a total description of reality. The problem of confronting the adolescent's model through the language he uses is that it is always disguised and distorted in some way. If he says, "I'm unhappy," the therapist might respond with "About what?" and in turn he might say, "About everything." The questioning could become specific, such as identifying situations that do make him happy, thus recognizing the generalization. The fact is that he may be generalizing in a limited number of situations involving family, and the depression involving ambivalence to depression about "everything."

The process of confrontation involves understanding the particular defenses that the adolescent is using. For example, the borderline adolescent might make such statements as "The other kids make me angry." This again is a generalization and probably a distortion of a few incidences. The therapist might respond with, "Tell me which kids," or "How can anyone force you to be angry?" An answer to these questions would force some of the deleted material from the model to be restored. What you might want to do at this point is to connect the adolescent with the experience of getting angry and with its source (probably repression). This might be a slow process, but unless the model is clarified, therapy will be lost in the adolescent's language. One way a perception can be distorted is by changing the locus of control whereby someone else is made responsible for something that happens to the adolescent rather than taking responsibility for it himself. The adolescent might say, "My parents make me angry," implying that the cause came from outside of himself and his anger is in no way his responsibility. There are a number of avenues open to the therapist to pursue this situation. You might ask if there are examples of situations where this particular behavior occurs and the adolescent does not respond with anger. This uses the individual's own experience to challenge his model.

The language of the borderline adolescents in a therapeutic situation will contain many clues to the premises of their perceptual model. Being able to recognize these premises and appropriately confront an individual is what makes a good therapist, as opposed to merely a friendly figure who can talk to the adolescents. For example, if the adolescents were to say, "Everybody is against me," the inclination of many people would be to accept the statement as it stood or to do a general confrontation by telling them that it wasn't true. It would in no way put their perceptual model to the test.

It is helpful for the therapists to ask themselves if what the individual has just said is linguistically complete. Could the statement be made more complete in a more elaborate statement? If he said "I'm angry about what is happening at home; they don't want me there," several statements are made that you are expected to accept. The adolescent is saying that he is angry because his parents make him that way and furthermore they reject him which means he is justified in rejecting them and blaming his behavior on them. The assumption is that if they make a miraculous change everything will be alright.

As therapists, as well as human beings, we are taught to fill in the deletions and ignore generalizations in other people's language without requiring them to do it for us. We can readily infer what the borderline means when he says "running has never helped." He should have to specify what it is he has been running from and just what it is that it never helped. Your task is not only to confront the defenses, but to help the individual restore deleted material that fits his perceptual model.

I would suggest that you listen carefully until you can identify key phrases that represent parts of the model. They will leave a question unanswered unless you supply the answer by making an unwarranted assumption about the intended meaning. You should follow an easy, logical questioning routine in a nonthreatening, nonaccusatory manner, asking for clarification and references for material that has been deleted or distorted.

When the borderline adolescent resists clarification because of the difficulty of supplying the material, you have two choices: Either back off and try again later or confront by supplying the deleted or distorted material from your knowledge of borderline dynamics and the particular case. If you choose the latter you have inevitably provided some interpretation, which may or may not be appropriate at a given stage of therapy. This should be a slow and laborious process and not one to be rushed into in most cases. A critical part is the therapist's good judgement and experience; inappropriate confrontation will jeopardize the therapeutic alliance.

In conclusion, I would like to note that the use of linguistic analysis can be a very powerful tool when used in conjunction with an in-depth understanding of the borderline dynamics and the two-factor model. When used without good clinical judgement and patience, not to mention understanding the dynamics of the case, it can resemble an inquisition or something more appropriate to a police interrogation than to the psychotherapist's office. It is also quite possible for the more inflexible therapists to become quite engrossed in the technique of linguistic analysis and ignore the borderline concepts.

Part II

INTRODUCTION TO CASE STUDIES

In this part I will be presenting fifteen cases that represent the continuum of acceptance and rejection—starting with Total Rejection and ending with Low Rejection adolescents. All of these cases are divided by chapter in terms of the four categories in the two-factor model.

The cases are not presented in the detail that the reader might desire because the purpose has been to present information in a format that provides the essential information that a mental health worker could conceivably gather on any adolescent in their charge. Even though the information may be insufficient for some purposes, it is possible to gather information that will allow the therapist to proceed in an effective manner. Because of space limitations and the objectives of this book, relatively little space has been devoted to treatment and psychotherapy.

Chapter 10

TOTAL REJECTION CASES

The three cases presented in this chapter are representative of those severely disturbed adolescents who perceive total rejection from their family, but each differs as far as other factors are concerned. The first, Betty, illustrates utter despair turned into perpetual attention-getting and self-destructive behavior, but lacks the stress and severe depression of the borderline adolescent. The second case, Rick, represents the most destructive of all possible early developments with an early psychopathic resolution. The third case represents a rather rageful abandonment reaction with no hope of retrieving the lost parent. With Buddy we see very aggressive behavior and delinquency as a method of dealing with depression. Yet there is no serious threat to others—just rageful destruction of property typical of Total Rejection adolescents with frequent early separations in their history.

All three cases are adolescents with normal intellectual ability. None of them has known neurological factors that might account for their behavior. However, Rick did have perceptual distortions and a verbal WISC–R score that was some 40 points higher than the performance subtest.

Case #1 Betty

Betty came to our program from a juvenile correctional setting after attempting to hang herself. She had difficulty in functioning in a peer-oriented environment, where she would resort to physical intimidation, physical complaints to staff, attention-getting and self-destructive acts.

She was 17 upon admission to our program, but she reminded me of a 2-year-old in search of a symbiotic union. Interestingly enough, she had no real delinquent history other than running away and some prostitution, despite the fact that she was considered somewhat notorious in the correctional setting. She was originally removed from her parents' home because of severe physical and sexual abuse by her father.

Developmental History

Betty came from a family of 6 children where she was the third from the oldest child. The family was intact although the parents had been divorced and later remarried. The father worked but contributed only marginally to the support of the rest of the family. They were well-known to the authorities because of the many quarrels and domestic violence, and the father was known for his abuse of the rest of the family. He went to such extremes as chaining the children in the basement and beating them. Reportedly the mother on occasion encouraged his sexual abuse of the two girls.

Betty's early development is somewhat clouded because she consistently distorted the facts in such a way that some of her fantasy found its way into the record. She preferred to believe that her real parents were killed in an automobile accident when she was 2 and that she was then adopted by her present family. This fantasy is part of the fact that she clearly rejected her family at the beginning of adolescence. She also refused, as do all Total Rejection adolescents, to accept anyone else as her parents, which accounts for her runs from numerous foster homes. She still visited her family on occasion but these were made as reaffirmation of the rejection. When she spoke of her family it was as though they had vanished.

The first year of her development was adequate as far as can be ascertained. Sometime during the second and third years there were at least two extended physical separations from the mother with later separations from the father, who was in and out of the home at this time. The level of care throughout the early years was physically marginal and certainly not nurturing. The physical abuse did not become excessive until latency, at which time Betty acted out a great deal.

FAMILY PATTERN

On a 14-factor scale that was used to rate families in our study (see appendix) this family scored negatively on all of them, with the exception of borderline characteristics. Betty's perception of her parents was not ambivalent.

I believe the parents were very psychopathic. This is unusual because it applies to the mother as well as the father. They indiscriminately used and abused her while at the same time supplying a certain amount of minimal physical support. The result was that Betty was like someone left out in the cold who seeks out every bit of warmth no matter where it is. When she got it she took off once again with no attachment.

In some ways the family pattern is descriptive of the Severe Rejection group, but there are insufficient redeeming features in order to dangle the carrot of acceptance in front of her. In that sense it was no longer a particularly frustrating environment; she showed none of the internalization and rage repression of the severely rejected adolescent. What internalization there was seemed to come out as psychosomatic complaints.

PERCEPTION OF ACCEPTANCE AND REJECTION

Betty perceived total rejection from her parents. As she said she occasionally went home if there was a need for something, but she was passive around her family and allowed herself to be used sexually or in any other way. This was in keeping with her self-destructive, helpless 'poor me' approach to life in general.

RESOLUTION

Betty had no solid resolution; or perhaps it would be fair to say that her resolution was to appear very unresolved and vulnerable. She was a very good survivor who could correctly read her environment well enough to get along in a relatively good style when she chose. When she was coming on as the prostitute or lesbian hustler she would dress and act the part; or when she was doing her 'down and out' routine she could dress in a way that left no doubt about what she was trying to say. Her use of drugs and alcohol also varied accordingly. They were primarily used as part of her long-term, self-indulgent and self-destructive style, but not in an acute depression-relieving way that is found in the more borderline adolescent.

When Betty was confronted there was an element of depression but it was as though it was perpetual and not defended against. You did not produce the despair and deep abandonment depression of the borderline adolescent. Betty would simply go on at great length about the horrors of living with her family until it had produced depression in those around her.

TREATMENT

Betty stayed with the program until she was 18 whereupon she more or less "hit the road" as nearly all Total Rejection adolescents do. They cannot seem to stay in any alternative placements no matter what they are. She continued to check in with certain people every few months. Her style of dress and general level of care would vary greatly. She always seemed to have money and would not demand anything except a little conversation and friendliness.

I dealt with Betty in a few individual sessions and in a group where she was always cooperative and at times an effective peer leader. She seemed to show some insight around the stress and ambivalence of the more borderline adolescent girls. She was always willing to talk in the group or individually, but it seemed to be a form of prostitution in that I felt she would say or do anything appropriate for a little attention. I do not believe that she ever had any intention of making major changes, because it would not be in keeping with the Total Rejection perception. Her parents were responsible for damaging her and to be successful would have removed that responsibility from them. Some of the later information about Betty came from another adolescent (case #9) who had been a friend of hers in the program. During a recent conversation with this borderline girl, who had taken great strides toward whole object relations, she said: "Betty was here again. I hope you know she's not going to change. She's always going to be the same old Betty. I know because I'm pulling away from her."

CASE #2 RICK

Rick is an example of what can happen if you put most negative early developmental factors together in one individual. He was referred to the program at the age of 16 from a juvenile correctional facility where he had been off and on from the age of 12. Originally he had been sent there for attacking his sister and for generally being out of control. He was notorious among agency personnel because of his impossible behavior and his inability to last in any setting.

Developmental History

Nothing is known about Rick's natural parents except that his mother did little to care for him. Within the first year of life he was hospitalized several times for extended periods for a variety of physical problems all stemming from a lack of care and abuse. He was dehydrated and seriously ill on at least least two occasions. Finally when he was around 8 months of age he was placed in the first of several foster homes. Another separation followed at around 15 months of age. Little is known about the quality of these foster homes, but there were some continuing physical problems that plagued him. Another separation followed at a-bout the age of 3, which was described in detail in the casewor-ker's report at the time. When he was informed that he was going to a new home and that they were going to adopt him he said nothing, but took great pains to collect his few belongings and calmly marched off to the waiting car with no sign of emotion or farewell to his foster parents.

Rick's adoptive parents were well-intentioned people who tried to care for him as best they could. They had two older daughters and periodically took in foster children. Rick would become angry and attack any of the other children at the slightest provocation, because he was jealous. On more than one occasion he physically assaulted his mother over some slight provocation. This pattern of angry acting out and inability to control his impulses continued in school, although academically he had little difficulty. He was impulse ridden, angry and paranoid. He never made an attachment with anyone in the family despite his many years there, and the crowning blow came when they took in another foster child to share his room. Rick took this as a sign that he would soon be gone and his behavior escalated to the point that the family was fearful.

At the age of 11 Rick was placed in a maximum security ward for adult offenders in a state hospital because there was no place else to put him. At the age of 12 he was transferred to a juvenile correction facility thereby beginning what would prove to be a long and frustrating task of trying to place him in foster homes. During one such placement he hit his foster father on the head with a hammer causing him to fall from a roof; Rick complained that the man was making him work too cheaply.

Family Pattern

Rick never gave a thought to his natural or adoptive family, except to occasionally express anger toward everyone for abandoning him. However, his anger was devoid of any real feeling about the matter. He would usually express it in the context of complaining about someone for not being fair to him at the time. His adoptive family was probably quite accepting for the most part but, because of the severity of the damage by the time they got Rick, I doubt that it made much difference.

Perception of Acceptance and Rejection

Rick perceived Total Rejection by his natural mother and by his adoptive parents since they had made no move to contact him in many years. He, in turn, seemed to have totally rejected them. It is important to note that the resolution in this case is so psychopathic that there is no degree of abandonment depression or lingering fantasy of being rescued by the parent.

Resolution

As a result of the very early separations and repeated abandonment, Rick developed an early psychopathic resolution that outweighed all else in its significance. There was never any attachment to a maternal figure beyond a very tenuous one that was broken off by another separation. As a result he could never form anything beyond a brief clinging attachment to some authority figure.

Treatment

Rick spent over one year in a residential treatment program and was finally returned to a correctional setting little improved. He was released from that setting twice, only to commit some crime and be returned. Finally he was sentenced as an adult and sent to the same maximum security setting where he had started out at the age of 11.

I believe that Rick's case illustrates the powerful effects of a negative first year of life. He was an individual so full of paradoxical factors that seem to occur only in adolescents with first year disruptions.

Rick was like a humanoid devoid of certain critical human emotions, such as trust, and empathy, and he was perpetually infantile in his world view. He was, above all, oriented only to the moment and impulsive about getting what he wanted. He claimed, with a great deal of conviction, that he did not have control over his impulsive behavior unless I, as the therapist and authority figure, supplied that control. For example, he had for years made crude sexual advances to females any time there was not an adult male around. I calculated that he had escaped from institutions over sixty times and never failed to get caught almost immediately. Frequently he would run in a circle until he ended up where he started. Rick was of small stature, but he liked to lift weights and was very strong for his size. Frequently when things did not go his way he would become aggressive; a dangerous combination you would think, yet there was never much anger or drive behind the acting out. It was as though he could not internalize or store up feelings of any kind but would constantly vent. He could not be depressed because he would convert that rapidly to anger and project it on his immediate environment. Rick was a good distance runner so I would take him along with me frequently on long runs. I was the authority figure so that I could let him run for a distance on his own. He would return proudly and say, "See, you can trust me." He was once running ahead of me and came to an intersection that was quite busy. I told him to go on across but he became confused in the traffic and ran back and forth in the street until he became panic stricken. His perceptual distortion and judgment were so faulty that he literally could not decide when to cross the street. Another incident that took place two years after he was out of our program illustrates his incredible ineptness. He tried to rob a post office and threatened the woman clerk. He then walked out of the building; she followed him, grabbed his coat and told him to sit on the curb until the police came, which he did.

Rick made slow progress in the program, as long as there was a strict behavior modification program that monitored his behavior around the clock, and providing it was administered by myself or one other staff. The moment the strict controls were off he would disintegrate into anger and acting out and then blame everyone else for not controlling him.

He could discuss his situation intelligently and without emotion, except for the projection of periodic anger at various sources. He was quite intelligent, although he did have a tremendous 40-point discrepancy between his verbal and performance scores on the WISC. He passed his high school equivalency test at age 16 with little difficulty and read quite widely.

Was Rick a dangerous psychopath? He was too damaged and inept in my judgment to carry out anything that was not pure impulse. On the other hand, I have no doubt that if someone put a gun in his hand and said shoot he would, providing that person represented some authority. The combination of paranoid fear and psychopathic resolution is such that no act would be impossible under the right circumstances. Rick was quite typical of the psychopathic Total Rejection adolescent with his great fascination with power, Nazi emblems, biker emblems and so forth. I believe that the most significant aspect of this case is not the rejection or even the psychopathic resolution, but the fact that Rick is representative of a degree of psychological damage that only occurs with the adolescent who has had the severe first year disruption in his development. In fact it seems to be only this element that sets adolescents like Rick apart from others who may share the rest of his developmental pattern.

Case #3 Buddy

Buddy was sent to residential treatment for being out of control and busting up every foster home or group home in which he had been placed. If anything he was more explosive than Rick and only slightly better at internalizing stress. He was 15 years old and of Spanish and American Indian background.

Developmental History

Buddy was in a series of foster placements until 18 months of age, finally being placed in an adoptive home that was far from being stable. His adoptive mother died after heart surgery shortly before his seventh birthday. After his mother's death his father tried to keep the family together, but he had been raised in foster care himself and possessed inadequate parenting skills. He was very inconsistent and somewhat indulgent with his son. Buddy and his younger sister were placed in temporary foster care on several occasions because of the father's difficulties and depression.

Buddy was 9 years old when his adoptive father remarried a woman with 6 older children all of whom were living with her. He was apparently sexually abused by some of the older children. When he was 10 years old his father committed suicide. The stepmother continued to care for the children after the father's death for approximately one year. She moved to another state and took all of the children with her, but shortly thereafter returned Buddy to be placed in foster care. From that time on he was placed in a series of homes, and finally a treatment setting was the only choice remaining because of his aggressive and self-destructive behavior. Buddy was of normal intelligence, very charming and appealing when he chose to be. His most outstanding problem was his anger which could erupt with no warning. He was strong for his size and had the potential to do great damage but, as is the case with most rageful totally rejected adolescents, they are not the ones who end up seriously assaulting others.

Family Pattern

The rage that was so evident with Buddy came from having lost two families. There are a number of cases that I have dealt with where the rage from the loss of the parent through death seems particularly strong and inwardly directed. I do not think that he had ever mourned or dealt with the losses. The most rageful, self-destructive, and generally impossible to treat severely disturbed adolescents are those that have lost a parent through death during critical periods of their development.

Resolution

It is difficult to describe Buddy's resolution except to say that it appeared to be moderately psychopathic. One could say that he was dealing with enormous abandonment depression which would seem to be an understatement given his history, but on numerous occasions I confronted him around his behavior and never knew him to respond with anything other than anger. Yet there were certainly far more human qualities and feeling expression than was the case with Rick or even Betty, for that matter. I suspect the difference has to do with the age at which the resolution was formed. In Rick's case it was formed by the age of 3; in Buddy's case it was more likely to have been sometime after the death of his father.

Treatment

Buddy made progress in the nurturing environment of the treatment program in many respects and was well-liked by the staff despite his aggressive behavior. He would go to great lengths to run from the program but would soon contact us and let us know how he was doing. He would always return and rarely got into trouble while on one of these runs. Finally he was discharged after one of these extended absences, but he would phone and let us know how he was getting along. It is interesting that he would usually give a positive picture of how he was doing, which is contrary to the negative picture given by a borderline adolescent while on one of his depression defending runs.

The Total Rejection adolescents drift around because it is impossible for them to make attachments beyond the most primitive level. Buddy finally checked into a motel and proceded to tear it up and wait for the police. This pattern of rageful destruction by totally rejected adolescents is very common and I cannot recall them doing serious damage to any individual in the process. I once had a youth who tore up a grocery store and robbed it. He dialed the police and told the clerk to call them while he sat there and waited. We will discuss the more violent cases under the ambivalent and low rejection cases, but one would logically think that they might occur with adolescents like Buddy. I have no doubt that severe aggression toward others would have materialized if there had been the strong indulgent or symbiotic factor added to this negative and destructive pattern.

The Total Rejection adolescents will typically survive for up to two years on their own because they cannot attach anywhere else. They will use the staff that they have been somewhat close to as though they were friends and drop in to visit periodically or phone. Sooner or later they do something to deliberately place themselves back into some institutional setting. One must assume that it is ordinarily quite deliberate.

I am prompted to conclude that few of the Total Rejection adolescents with developmental histories and other factors as negative as those described here can survive for any extended period outside of some institutional care. Unfortunately cases such as the ones described here are not unusual—I certainly did not select them on that basis. As the progress and failures of these adolescents are followed in the future we should certainly obtain some interesting results about the paths taken by the Total Rejection adolescents as they become adults.

Chapter 11

SEVERE REJECTION CASES

In this chapter four cases representing examples of the adolescent's perception of Severe Rejection will be presented. In keeping with the idea that the two factors of acceptance and rejection are on a continuum, the cases here are presented from most severe to least severe rejection. As such, the first case in many respects has more in common with Total Rejection than the last case, which has largely borderline features. These differences stem from the inclusion of other factors into the clinical picture, such as early development. The similarities between the cases has to do with the similarities of perception and the adolescent's need to deny, distort, and defend against the threat of total abandonment. It is this group that will be most likely to be misunderstood, mistreated, and to be treatment failures because of our failure to understand the nature of the perception of severe rejection.

CASE #4 JOHN

John was referred to our program at the age of 16 from a correctional setting where he had been sent for sexually molesting a 4-year-old girl, and for various other crimes. This case is very similar to that of Rick's Total Rejection, but it illustrates what happens when you add Severe Rejection from the mother to the other factors. Here we begin to see more borderline features and the beginning of ambivalence, although in the case of John, I believe, the diagnosis is still psychopathic resolution.

Developmental History

There are extensive comments from a pediatrician, when John was between 6 and 10 months of age, indicating that he had been neglected and abused to such an extent that the doctor felt obliged to report it. John's mother had a psychiatric history; she supported the family while John's father, who was middle-aged at the time, stayed home to care for him and his sister, who was 2 years older.

The level of care may have improved somewhat after this, but about the age of 3 John's father began to sexually abuse both he and his sister, while the mother was working. At about the age of 5 John was placed in foster care, and about a year after this he was placed in the first of what would turn out to be many years of residential care and treatment. His father soon disappeared from the scene and the contacts with his mother were few and far between; those that did occur were labeled as erotic, sensual and totally unsatisfactory by the workers at the time. She took the daughter home to live with her, but would not keep John because he was described as a behavior problem. By the age of 9 he was described as totally uncooperative; charming at times, infantile and very manipulative of adults.

John's mother, at the time I first met her, was interested in her son's welfare, although she communicated great discouragement that anything was going to be done. Her affect was abnormal, although I felt that her depression had more to do with just being worn out from many years of work and the life style she had lead. After one session with her son she got up and walked out without so much as an acknowledgement to her son.

John was always very infantile, playful, and manipulative under all circumstances. He reminded one of Rick in most respects; however, he was rarely angry and assaultive except in a semiplayful way. He would constantly bother and cling to some of the more maternal staff as a 3-year-old might. Despite his history of sexual assaultiveness, and his strength, these staff members were protected from any assault by other male patients.

John was similar to Rick in his relatively high intelligence, the severity of his early development, and in his considerable physical strength. They were also similar in their inability to use this strength in any seriously aggressive manner.

Family Pattern

The family pattern was one of Total Rejection from the father and Severe Rejection from the mother. The acceptance that did come from the mother was highly sporadic and infrequent, but when it was forthcoming it was erotically tinged. John's pattern of behavior, the few times that he did try to live at home, was to project or internalize feelings until he exploded in some bizarre behavior involving sexual aggression and drugs.

Resolution

I cannot remember John ever acting depressed no matter how much he was confronted; for that matter he rarely acted very angry for more than a moment. His resolution was to deny feeling anything at all. He would not project the confrontation back angrily as most psychopathic youngsters will do, but only jokingly, which throws into question whether that is a correct label to apply to his resolution in the first place. In any case, dealing with the rather enormous stress by this method would never work for John because he was a lively, intelligent, and, in many respects, a very sensitive adolescent. This meant that he had to keep everything on a superficial, infantile level at all times.

You always had the feeling with John that with a little more work you could penetrate his shell through confrontation, although we certainly never did to any significant extent. Perhaps the difference between the early and later resolution is suggested by the difference in John and Rick's draw-a-person responses. Rick's drawings were of a large, severe looking face which covered the entire page in bold strokes; a type of drawing common to psychopathic adults. John's drawings of a person were half inch high stick figures drawn lightly in the center of a large sheet of paper.

John remained with the treatment program for over one year and was discharged to his home with his mother and stepfather. Given where he started from in the program, he made progress by completing his high school equivalency and handling freedom outside and on passes home. The treatment might be called almost parental; it was a tight structure with monitoring of his behavior, gradual freedom and separation, and the development of a degree of trust in certain staff members. Many sessions in therapy were attempted with John, but he would deny all insights and always come back to the immediate situation. It was more than mere avoidance of issues or underlying depression, it was as though he was saying, "I just want to start over again and be parented."

Given the severity of his problems, we had no great expectations about his success after discharge. He got a job and did better than expected for a period. When he came back to visit he was well dressed (which was unusual for John), quiet and polite, quite unlike what he had been in the program. He gradually became more agitated with his freedom and lack of structure on the outside. He had, in a sense, been deprived of his only outlet for stress by being unable to act out in an infantile, mildly aggressive way. Without this he was essentially being asked to suppress all feelings. This was not abandonment depression in any true sense because general agitation and paranoid fear predominated over depression. As such the acting out was not directly self-destructive, as it is inclined to be with the more borderline adolescent, but tended to be more indirectly destructive as with the Totally Rejected adolescent. He got into heavy drug usage, which had the effect of breaking down his resolution to suppress feelings, and the result would be bizarre acting out involving sexual aggression against children and the psychopathic-like fascination with guns which he would steal.

John was involved in stealing guns and a motorcycle, and rode around until he was caught. Finally he went through this sequence and barricaded himself in his house prompting the local authorities to call out the SWAT team. Of course he never did more than fire the guns into the air, but he did a convincing imitation of a very dangerous individual. Not surprisingly, all of these incidents were preceded by a pattern involving his mother, a girl friend, or in one case, visiting his natural father. Only time will tell whether anyone as psychologically damaged as John can ever function outside of a secure setting. One can only speculate as to the type of treatment environment that would have to be maintained for a very long time in order to have a chance at effective treatment.

CASE #5 LARRY

Larry was sent to our program at the age of 14 after attempting to burn down the foster home he had lived in for 7 years. The act was preceded by a short period of bizarre, psychotic-like behavior and great stress directly related to the fact that his mother began contacting him after an absence of several years. Larry represents severe pathological rejection that illustrates the power and attraction of even minimal hope of acceptance from the mother. It is indeed the most powerful and motivating of all forces. It is similar to John (case #4) in this respect, although Larry did not have the negative first year of development, and his mother, while far more pathological than John's, was more assertive in her acceptance when it did occur.

Early Development

Larry's early development is one of the most negative of all, although the first year of life was at least minimally satisfactory. The family was well-known to welfare agencies at the time of his birth and the records were extensive.

During the second year the father left several times, and on at least two occasions the mother left for a long period, leaving Larry and his siblings in the care of relatives. This pattern of frequent separations, alcoholic violence, and the beginning of physical abuse took place during his third and fourth year of development. Larry had a brother one year older and another 4 years older. There was also an older sister and a younger sister.

When Larry was 4 his father was sentenced to prison. Shortly after this he and his older brother were starting fires in the house and neighborhood. By the time he was 6 he and his brothers were placed in a foster home. They were removed from at least two homes because of their acting out and interference from the mother. It was here that a pattern began; there would be violence in the home, the children would be placed in protective custody, things would settle down at home and then the mother would insist that the children be placed back with her again. The children would act out in such a way that they would eventually be placed with her because of the difficulty of keeping them in foster care.

Little is known about Larry's natural father except that he was regarded as an habitual criminal with a record of violence. His mother had been diagnosed as a paranoid schizophrenic; her affect was clearly disturbed with emotions that seemed totally inconsistent with the content of what she was saying. There was never any indication of depression.

Within the foster home Larry was the youngest of several children and he put himself into a very dependent and sometimes infantile position. He was demanding, manipulating, and quick to take anything that did not go his way as rejection. Throughout latency he remained in a quasi-symbiotic relationship with the foster mother that created great dependency. At no time did he accept her as a replacement for his natural mother.

Two things seem to have conspired to prompt the acting out behavior just prior to his fourteenth birthday. First, it is the most frequent age period for acting out in adolescence and, second, his mother began a campaign of calling, visiting, and interference. Severe rejection along with abuse seem, in particular, to create a carrot to dangle in front of the child that is very powerful. Tremendous stress was created that Larry had no acceptable way to process but in a psychotic-like reaction that lead to the fire, which he saw as a means to get himself placed at home. Although I would emphasize that this was not a conscious deliberation on his part. He chose the first perceived rejection from the foster mother as the instigation for the fire.

Family Pattern

The family pattern in and of itself was not borderline, but rather a combination of delinquent (without much indulgence), violent, psychotic, very unpredictable, and, above all, severely rejecting. Larry would not dare to strike out against his mother for fear of physical retaliation and total rejection. The next older brother acted out through persistent delinquent behavior and aggression, and the oldest brother had been frequently arrested for bizarre sexual acting out and robbery. Here we can see the fire-setting and sexual acting out coming from the same basic parental pattern. It is interesting to conjecture that the result may have been a more violent acting out if there had also been the indulgence or symbiotic relationship with the mother.

Perception of Acceptance and Rejection

Larry perceived severe rejection from the family in general and not simply from his mother. He would be indiscriminately physically abused without provocation just as he would be accepted home without any basis in his actions to justify it. His mother was unpredictable which kept Larry attached firmly as if by some invisible umbilical cord. Just when it appeared that he might be angry enough to reject her she would be seductive to get him back and then pull the rug of support out from under him. Her pattern with all the boys was to ignore them when they were locked up (except for the oldest who was somewhat indulged) in treatment and begin contact as they got close to release to make sure they would return home. The power of this pattern comes from the intermittent nature of the acceptance from the mother. It becomes even more formidable when the abusive and violent nature of the pattern produces a profound fear and paranoia in the adolescent.

Resolution

Severe Rejection does not ordinarily produce a firm resolution to the stress which necessitates the need for indirect methods of acting out against the parent. The primary defense is projection and denial as well as a clinging, demanding dependency whenever possible. The tremendous stress created must be largely internalized until it can be vented via indirect methods. One means of denial and probably minor ventilation of aggression is through almost constant manipulation of the environment and various clandestine acting out.

The resolution is to distort and deny the relationship with the mother. Identification of the problem would be very threatening. The fact that no clearly identified resolution to the stress exists, does not necessarily mean that they are unresolved and open to the proposal of a more adaptive resolution and treatment, because to do so would threaten abandonment. Their rather inadequate defenses are shallow but firm and can take time to penetrate.

Larry may be said to have split object relations, but it was almost entirely of the withdrawing part mirroring the split in the acceptance and rejection. As such, there is a certain pathological intactness that is unique to this type. In order to internalize the paranoia and stress, rather firm defenses are required to protect the ego structure; there is not the rapid and frequent swings as in the more borderline adolescent. By contrast with the Ambivalent Rejection adolescent, one sees the paradoxical situation of greater reality perception in any situation that does not involve the mother, and more stable patterns of behavior in this adolescent. Larry had developed very subtle forms of acting out in such a way that it was only after a considerable period of treatment that he was inclined to act out self-destructively in a more borderline fashion.

Treatment

Treatment for Larry was very long and arduous with many false avenues that both he and the mother lead us down. He had virtually no contact with his mother during the first year of treatment, despite the fact that she lived only a short distance away. When it got close to discharge he would regress severely and act out either through running away (he did not go home, unlike the borderline adolescent) or by attempting to start a fire in the program. During these periods of stress he would regress so much so that his behavior could become quite bizarre and psychotic-like.

Individual treatment for Larry was a modified form of what I would do for a more Ambivalent Rejection borderline adolescent; the difference being a stronger emphasis on the relationship with his mother and to attack his distortions and denial more vigorously. It got to the point where he referred to therapy as brainwashing, which in many respects it was. The lethal nature of the family situation and his relationship with his mother was reviewed repeatedly, interspersed later with direct contacts with her. These contacts were used as reality examples of what we talked about in therapy sessions. To try to force him to go elsewhere than home would have lead to another fire in his panic to get to his mother.

Larry was intelligent and understood the information that was given to him even when he chose to deny it. I have previously described one of the sessions with his mother where she confronted both Larry and the therapist about the fact that she had ultimate control over all her children and not the therapist. She was adamant in insisting that Larry was going to fail again after he left the program and there was nothing we could do about it.

Larry left the program and returned home followed by intermittent readmission on a brief crisis basis following some violent episode. On one occasion he escaped through a bedroom window pursued by his mother with a knife. For many months he came back for sessions with the therapist and showed steady progress in the development of a more clear whole object relation. He became quite philosophical about the family situation and found a good deal of sick humor in the whole thing. During these sessions he would recount the events at home and provide long accurate descriptions of the family dynamics. He learned to understand the bind he was in quite well. During the next 18 months he was able to get himself out of the home for brief periods, such as a stint in Job Corp, but would return to the family again. He managed to successfully avoid trouble with the law and had developed alternative places to stay for brief periods when the pressure became too great at home.

CASE #6 HOLLY

Holly was referred for treatment after stabbing her grandmother with a pair of scissors; she had also inflicted wounds on herself at various times. She had been supporting herself as a prostitute, and although she was still 14 at the time of her entry into our program, she looked 30 years old. She had spent much time in a juvenile correctonal facility where she was regarded as incorrigible; she was at times the loudest, toughest acting, and most vulgar female I had seen in the treatment program. She was very attractive when she chose to be; her appearance would vary from dressing like a prostitute to the disheveled look of the totally rejected adolescent. Holly had a slight speech problem and her intellectual ability was within the low normal range; at one time she was thought to be mentally retarded.

Holly's case illustrates that one should not jump to conclusions about an adolescent without first doing a thorough study of the factors involved, and by trying a confrontational approach. It illustrates how an adolescent can move from one category to another in the acceptance-rejection continuum and confuse the clinical picture. It shows the importance of concentrating on borderline dynamics and the individual's perception of rejection as opposed to more superficial acting out. It was, in fact, the latter—the resolution—that had lead to her diagnostic classification as hopeless. Holly had been variously diagnosed as schizophrenic, sociopathic, and as having a severe personality disorder. She could, under stress, decompensate into a state where she could be dangerous to others. She was extremely morbid, as is often true of Severe Rejection adolescents; she was depressive and talked frequently of death. She often carried concealed weapons because she was afraid of being harmed.

Developmental History

Little is known about Holly's natural father other than the fact that he was thought to be very sociopathic and left the family when she was about 2 years of age. Within one year the mother had remarried the stepfather who remained with the family. As far as can be determined the first year of Holly's development was satisfactory with difficulties beginning during the separation-individuation stage of development, climaxed by the separation from her natural father. Mother provided little support and attention during this period and was borderline herself. The stepfather moved into the situation prior to Holly's third birthday further adding to the problem because he was seen as a fearful, threatening object and as someone who pulled her mother away.

The situation was further complicated by the birth of a brother when Holly was 1 year of age, followed by two siblings born to the mother and stepfather when Holly was about 4 and again when she was 7. She began experiencing difficulties in school by about the fourth grade. She was fearful and morbid by this time with fantasies of killing her stepfather and burying him in the backyard. She was already carrying weapons for protection at this early age. In addition, in true borderline fashion, she was mother's confidant and sister, who had some responsibility for siblings as the oldest child. Mother was unpredictable and impulsive at that time, although there were definite suggestions of an early symbiotic attachment on Holly's part. More than likely she saw the entire situation as very threatening and her mother as being defenseless against a rageful father figure. It was also clear that her mother could be very withholding of libidinal supplies and attention without much warning or provocation.

The stepfather was well-intentioned but clearly seen as the ogre in the situation by both Holly and her mother. He was immature, did not know how to relate to Holly and was prone toward angry rages without directly assaulting the family. Mother would use him to some extent as a means of control over Holly who took this as a real danger and a threat far beyond the reality of the situation. By the time she was 12 she was considered to be out of control and dangerous.

Family Pattern

The family pattern is Ambivalent Rejection for the most part although the combination of violence and the early pathological element surrounding the natural father also gives the situation many Severe Rejection elements that were in fact exaggerated by Holly, as far as her perception was concerned. Because her behavior became so severe and the family felt somewhat at risk anytime she was at home, they did reject her outright. This in itself is very unusual for a borderline family and tended to alter the clinical situation. After Holly entered the treatment program her parents moved and left no forwarding address; they were skeptical that she could get any help at this late stage.

Perception of Acceptance and Rejection

Holly never mentioned her parents and acted as though she accepted the rejection—as such, she physically looked like one of the totally rejected adolescents. She was going to prove that she was the worst and the most vulgar female in the program. She always bore a hard, determined expression to cover up any depression that might have been present. She made it clear that she viewed herself as a "loser." But in looking through her previous records in the correctional setting and elsewhere, there were many things that struck me as being a Severe Rejection pattern, e.g., morbid fantasy, interest in artistic expression, paranoid fear, fascination with death, and so forth. While these things do occur with the Total Rejection adolescent they are usually not predominant features. As it turned out the Severe Rejection pattern predominated throughout much of her childhood, as far as her perception was concerned.

Resolution

Holly appeared to be highly resolved with such a tough front that no one could penetrate it. She would explode in a rage much like the Total Rejection psychopathic adolescent except that she would cry, which I have never seen the psychopathic adolescent do during one of these acting out periods. Also in exploring her delinquent history I noticed that it was not as extensive as I had thought and it was quite goal directed. Keeping in mind that the Total Rejection delinquent pattern is rarely goal directed but rather one of outrageous displays of aggression and attention-getting. Holly had mainly confined herself to shoplifting (which she claimed her mother taught her to do), prostitution and some threatened aggression. The latter, when closely examined, seemed to be of a borderline variety and stemmed from fear when escaping a situation and being thwarted.

Treatment

I did not deal with Holly until after she had been in treatment for several months. The first time I had a session with her I was met with the usual suspicion and choice words reserved for the male staff, but she came to my office willingly. I began with my usual approach to an initial session, which involves a very mild confrontation of going over some of her history and the reasons she might have done some of the things mentioned in her record. In Holly's case the result was rather dramatic; her face softened and she started to cry. Then she began to talk in a soft voice that I had never heard her use before. It was obvious that she was incredibly shy and afraid of men. She acted very surprised that I would give her any attention without wanting something from her.

I did not have a lot of sessions with Holly after that, but each time she talked freely and acted most grateful that I was spending time with her. She admitted that she felt rejected by the lack of contact with her parents and she felt that she was a terrible, hopeless person. In my opinion Holly would have gotten nowhere unless the issue with the parental rejection was pursued. I finally traced down her parents at their new home—which fortunately was within driving distance—and had a session with them, unknown to Holly. They were reluctant to renew contact although her mother wanted to and was very upset by the situation. I explained to them that I felt strongly that Holly would find them after she left our program, no matter where they were, and end up on their doorstep. There was little doubt about this because it is a pattern that all high rejection adolescents will go through until they have either accepted the rejection or worked it out with their parents. Under this sort of intimidation the parents decided that they would rather work with me as the mediator in the situation.

Holly ran from the program shortly before she would have been released, which is in keeping with the borderline adolescent. She was apparently fearful that she would not have been sent home to her parents, which was probably true because the social agency responsible for her, as well as her parents, were still fearful of violence. Since she ended up on their doorstep after the run, as predicted, they took her in and I had further sessions with them and Holly. She stayed with her parents for a few months before moving out with a boyfriend. She finished her high school equivalency and made slow but steady progress in all areas.

Once the contacts and the sessions with the parents began,

along with supportive individual sessions, Holly changed in a number of remarkable ways. She no longer used the tough defense or resolution and became quite an unresolved borderline adolescent who was open to treatment. She changed physically in that she looked younger and softer. She pursued her interest in art while in the program which developed to the point that she had a professional exhibit of her work.

CASE #7 DEBRA

Debra was an attractive blonde, 15 years old, referred to residential treatment because of overdosing with drugs and a variety of self-destructive behavior. She was very vibrant and alive on the one hand and intensely depressed on the other; she is an example of splitting carried to an extreme even for a borderline adolescent. She is, in fact, an example of what would happen if you combined strong elements of both Severe and Ambivalent Rejection.

Developmental History

Debra's first year of development was adequate, as far as could be ascertained. Sometime during her second year her mother abandoned her while her father was away and she was placed in the first of many foster homes. She never saw her mother again and her father remarried. From about the age of 2 until nearly 8, she remained in a series of foster home placements, the quality of which varied considerably. The last home was negative in many respects, with the parents being alcoholic and somewhat abusive.

Throughout the latter few years of these foster placements, her father visited regularly and indulged her with gifts and promises that he was going to take her home with him. Debra's father was married six times; the marriage to her mother being the fourth. He had a history of antisocial behavior and presented himself as a very sociopathic individual with relatively good ego strength who was able to support his family in a middle class manner.

Very little is known about the mother except that she was a

dancer and made no attempt to get her daughter back or make contact through the years. After Debra went to live with her father, when she was 8, she came to consider her stepmother as her mother. This woman was supportive of Debra, but heavily involved in her own career as a police officer. When Debra was 10 her stepmother left and maintained minimal contact from that time.

The father dealt with Debra in a very ambivalent manner. He had always indulged her in what she saw as an attempt to persuade her to live with him. Once in the home, this pattern continued to some extent; however, the other side of the father's personality also became apparent. He was violent, threatening and abusive at one time, and indulgent at another. When Debra was about the age of nine, he began sexually abusing her. She was made to feel grateful to her father for rescuing her from the foster home, and she clearly both loved and feared him. After the stepmother left the home the sexual relationship between Debra and her father increased. He stated on many occasions that she reminded him of her mother, which was a mixture of love and hate. She came to feel that she was a "tramp" just like her real mother.

The behavior pattern of the Severe Rejection child contributed to the problem after Debra went to live with her father. Her level of trust was nonexistent and her self-concept was extremely low, which all conspired to produce limit testing and angry behavior toward anything that appeared as a rejection. As Debra stated it, "I limit test to see if you really love me." Not long after she moved into her father's home, he and his wife left Debra for the weekend in the care of a baby-sitter. While they were gone, she started a fire in the attic and shortly after this she was placed in a residential school which she was kicked out of after two months. This pattern of Severe Rejection is not a borderline response to latency age development.

When Debra was 12 years old her father remarried a woman with two children of her approximate age. She did not get along with this stepmother, feeling that this woman was a threat and infringement on her tenuous relationship with her father. She began to get into heavy drug abuse which the father reacted to by putting limits on her freedom; depriving her of material things and being physically abusive (often in conjunction with sexual abuse). This lead to even greater dependence on drugs, as a way to deal with the stress and depression. It is interesting to note that she never sexually acted out with anyone except her father.

The discrepancy between the sexual relationship with the father and the increasing physical and verbal abuse increased the conflict and stress to intolerable limits. The use of drugs became suicidal. She told a psychiatrist about the sexual abuse. The result was a lot of publicity which increased her guilt to impossible dimensions.

Family Pattern

The family pattern in this case is not particularly borderline in its dynamics. A borderline pattern is produced in Debra if you consider the entire history of Severe Rejection, abuse, Total Rejection, indulgence, and ambivalent behavior from the father. One result of this unusual family pattern is that it provided an exterior facade of intactness for Debra that was not representative of the internal emptiness. As a matter of fact this, in and of itself, was a source of stress for her because she recognized that everything looked so good on the outside to others (both in terms of her as a person and as a middle class family) but no one could see how bad it was on the inside.

Perception of Acceptance and Rejection

Debra's perception was certainly that of the severely rejected adolescent, although it was mixed with a good deal of ambivalence. One might say that Debra received high stress from two different sources: The borderline stress coming from the ambivalence of her father's behavior toward her, and the stress that comes from the disparity between very Severe Rejection on the one hand and a sporadic indulgence on the other. The result of course was that Debra used a splitting defense. Everything was in extremes and contrasts; even her beauty on the outside was contrasted with what she perceived to be deep ugliness inside.

Resolution

Debra's resolution or lack of it is representative of the history it reflects; it is widely varied and very superficial. One moment it seems to be the shell-like structure of the Severe Rejection adolescent and the next the unresolved borderline crisis. Some form of resolution was forced very early in her development when she was forcibly separated from her mother and father. This could not be solidified into a psychopathic resolution; probably because it happened during the separation phase of development and because of the nature of the foster care which immediately followed. I suspect the intermittent involvement of her father also kept it from solidifying. Her resolution, if you want to call it that, was to be frightened, impulsive, acting out, never thinking beyond the immediate and, above all, not to trust anyone too much. During latency she could vent her rejection and anger in indirect ways, such as fire-setting, being manipulative and devious, as most Severe Rejection adolescents are at this age. At pubescence, the second stage of separation-individuation, began the borderline conflict and the sexual relationship with her father necessitating a more borderline acting out through drugs and self-destruction.

The split object relations are more differentiated in Debra's case relative to most borderline conflicts. The divisions into goodness and badness, rewarding and withdrawing, are very clear both literally and symbolically, but always in a nondelusional, nonpsychotic fashion. There is a real practical basis here rooted in her developmental history. As one adolescent girl with a similar highly rejecting history said to me, after observing psychotic episodes in a borderline adolescent, "When you had to scratch around to stay alive and survive like I did, you can't be a complete flake." Indeed what seems to be universal among the more rejected and abused adolescents is this pragmatic, observer of the environment, survival side even under enormous stress conditions. When they do act out directly or become psychotic it is not gradual, but a sudden onset under enormous pressure like a dam finally giving way. Debra's situation can be described as not so much fear of abandonment but the deadly certainty that abandonment will always occur.

Debra would talk openly about the good and bad parts of her as being clear entities that represented two different versions of herself; one part tells her to do such acting out as cutting on her arms and that if she does she will feel better. In true borderline fashion she felt a great and immediate sense of comfort and relief after she did act in some self-destructive fashion. This can be seen as the rewarding part which demands dependent regressive behavior. There is considerable self-hate here—much more so than in most borderline adolescents—because of the abuse and repeated rejection. One voice tells her that she is bad, evil, and that she will never make it successfully, and her only salvation is to harm herself. She realizes that the voices are not real except in the sense that she believes what they are saying to her. Of course the other voice tells her what a fool she is to be acting out and in a sense echoes all the objective, positive messages she hears from people around her.

Some idea of the conflict of voices is found in the following illustration. One of her objectives is to be a model. Upon visiting an agency she was told that she had many attributes necessary for the job and received a lot of praise. Shortly after she felt compelled to cut her arm very severely because the voices told her that she was no good and this was the only way she would feel better. One part represents the early rejection, the abandonment, and the unpredictable violence, but beyond that there is the voice of the pragmatic, ethical and reality-oriented Debra. These two images are very well-formed to the point that they may be somewhat representative of multiple personalities. However, there is a considerable reality ego operating in the sense that she is capable of observing the two sides.

Debra's drawings are interesting because they are representative of the Severe Rejection group of adolescents. They are characteristically detailed and well-executed showing a degree of talent not usually found in the other groups. These drawings are often done as part of a journal she keeps every day. This represents an unusual combination of two levels: 1) The Severe Rejection borderline adolescents are more likely to choose drawings as a means of expression, (2) The Ambivalent Rejection borderline more often use writing as their expression.

Treatment

Debra's depression was more difficult to deal with therapeutically than most borderline adolescents in the sense that her history was so negative and rejecting that there was a sense of legitimacy to the depression. She possessed that sort of pragmatic view of her own background which seems to occur only with the more severely rejected adolescents, whether they have the splitting borderline dynamics or not. The advantage to this, from a therapeutic standpoint, is that she also had a greater degree of reality ego to work with that could integrate the split parts in a way that the more ambivalent rejection adolescents could not.

Because of the reality of abandonment, as opposed to the fear of it occurring, the relationship with the therapist probably became even more critical than with other borderline adolescents. There were really no other positive or accepting aspects in her life to rely on at first and thus the therapist became the only available life preserver to keep her afloat. She was quick to take anything as a sign of rejection and a considerable amount of transference acting out—even to physical proportions—took place.

Because of her lack of a firm resolution, and the severe rejection, the depression was always near the surface. This, combined with the reality ego meant that she did quite well in a therapeutic setting as long as the therapeutic alliance was intact. It was necessary to allow her to be very dependent during much of the course of treatment. She could combine or integrate the split parts relatively well, and developed a reasonable degree of whole object relations after many months of intensive psychotherapy.

Chapter 12

AMBIVALENT REJECTION CASES

The focus of this chapter is on case examples of Ambivalent Rejection adolescents. Keeping in mind the continuum of acceptance and rejection, the four cases presented here cover quite a wide range. The first has many Severe Rejection factors so much so that the distinction is rather blurred. On the other hand, the last case presented is of a relatively high acceptance and as such has more schizophrenic features in the borderline dynamics than any case presented throughout this entire section. Case #9 is in the middle because it represents the maximum Ambivalent Rejection and borderline symptoms. From that point on, if we consider that to be an apex of ambivalence, the cases get into more of an acceptance and indulgence factor, or as we shall see in the next chapter, the element of symbiosis.

CASE #8 TED

Ted was referred for treatment just as he turned 12 years of age because of failure to get along in several other placements; also for bizarre, self-destructive behavior, such as walking on the ledge of a tall building. He was also particularly prone to attacking females including his mother. He was successful in at least one residential placement, but when he was sent home to his mother, he once again became aggressive.

Ted was a good-looking, charming, and pleasant young man who could be a leader among his peers. He had never showed delinquent behavior for more than a short period of time and was a good student of above average intelligence. On entering the program he felt he had no problems except his temper and not getting along with his mother, who, he insisted, cared for him very much.

Developmental History

Ted's natural father was deported to his native country just prior to Ted's birth and the family had no contact since that time. A stepfather came into the home when Ted was approximately 3 and left when he was 6. He was very physically and verbally abusive toward Ted, although I am uncertain to what extent.

Throughout most of Ted's early development he and his mother lived with the maternal grandmother who was a real matriarch and driving force of the extended family (she quite literally drove her children crazy!). Mother's life before and after Ted's birth was a perpetual series of moves in and out of her mother's home in an attempt to separate herself from her influence. Ted was always caught in a tug of war between the two women. For long periods after his mother became angry and stormed out, she would leave him in the care of grandmother. The grandmother indulged him as a means of getting back at her daughter. Ted would then prefer grandmother over mother, which would set her off on a rageful, punitive display as she tried to get back at both Ted and her mother. Ted was not always the innocent victim of this triangle since he was very good at playing each against the other, extracting maximum benefit in material goods and attention. This pattern continued even during the time he was in the treatment program; his mother saying she would not visit as long as Ted was allowed to have visits with his grandmother. Grandmother, of course, never missed a visit each week; Ted would enter the room and demand money, whereupon she would open her purse and give him what he wanted.

The grandmother was one of the most incredible women I have ever met. The first time I saw her I did a double take because she looked and talked like Brenda's grandmother (case #9), but she was even more destructive and pathological. They both ruled the extended family in an autocratic manner using economic means and psychological terrorism. The grandmother presented herself as the 'salt of the earth' and an island of calm amidst violent and irrational behavior in the family. She described shoot-outs between her former husband and the children. She presented herself effectively as a martyr and extremely rational and reasonable in comparison with her very "crazy" daughter.

The comparison with her daughter was valid to be sure as she was one of the most irrational and severely disturbed mothers of all the cases described. I believe she was quite psychotic with considerable paranoid schizophrenic tendencies. I personally feel uncomfortable with paranoid schizophrenics and this woman was one of the most enraging people I have ever encountered.

Ted's mother was similar in many respects to Larry's mother (case #5) and in that sense very characteristic of Severe Rejection. You must also add the rather constant indulgence from the grandmother, because she played a key role in his early development as well as in later contact, to such an extent that his total perception was still quite ambivalent. It should also be noted that the combination of the indulgent pattern and the role model of violence allowed him to act out his frustrations through aggressive behavior toward others. He would act out toward his mother only under the most extreme provocation; the rest of the time it was carefully sublimated and indirect as in the Severe Rejection adolescent.

Another difference from the usual Ambivalent Rejection individual is that Ted was acting out in latency, as is true of the Severe Rejection case, to the point that he was in a residential program for a period of time.

Family Pattern

The family pattern is a complex one to be sure but largely in the Severe Rejection category. The abuse, absent father, highly pathological mother, and the general use of violence as a method of acting out certainly place it in that group. In addition, the rejection and acceptance cycle tends to be more like the Severe Rejection pattern and not the borderline group.

Perception of Acceptance and Rejection

Ted saw acceptance from his grandmother through her indulgent pattern. At least initially he felt that she was a benign individual who gave him everything he wanted, but he was smart enough to see that she did it in part to get at his mother. It was also his way of getting back at his mother as well, so he had something in common with his grandmother; a mutual pact, so to speak. But as is often the case with indulgent, highly accepting patterns without symbiosis, he had no strong feeling for his grandmother and felt little reluctance at not being able to see her when he started dealing therapeutically with his mother.

Ted's perception of his mother was quite another matter than his perception of his grandmother. When asked about this he would say, "Of course she cares about me, look at the way she is always trying to get her hands on me." But he would add, "I know she hates me, too; maybe even more than she loves me. That woman is crazy, you know!" Her acceptance of him was intense but highly intermittent. But it is fair to say that he perceived a highly ambivalent acceptance-rejection pattern between the two of them.

Resolution

Ted initially had a fairly structured if superficial resolution to deal with the stress—certainly more so than most Ambivalent Rejection borderline adolescents—by his periodic aggression and indirect methods of acting out. Part of this included his denial that there was really a problem at all much like the Severe Rejection adolescent, along with assurances that if we could just let him he would work everything out. He used his appealing nature and social ability to come across as a normal young man and thus deny the depression around his feelings of rejection and conflict. When confronted about this he became quite unresolved and appeared to be a definite borderline adolescent who was very open to treatment.

Treatment

Ted's case should remain a lesson to all of us who deal with severely disturbed adolescents of how not to handle a case after discharge. While I was not personally involved in one to one psychotherapy with Ted, I was involved with the interaction around his mother and grandmother. It was so complex that it was never really comprehended by those who had the responsibility of dealing with Ted after he left the program.

As predicted, mother began to contact and visit as soon as she found out that Ted was going to a foster home. This of course is in keeping with a Severe Rejection pattern mother and very similar to case 5. Ted understood the family dynamics well enough and with strong therapeutic support he confronted her with what she was doing and succeeded in at least temporarily gaining control of their relationship. He made it clear that he wanted to see her only as much as he felt comfortable with, to which she responded with every conceivable form of guilt inducement, rageful temper tantrum, and threatened rejection. It literally got to the point that she said "God will get you for this." (She was very religious at this point.) Ted wanted to control the degree of contact and be responsible as we had taught him to be. Over a period of two years after Ted left the program and went to live in a foster home there was constant interference in Ted's ability to control the situation by representatives of social agencies, the foster parents, and the court. I suppose the tip-off of what was to come came just after he left the program; there was a court hearing which included a large number of people interested in the case in one way or another. Everyone except Ted was brought in to testify about where Ted should live (his mother was trying to gain legal custody). Afterward he came to me and said, "Don't they understand that all I want is to be able to see her when I want? I don't want to live there."

The attitude of those in control was: We know what is best for you and will maintain the control over when and where you may have contact. This is always a great threat of either ultimate abandonment or of being cut off entirely from the mother. In fact, these legal agents can gain control as every adolescent knows and few social agencies and courts seem to understand. If you act bad enough they will have no choice but to lock you up or send you home.

For at least one year Ted did very well in the foster home and in school, where he starred on the football team and was very popular. But gradually he was placed in an acceptance-rejection bind that lead to acting out. The foster parents were resistant to his contacts with his mother because she was so obviously "bad" for him. Ted liked them very much but saw it as trying to buy him away from his mother just as his grandmother did and as a potential threat to totally cut off contact. The social agency representative and the court went along with the foster parents by rigidly controlling contact even as Ted got older and was showing how responsible he could be at controlling the contacts. His mother, being a basically intelligent woman, handled everything by being passive, but showing she cared by persistent legal pressure. The result was that acting out increased to the point where Ted was placed in a group home and then finally in his own home with his mother because there were no alternatives left. At this point the social agencies made it clear that he had burned all his bridges behind him by his behavior and of course he was then totally trapped in his mother's home. After a short period of time he ended up assaulting her severely enough to be sent to a juvenile correctional facility.

CASE #9 BRENDA

Brenda, a 17-year-old, was brought to our program in an extremely regressed and agitated state because of self-destructive behavior, such as drinking toxic liquids, cutting herself, and overdosing on street drugs. She had been living on the street for months—nothing was too bad for her including eating from garbage cans and living as a prostitute in dangerous areas of the city. Upon entering treatment she would act out by hitting herself against the wall until she required physical restraints. She had previously been hospitalized on several occasions. Brenda was of low normal intelligence and very behind educationally since she had not attended school for several years. Initially she refused to have any contact with her parents or any family members and would accept no phone calls. She would sit around and rail against them, followed by a bout of severely self-destructive behavior.

Developmental History

Brenda was the oldest of five children. From all that could be ascertained her first year of development was satisfactory from a care and nurturing standpoint. Her mother was quick to push her into the separation stage because of her own borderline problems and the fact that Brenda's brother was born when she was 12 months old; followed by a sister when she was 3. Her mother stated that she loved kids until they could walk and then preferred to have little to do with them until they were much older and more reasonable. There was a pattern of threatened separations from the mother followed by brief but traumatic actual separations where Brenda's mother would be gone for an hour after an argument. In other words, there were no long separations, but a pattern of fighting that seemed to be perpetual but not serious.

Throughout childhood Brenda had many fears and anxieties that were normal for the age she was at, but tended to be unresolved and to persist into adolescence. Being the oldest she began to find her place and regain some attention from her mother by taking over some of the household tasks and care of the younger children.

By the age of 12 Brenda was heavily into the drug culture and running from home for brief periods of time. She had particular difficulty with her father who reacted very negatively to her developing sexuality. She had many sexual fantasies about him, which were mixed with reality. He had always been very physical with her both in a punishing way and in a sensual and erotic manner. Her need for his attention was so great she became very confused about their relationship. This case served as a warning to me to be cautious about reaching conclusions about the sexual relationship that might exist between the father and the borderline daughter. Brenda was convinced that her father had sexual relations with her when she was 12. This was investigated and turned out to have no real basis in fact. I was involved in a long confrontation with Brenda and her father around this issue. Their relationship had been so arousing, erotic and sensual that reality had become quite mixed with fantasy and her fears. I also learned from this case that the degree of sexual ignorance can be great even when one has worked as a prostitute, as Brenda had done periodically on some of her runs from home.

Family Pattern

This family contains all of the characteristics of the borderline family. It is pathologically intact with no separations, and heavy involvement of the maternal grandmother who controlled the family economically.

The acceptance and rejection swings in this family were extreme and frequent coinciding with Brenda's destructive binges and clinging defense. Her family responded just as dramatically by dropping support for independence (for example, by taking her car away from her when she had been successfully employed for some months and was dependent upon the car) and welcoming her home once again when she failed.

I visited the home on one occasion after Brenda was released from treatment. There was a sense of depression and foreboding about the atmosphere that struck me. The parents greeted me with fixed half smiles, while the children sat around looking severely depressed and fearful of moving lest something terrible would happen.

Brenda's father had a great deal of difficulty adjusting to the loss of his own father. When he first married her mother he insisted that she not leave the house without him and that she wear only high-neck sweaters so as not to reveal herself. He was loud, physical, outgoing, very loving toward Brenda at times, and always unpredictable and explosive. He could be unusually harsh and critical of her for something very minor, yet pack up the entire family to visit her when she was in the treatment program. Brenda complained that he, more than any member of the family, was only nice to her when she was hospitalized or in residential treatment somewhere. Later when she had a child out of wedlock he was the first to want to bring her home and said to her, "Remember, the baby always has a father." It seems clear that the father demonstrated a high degree of borderline characteristics.

Brenda's mother was a rather thin, anemic-looking woman who appeared older than her years (she had Brenda while still a teenager). Rather than the emotive animated style of the father she was quiet and usually seemed depressed. Her affect was usually restrained and at times mildly inappropriate. One had the impression that she could have had a severe depressive illness. She always said the appropriate expected things about her daughter, but without the affect you expected and it was never in keeping with the severity of the problem.

The grandmother was hardworking and to a considerable extent the economic support of the family. She was pragmatic, usually reasonable to those outside the family and almost constantly critical of Brenda and her family, although she was also very indulgent of all of the children. Yet she took considerable abuse from Brenda, such as having money stolen and her house used in inappropriate ways. She made it very easy for Brenda to act out against her.

Brenda's sister, two years younger, also experienced problems, and ran away from home. Unlike her sister though she seemed to be breaking away from a symbiotic tie with the mother, which had been somewhat desperate given the depressed state of her mother.

Perception of Acceptance and Rejection

Brenda perceived her family with great borderline ambivalence; the swings were exaggerated, erratic, and quite unpredictable. She outwardly rejected them when she was hospitalized; ranting and raving against them and initially refusing any contact. But the family waited that out because she was hospitalized and not independent. With the first weakening in Brenda's resolve they brought the entire family to visit and proceeded to talk about her in her presence in a joking and provocative manner. The family atmosphere during such visits was in marked contrast to the observation I made in the home.

Like nearly all Ambivalent Rejection adolescents Brenda was driven to the point of utter frustration and rage by the unexpected caring and attention of her family and then the sudden withdrawal when she made any progress toward independence. She fantasized mass homicide of her entire family, which was the theme of many of her drawings. She would be driven to the point where the rage was so great she would slip into a psychotic-like state with distortion of reality.

Resolution

Brenda represents one of the more unresolved borderline adolescents; her only resolution for coping with the considerable stress was through self-destructive acting out. When she ran from the treatment program on one occasion she hitchhiked repeatedly in a triangular route with no idea where she was going or what she was going to do. This made her treatable in spite of the severe nature of the borderline regression.

Treatment

After running from the program shortly before scheduled discharge, Brenda went to live with her grandmother and then later with her parents. During this time she kept in regular contact with her therapist. She gradually moved out on her own, had a child and was relatively self-supporting. Her use of drugs and alcohol subsided to a very minimal degree and she achieved a certain distance from her family that she felt reasonably comfortable with. There was a tremendous improvement in her integration, her splitting type of defense and the development of whole object relations over the course of about two years after discharge from treatment.

One of the objectives of treatment was to provide her with family dynamics information which she consistently rejected at first but later used to good advantage. She would visit or call up her therapist and casually discuss what was going on in the family. She would always end such a discussion with a sardonic laugh and say something to the effect of, "Well, that's my family; I can understand them but I sure can't change them." The whole object relations shows up in these discussions where she shows a degree of empathy instead of anger and can put herself in the place of other family members.

The role of the baby in Brenda's case should not be overlooked. Having a child, of course, represented someone who was dependent on her and cannot distance himself until he in turn reaches the separation-individuation stage of development. This, of course, is why the borderline mother has a child during her own adolescence. Brenda has shown a great deal of concern about not repeating the problem in her own child and has made some real efforts to prevent that by educating herself about child care. One factor in Brenda's relative success is the fact that she is a very strong and dynamic individual. When that energy was put into self-destructive, regressive behavior she was one of the most difficult cases, but when her resolution was to be successful she put the same energy into that. Perhaps her resolution can be stated by something she said to me about two years after leaving the residential treatment. "God! I'm tired of being borderline; of my crazy family—all my energies have gone into it. I'm going to do something for myself for a change."

Case #10 Linda

Linda, an attractive blonde, was 15 years old when she was first sent to a residential program after one previous hospitalization and a suicide attempt. She was a very regressed, acting-out borderline adolescent, who had previously been diagnosed as schizophrenic, largely because of the fact that she would be mute for periods of time and often seemed preoccupied with her own thoughts and reality. When she first came to the residential program she spent considerable time curled up in the fetal position and kicking at anyone who came near.

Developmental History

During the first three years Linda was cared for much of the time by her grandmother as her mother found it difficult to manage the children because she was depressed. The depression was severe enough that she would totally withdraw for periods of time. When Linda was about 3 the family moved a great distance away when the father was in the military. This move away from the grandmother was quite traumatic; she reacted by withdrawal and temper tantrums for about one year. During latency Linda spent much time taking over for mother since she was the oldest girl and there were 4 younger siblings.

When Linda was 11 years old she planned her first run from home with the intent of going to San Francisco and starting a new life. Her reasons were to find a new home that would care for her, while getting a job so she could be independent. While this of course was unrealistic it was not to Linda at the time. She had cared for her siblings and had been the responsible mother figure in the home; surely she could be responsible for herself.

During the years of adolescence the problem gradually worsened with acting out confined largely to wandering away from home. Leaving home often consisted of nothing more than skipping school and staying downtown. She was not involved in the use of drugs or alcohol and she did not act out sexually although it was part of her fantasy. The family was very accepting in many respects, as well as very middle class, religious, and had high moral standards. Since there was no sexual abuse or any reason to act out against the values of the family, Linda acted out in a very restricted fashion by the creation of her own rich fantasy world. I belive it is important that the family was consistent in their values and did not present Linda with a conflict in this area.

Linda's method of acting out included running, taking an overdose, and creating her own fantasy. She became quite proficient in the use of sign language for the deaf and on several occasions managed to convince experts that she was, in fact, deaf.

Her mother, while very well-intentioned, was angry and resentful of her daughter because of the problems she had caused the family and because of the responsible position she was in while taking over some of the mother's functions. She was in a sense saying to her daughter, "I'm sick too, I have problems you don't understand, but you're the one who gets all the attention." I believe that this feeling often exists in parents of the borderline adolescent but is rarely stated outright by the parent.

Linda's father was a professional who approached his daughter as though she were one of his patients. He could be intimidating because he was intellectual and analytical—he would usually bring his briefcase and take notes about everything that was said. He had an affect problem but without obvious depression. There was a history of schizophrenia on his side of the family. I began to see him in a somewhat sympathetic light because he would never be able to communicate with Linda in the way that she wanted. I think more was accomplished with this family (they had been in family therapy on many occasions without success) by taking an intellectual approach that made them feel less threatened and defensive. I spent several sessions covering the dynamics and developmental history, including their own, and followed this up with having Linda conduct her own sessions with me present. The result was that both parents made a conscious effort to interact in a modified form with their daughter. The content of the communication changed, but of course the affect with which it was said, and thus the perception that Linda had, was altered only slightly.

The problem in one sense was simple: neither parent had enough libidinal energy to spread around six children—and perhaps not even to one. Their home was a constant competition for parental attention and affection. This was a very high stress situation for Linda because of the conflictual situation where fairly high expectations were present along with guilt and frustration of not being able to meet them. She was very angry at the lack of time and attention she received and the way in which it was given when it was there. This meant that Linda could not act out in many ways that defied family morality and standards. She was caught between getting angry at them, so much so that she would run away and they would have to come and get her, and her feeling of responsibility and guilt. One partial solution was to develop her own fantasy world similar to a fairy tale that was not delusional—she simply preferred it to reality.

Family Pattern

The family pattern was clearly ambivalent. It was closer to a schizophrenic pattern than any of the other cases discussed because there was more of the double-bind quality that included a proscription on the methods of acting out. It was a family with no physical separations (except from the grandmother) and the threat of abandonment was not used to any great extent. Rather it was a question of withholding, withdrawing and insufficient libidinal supplies from the mother which belied the high acceptance and high expectations.

Perception of Acceptance and Rejection

Linda perceived her parents in terms of ambivalence, and her own behavior was a mirror of this perception. If you were to observe Linda in treatment you might have assumed that she had the most rejecting parents of any of the adolescents. Her reaction was similar to Brenda's (case #9) in which there was an extended period of trying to totally reject them, followed by a period of making contact which in turn lead to the ambivalence of "I love them, I hate them." What she was acting out, of course, was the fact that the messages were so confusing and she felt considerable guilt. With a case such as this the therapist can gain credibility by demonstrating that you understand the confusion of the family and can step through the looking glass.

Resolution

Like most highly Ambivalent Rejection borderline adolescents Linda was very unresolved. Her approach to coping with the high stress was not very firm even though she had to be highly sophisticated in her methods because of the limitations placed on what was available to her. Primarily she dealt with this by being very defensive, and manipulative in keeping with the fantasy she perceived. Her lack of trust came from the fact that she was certain that no one could understand the world as she perceived it—the Alice In Wonderland existence that she perceived and no adults could enter. Once she did trust somewhat, in a therapeutic setting, the depression was there in massive amounts.

All of Linda's defensive acting out was designed to gain attention for her plight; that which would get her some understanding even if she had to create a fantasy to achieve it. For example, she ran from home and traveled to a center for training teachers of the deaf. Here she successfully gained a lot of attention by convincing them that she was deaf and could communicate only by sign language, which she was very proficient in using.

Treatment

Linda was with our program for nearly one year and it was not her first residential treatment. I did not become involved closely with the case until the latter part of the time she was with us, but for a brief period it was quite intensive. Linda represents a borderline adolescent with some schizophrenic features accounted for by the high stress, ambivalence and high acceptance along with proscriptions on methods of acting out. However, rather than totally internalize the conflict in a psychotic fashion, she substituted a rich fantasy world of illusions.

Split object relations were obvious and everything was a part of the good or bad and rewarding and withdrawing parts. Even the manner of dress was a part of this splitting. She would regress and hide in large overalls (always clean and neat) while at other times she wore attractive clothes for which she would be amply reinforced because she was very attractive.

Linda followed a pattern on nearing discharge that is quite familiar for the Ambivalent Rejection adolescent. She changed her mind frequently as to whether she wanted to return home after leaving. Trying to force her elsewhere would certainly have provoked her into severe acting out. Not giving the adolescent some control and responsibility for this decision allows them to project all the blame back on the therapist and removes them from being responsible for their own lives. Linda chose a group home placement and then ran just before discharge and put herself in a position where she would return home. Her father flew to another state to pick her up and brought her home where she remained for several months. What followed were several other runs of great distance from home all involving some form of her fantasy. She would return home each time and try to extract more attention and some increase in the libidinal supplies available to her. As it would decrease, her depression and anger would increase. On the positive side she was no longer self-destructive during her absences from home or while at home.

Linda finally checked herself into a different residential program for adolescents and stayed there a few weeks on a voluntary basis. After this she lived with her grandmother. She made steady progress and seemed more willing to accept her family the way they were. She began to concentrate more on her own life and interests and looked elsewhere for appropriate support.

CASE #11 KYLE

Kyle was 16 years old when he was admitted to the residential program from a correctional setting, where he had been sent for car theft. He was referred for evaluation because he had been acting in a bizarre manner and had set a fire in the kitchen of the institution.

Developmental History

Not much is known about Kyle's first two years, but they were probably adequate in most respects. His natural father separated from his mother at that time and she remarried soon after. What is clear is that there was no adequate relationship with his mother during the separation-individuation stage of development and he clung to her in a symbiotic relationship inspired more by her unpredictableness than anything else. He had a brother approximately two years older than himself, who was apparently subjected to more rejection.

Kyle cared for his mother, who was an alcoholic. His earliest memories are of worrying about her because she was so drunk and would do things like deny that he was her son. When he was 10 his mother was hospitalized and then left for good; separating from her husband (Kyle's stepfather) and refusing to take Kyle with her. He was also prevented from going to her by the stepfather, such that Kyle always blamed him for coming between he and his mother. Even after she had moved away she would return briefly raising his hopes that they could be together again. She would suddenly call him on the phone and verbally reject him.

Kyle's stepfather was a businessman of some standing in the community. He was religious and conservative and not one to display feelings openly. He tried to deal with Kyle by criticizing his behavior and giving him material things when Kyle demanded them. He also tried to deal with the issue of his mother by telling Kyle how bad a woman she was and why he could no longer be with her. But Kyle felt that despite all of the things he had done to his stepfather he was still largely accepting of Kyle. This was essentially accurate as it turned out because he went to great lengths to take his son back. Here you have the phenomena of the adolescent ventilating dislike and rejection onto the parent who is most accepting and indulgent. He would never admit until he had been in therapy for a period of time that his mother was rejecting of him.

Unlike most borderline adolescents all was not well during the latency age. First of all the mother's behavior was simply too ambivalent—both extremely symbiotic and rejecting. It would have been impossible for Kyle not to react negatively to this since being responsible for his mother was an impossible task. The mildly rejecting consistency of his father, along with indulgence, only contrasted with the mother's behavior toward him. Kyle was having trouble in school by being branded as different, weird, and having some learning difficulties despite his high intelligence and verbal abilities.

The basic severity of the borderline problems and the utter panic at abandonment can be emphasized by the fact that a loss and rejection occurred at the age of 2 and again at 11 years of age; each early in the separation-individuation phase of development. This in and of itself suggests the severity of the borderline dynamics in this particular case.

Family Pattern

The mother's behavior in general was more typical of Severe Rejection in at least some respects, although there was the symbiotic element. In addition to the alcoholism her behavior suggests a psychotic pattern, although I did not actually work with her and cannot be certain of this. The indulgent pattern where Kyle would use manipulative escape from consequences probably comes more from the father than from the mother. At least a part of the stress of ambivalence in this case comes from the disparity between the two parents.

Perception of Acceptance and Rejection

Kyle was typical of the Severe Rejection borderline adolescent because he denied the level of rejection he perceived until well into confrontive treatment. Initially he summarized his mother simply by saying that she was an alcoholic who was out of his life. He projected all the rejection and blame onto his father who, he said, was the source of his problems. His usual procedure was to use his considerable verbal skills to get everyone away from the subject of his mother. The abandonment depression was so extensive that he had developed a sociopathic style of defense involving denial and projection as well as delinquent acting out in grossly attention-getting ways. Being the bad kid who needed help was clearly his way of fending off the depression and of activating the rewarding unit. This did provide some attention from her via the telephone and letters, but, perhaps more important, it solicited great attention from 'mother substitutes' in the community.

Resolution

We have already discussed most of Kyle's resolution. He was in many respects an unresolved borderline in the sense that he did not intellectually defend a resolution and admitted that he needed help in finding better ways to cope. However, the abandonment depression was so intense that he had great reliance on the defenses he had. His defenses were aided by his considerable intelligence and cleverness. He had some of the usual borderline defenses, such as drugs and alcohol but they were relatively minor. The symbiotic development seemed to be more important here because he defended against depression by developing a fantasy of being a special person, of being omnipotent, and requiring special attention. When he was in one of these states he was a confident and powerful person. In one sense, he had developed a very impenetrable narcissistic defense. When he was in this state he could care for his mother, his girlfriend, and himself; he was the omnipotent helper and caretaker. Thus he was either omnipotent or he was the child being cared for by the maternal figure. He would switch from one to the other just as soon as he was caught by the authorities for one of his acting out escapades.

Treatment

Kyle was one of the more difficult treatment cases because of the depth of the abandonment depression and the sociopathic style. Imagine a mother who at one time is dependent and symbiotic and at another overtly "crazy" and rejecting. Add to this high expectations of a middle class family that placed emphasis on money and getting ahead in the world. Kyle had to be something special even if it meant being in control of the pathological ego. The highly ambivalent behavior of the rewarding and withdrawing mother was mirrored by the swings in Kyle's behavior; he could switch in minutes from the highly intelligent, competent con artist to the whimpering, helpless 3-year-old crying for his mother.

While I believe that Kyle's primary diagnosis was borderline personality, his sociopathic tendencies were considerable. I do believe that his sociopathic behavior was used entirely as a defense against the borderline depression. On any confrontation topic, other than his mother, he would do a good job of fronting without much depression; when consistently confronted about her, though, the depression was very obvious.

Kyle was in treatment for about one year interrupted by one run from the program where he stole a car and was caught in Atlanta driving a Cadillac. He functioned well as long as he had the structure and the 'mother' and 'father' figure in the form of therapeutic staff giving ego support. He developed a considerable grasp of the borderline dynamics, so much so that he understood his own case very well. He was able to complete high school equivalency and then took courses at the local college and returned each day to the program. He was a good student and received good grades; particularly in creative writing.

After leaving the program he went to another state to live with his stepfather. Kyle got a job, and a girlfriend; and he was generally successful for several months. He then went to visit his mother who lived in another state. All during this time he contacted me regularly to check everything out. After the visit with his mother, which I did not approve of, although I knew it was inevitable, there started a downward slide and a rapid retreat to old resolution patterns. Kyle started a car-stealing spree that amounted to over 25 cars in two countries. He drove halfway across the country to pick up a girlfriend in a stolen car. They then took off on a cross-country spree of living well on stolen credit cards and new cars. She was picked up and hospitalized after a severe acting out episode (she insisted she did not know the cars were stolen). Instead of running away Kyle returned to the hospital with identification stating that he was a 29-year-old psychiatrist (part of his resolution fantasy was to be someone important like a businessman or a doctor). He managed to talk his way to her room but did not get her out. He called me sometime later, and he told me he was "somewhere in North America." He asked me if I would come and rescue him (his words) if he told me where he was and I said "no," that he should turn himself in to the authorities. This did not seem to bother him and he went on to explain that I was an excellent therapist and he had learned a lot, but that when it got right down to it he preferred his way of dealing with depression because it was a lot more interesting than anything I could propose. Since he was well-defended, at this point, he was very adult-like and talked confidentially.

Kyle was finally picked up after a high speed chase. Despite my protestations to the contrary he got off on a mental incompetency plea and was sent to the state hospital in another state. After three days there he stole the car belonging to the superintendent of the hospital and wrecked it after another high speed chase. When he was put in jail he regressed immediately into a pseudo-psychotic state yelling for his mother.

Kyle was never deliberately harmful to anyone else despite his sociopathic acting out. This is related, I believe, to the fact that there was no history of physical abuse and no model of violence. I also suspect that the degree of rejection and fear of abandonment from the mother was too dramatic and the indulgence from the father insufficient. His delinquency was certainly never goal directed, but always designed to defend against depression and to create new highs and fantasies.

I was of the opinion that a sentence as an adult offender was the only reasonable treatment at the time. He understood the situation and made a decision about how he would deal with the depression. As long as he was able to coerce his environment into supporting his acting out, I did not think he would ever work on any other resolution very seriously. But even at that I suspected that Kyle would be running the prison hospital, the library, or teaching creative writing to fellow inmates before he was there very long. It may be part of my own fantasy, but I believe that Kyle will yet be successful simply because he will tire of the inconveniences of his present resolution.

Chapter 13

LOW REJECTION CASES

This chapter will present cases that I consider representative of Low Rejection, where at least one parent was perceived by the adolescent as being highly accepting. The goal-directed delinquent most often would belong to this group, but it is not included as a severe disturbance of adolescents unless there are other features present. Excluding this group the Low Rejection category of adolescents is still the most varied of all. I have selected four cases that represent this variety.

It is in the Low Rejection cases where we find severe aggression directed toward others because of the great discrepancy between acceptance and indulgence on the one hand, and a rejecting, violent model on the other. Two cases are representative of this aggression (cases #12 and #13); in one there is a symbiotic borderline development and in the other there is not. The final case is one of no significant borderline development, but a good example of how aggression of a relatively minor variety comes about through inappropriate parenting, indulgence but no violent model.

Case #12 Cathy

Cathy, a 15-year-old, was sent to residential treatment for the near fatal stabbing of her mother, as well as for suicidal gestures and alcohol abuse. She was a very charming, dark-haired adolescent of American Indian descent on her mother's side. She was unusual because she was at no time a behavior problem while in treatment. She was invariably angelic and cooperative.

Cathy appeared very paradoxical because of the discrepancy between her behavior in most circumstances and the aggression displayed against her mother. The factors in her background were equally confusing as it was possible to view her as a Severe, Ambivalent or Low Rejection adolescent depending on just what one wanted to emphasize. This case is a good example of why it is essential that the classification be made only in terms of the adolescent's perception, and the other factors used only to further refine that classification.

Developmental History

Cathy was born into a family system where all the members lived in very close proximity to the grandmother, who was the hub of the extended family. She was the oldest girl and the middle child of five children all of whom were within one or two years of each other. As far as can be ascertained her first few years were uneventful except that the symbiotic period was significant because a definite symbiotic pattern with the mother continued. The early maternal pattern was one of solicitous care of the infant interspersed with periods of brief benign neglect—in other words, it tended to be either smothering or neglectful. This pattern would tend to produce some separation problems during the symbiotic stage of development. The birth of her sister when Cathy was 1 year old, I believe, further promoted clinging to the mother.

Cathy cared for her younger siblings and became a help to her mother in most household chores. Very early she developed a high level of expectation of herself to care for the family and be responsible. For many years she was the 'good girl' in a very acting out family. When she was 5 her mother and father separated, after considerable fighting and alcoholism. The separation from her father increased her dependence and clinging to her mother. A succession of mother's boyfriends came and went in the household and Cathy was very good at getting much attention from them by being cute and entertaining. A stepfather who came into the home when Cathy was about 7 was prone toward violence and bizarre behavior. There were a number of incidents, such as killing Cathy's dog for no apparent reason, and some violent sexual scenes. He also sexually molested her when she was 8, which was followed by rather extensive litigation. After this, the mother moved the family to Alaska where he followed them; after one year she moved back and lived near her extended family, a block away from the former stepfather.

Despite the various traumas in her development Cathy continued to be the 'good girl' in the family and responsible. Her younger sister was the one who acted out and had difficulty with her mother. When Cathy was in elementary school she obtained good grades and got along well with the teachers for the most part. Her difficulties began when she entered the seventh grade, where she started taking drugs and alcohol; by the eighth grade she hardly attended school at all. For two years she mostly stayed home with her mother and took care of the house. She got into increasing difficulty with acting out.

A series of events took place that are remarkably similar across cases of severe symbiotic borderline aggression. All of the factors or events seem to produce an impossible bind for the adolescent that results in panic and explosiveness because of the threatened withdrawal of the mother—it is the ultimate reaction to the threat of abandonment. There is a sharp increase in the use of drugs, alcohol and sex as alternate means of dealing with the depression. During this period of time Cathy's mother was undergoing some changes in her own life. At first she was never home but was involved in alcohol and new boyfriends; then she found religion and insisted that Cathy attend church with her regularly. Cathy soon took to religion like she did to alcohol because both were a part of her mother's life. But mother would suddenly bring home a bottle for the children after swearing off drinking and making Cathy do the same. But a short time later she had reversed herself again and was back with religion. She would come home and find Cathy having a party and become angry and she would try to physically enforce limits on Cathy. The actual incident of the stabbing involved the younger sister; a fight started with Cathy and the mother got into it to separate them. While Cathy, who had been drinking, started arguing with her mother, the sister went into the kitchen and returned with a butcher knife. She laid it down between Cathy and her mother, whereupon Cathy picked it up and stabbed her mother.

Family Pattern

The family pattern was heavily influenced by a subculture where alcoholism as an escape was accepted and where violence in some form was a regular occurrence. You could say that not only did the family have borderline characteristics, but the culture also was in a sense the large borderline family from which all members had enormous difficulty separating. Instead they usually accepted it for what it had to offer in terms of support and the satisfaction of dependency needs, and dealt with their depression through the use of alcohol and acting out.

The family was in some respects very middle class in their values. They set high standards for the care of very young children and placed value on getting ahead through education and improved job skills. Cathy's oldest brother was an honor student, an outstanding athlete with a scholarship to college and in training as a Marine Corp officer. In contrast the second oldest brother, who was one year younger (and one year older than Cathy) was AWOL from the Marine Corp and a school dropout. The older brother, though, frequently drank and got into fights despite his good record.

It is not an exaggeration to say that the entire family had an unusual affect and acted in a borderline manner. For example, the oldest son, who was doing so well, had a depressed affect and admitted to Cathy that he had suicidal thoughts frequently, while the one who was acting out and staying home was always smiling and outgoing. On the occasions when I saw the mother she was usually quiet, quick to put herself in a dependent role, and seemingly happy. Cathy usually looked more like her older brother only more fearful. This affect changed considerably while she was in the treatment program; she became more talkative and smiling, and seemingly happy even though she complained about being away from her mother. The younger sister looked angry, but because she was always acting out, had the most appropriate affect until she got pregnant (so she could be home with her mother). She did this while Cathy was in our program and out of the home. The next time I saw Cathy at home she looked more depressed than angry and communicated no more than anyone else in the family. At least one of the aunts, and perhaps two, had persistent psychotic episodes; they, too, lived in the neighborhood close to the grandmother.

Certainly the symbiotic clinging to the mother is in evidence, even though it was not always reciprocated by the mother. The borderline ambivalence is also in evidence although it seems to operate with less frequent but more dramatic vascillation than is usually found in the borderline family. Perhaps most important, the model of violent acting out was certainly prevalent throughout the extended family and culture. There are many of the unpredictable, violent, and threatening elements present of the Severe Rejection family. If you put all of these elements together you have a prescription for violence, at any threat to Cathy's precarious resolution.

Perception of Acceptance and Rejection

Cathy viewed her mother with considerable confusion and wondered why she could be so mean and rejecting of her on occasion, but there was basically no doubt about the symbiotic acceptance that was perceived. It was always perceived as threatening and tenuous, given her mother's unpredictable behavior. If I had any doubt about the Low Rejection perception—which I did at first—there was no doubt after watching the two of them together. Given that this girl had only a short time before plunged a knife into her mother's chest, their first meeting after Cathy had been in residential treatment was very interesting. Immediately they began talking as though nothing had ever come between them; they both smiled and laughed in a soft but animated fashion. They moved close and held hands throughout their visit while the younger sister frowned from the other side of the room. She was on her way to the group home at that time. The symbiotic attachment between Cathy and her mother seemed quite mutual and very strong.

Resolution

Cathy's resolution to the high stress was the symbiotic attachment to her mother and the mutually dependent relationship. She could function in her rather fragile world, with the depression under control, by relatively moderate acting out as long as her mother did not threaten that relationship by extreme ambivalence or threatened withdrawal.

Treatment

During the course of treatment, which only lasted about six months, the dependency relationship was temporarily placed on the therapeutic staff. With her resolution then in place she was delightful and quite a normal, pleasant adolescent who looked quite out of place in a secure-treatment program. She was under no particular stress because we were supportive and helped her meet her expectations of herself. Because under such circumstances she offered no threat to anyone, it was difficult to keep her in treatment longer.

Cathy had many of the characteristics found in the homicidal adolescents discussed in Chapter 8 (Threat of Withdrawal Borderline); she was constantly in conflict over the discrepancy between expectations of herself and others and her own behavior. She could be righteous, highly moralistic, and a perfectionist. She was not psychopathic in her resolution because it was relatively easy to penetrate the shell and uncover the depression, at which point she was vulnerable and workable in treatment.

The problem with Cathy's treatment was that she returned home before it had been anywhere near completed. She lived a great distance from the program so contact was very sporadic. She went back into the symbiotic relationship with her mother, seemed depressed and distant, but she managed to maintain herself in the long run with only minor acting out episodes. Shortly after leaving the program she made some attempt to separate from her mother by moving away to college. One thing she did gain from our program was her high school diploma and the realization that she was very intelligent. After a few days away at school she missed her mother too much and went home.

I frankly think that to have achieved a better outcome in Cathy's case would have necessitated radical surgery from her family and culture. This could only have been done by maintaining a highly dependent therapeutic arrangement.

Case #13 Lloyd

Lloyd at the age of 16 was referred to a treatment program from a correctional setting where he had been sent for kidnapping and threatening with a rifle. Lloyd is typical of a group of adolescents who is prone to severe violence reaction because, like Cathy, he is both a Low Rejection and a Severe Rejection pattern adolescent. He had no delinquent history prior to his arrest other than minor aggression and problems in school. His aggression is very similar to case 15 in that it stemmed from fear of a perceived threat and not simply from trying to impose his will on someone else. The difference in the two cases, however, is that Lloyd had a very clear violent, threatening model in his father and greater indulgence from his mother, which resulted in great stress that was periodically ventilated through aggression at some fearful thwarting object. Lloyd had few acceptable methods of ventilation because he was socially unacceptable to most of his peers; he was a loner and adult-oriented most of his life. These factors in combination are typical of the homicidal adolescent; the fact that he was not has more to do with circumstances than clinical factors.

Developmental History

From a very early age Lloyd was on medication for his hyperactivity. He also had some speech problems and a general learning disability, despite relatively high intelligence. There

were no known early separations from his parents. During latency Lloyd followed a pattern of having both peer and academic
problems in school, of having minor physical skirmishes, of being
picked on by peers, and of being quite tied to his mother who
would rescue him from most situations. He was indulged and
excused for his behavior, while at the same time living in a rather
frightening world of threat and rejection from his father. He
withdrew from people not in his immediate family and acted in a
manipulative fashion toward his mother.

Lloyd's mother seems to have had many of the characteristics
of what I call the delinquent mother in that she was indulgent and
reinforced inappropriate resolutions to stressful situations instead of making him deal with the consequences of his behavior.
This was almost always the pattern despite verbalizations of ethical standards that she herself would follow. I find it interesting
that she also physically fits the characteristics of this group which
tends to be older and overweight. This is in contrast to the
mothers of the adolescents in the other patterns.

Lloyd's father was a man of few words and most of them
angry. He would accept no responsibility or blame and immediately projected it angrily to Lloyd or his therapist. He was
convinced that we were plotting to remove Lloyd from his control
just when he needed him to help work on his farm. Lloyd picked
up his father's paranoia, but the biggest source of fear was the
father himself. In our last conversation the father said to me, "I
just hope that you and your family rot in hell!" Lloyd tried to talk
with him, but he just sat there shaking with rage.

FAMILY PATTERN

The family represents two conflicting patterns that create
stress. Lloyd would explode in rageful paranoia when it was no
longer possible to internalize. He had few means of expression
and coping skills for more appropriate ventilation of the stress. It
was the Low Rejection perception, or symbiotic indulgent factor
from the mother, that provided the trigger for acting out against
any thwarting object.

Perception of Acceptance and Rejection

Lloyd viewed his mother as accepting for the most part yet during the process of treatment he began to see how that acceptance always carried a price tag. A rejection element also crept into the picture during the latter few years when she left him to fend for himself with his father while she worked evenings. It is often the case that the adolescent is quicker to reject the parent who they perceive as accepting; thus Lloyd at least initially experienced little difficulty separating from his mother.

Lloyd consistently perceived his father as harsh and rejecting. There was some movement in terms of seeing his father as less frightening and as being very much like himself. But he could not dismiss his father quite as easily as his mother. The father remained very much a part of his thoughts and feelings and Lloyd knew that sooner or later he would have to return home and deal with him.

RESOLUTION

Lloyd never had any firm resolution, which made him somewhat more receptive to treatment. What resolve he did have was to hold it in until you exploded, to be manipulative and demanding of his environment, and to strike out aggressively when threatened or when the resolution did not work. And, above all, he would always feel justified defending himself against any threat.

TREATMENT

Lloyd's treatment lasted over one year before he was sent to a group home. Treatment consisted of a long slow building of more appropriate coping skills and of dealing with his manipulative behavior designed in part to avoid treatment issues. A heavy confrontation approach was also used around his anger and frustration. All variety of minor behaviors had to be dealt with as though they were representative of more violent behavior, that would, of course, only occur outside of a treatment setting.

Much of the therapeutic time with Lloyd was spent around his refusal to do something expected of him, or his trying to deny some immediate consequence or reality. He would work very hard to distort things, and avoid school work or anything in which he was not competent. However, when I got past this level it was rather easy to work with Lloyd because to a considerable extent he possessed whole object relations. He possessed a reasonable degree of ability to integrate the good and bad parts of his family situation to such a degree that I did not consider him a borderline adolescent.

Here we can consider the apparent paradox that the most potentially dangerous and explosive individuals are often those with less split ego function and better object relations. Once through his rather fragile exterior and defensiveness, he strove hard to understand and find a better resolution. The question will be whether someone like Lloyd can withstand the fear and threat of certain situations and avoid the panic and striking out.

CASE #14 SHARON

Sharon was a 12-year-old whose playfulness could instantly change to the seductive charmer who used her attributes to manipulate her environment very effectively. She was sent to a residential treatment program after numerous runs from her home where she would place herself in dangerous situations involving drugs and sexual acting out.

Developmental History

Sharon's early development was very good for the first year, but in a sense she never developed beyond the symbiotic relationship with her mother. Her mother stated, "I could never understand what other mothers meant when they talked about the terrible twos. When Sharon was that age she just clung to me and stayed by my side. I thought that meant she cared about me and that I had a good kid."

The natural father was alcoholic and prone toward angry outbursts. He separated from the family when Sharon was about 5 years of age, preceded and followed by alcoholic aggression directed at her mother. This caused Sharon to cling to her mother even more both out of fear and out of the need to protect her mother. She learned to both fear and be attracted to the father figure who threatened and rejected her one moment and who was very sensuous the next. She also came to view her own mother as a somewhat powerless figure against him.

Sharon's mother married while still a teenager in order to get out of the house and exert her own independence from her mother. On many occasions she stated that she never really regarded Sharon as her daughter but more as a companion and peer. Her mother seemed to possess whole object relations and was willing to work hard to help her daughter. She still had trouble acting like a parent with Sharon, although she apparently had no such trouble with her 4-year-old daughter. The stepfather came into her life when Sharon was about 8 and tended to stabilize the mother's own borderline characteristics. As a result she seems to have done a satisfactory job with her own belated independence and as such was more willing to let her daughter separate without great resistance.

Sharon's mother made it clear from the time that the stepfather entered the home that he was to act as a "big brother" to Sharon and not as her father. When she reached pubescence and began experimenting with drugs and sex, both parents were trying to set limits on her and act in the parental role. Sharon saw the stepfather as the villain who was changing her mother from a friend to a parent. It was not so much an interference with the symbiosis, which by this time was directed mostly from the mother to Sharon, as it was the interference with Sharon striving for independence.

In the latency age period, up until the age of 10, Sharon can be characterized as an outwardly model child. Sharon was quick to point out that this was not really the case since she could get away with whatever she wanted to, but was clever about it. She had always been confident that she could convince her mother of anything. Sharon's sexual development was precocious and latency ended rather early. The first signs of sexual development were taken as a signal for separation from the mother and this she did in rather dramatic fashion. Her runs involved the seeking of drugs, sex and excitement, as well as some independence from her mother. At first Sharon could see nothing dangerous about her behavior—she was omnipotent and special and nothing was going to happen to her. There was certainly the constant seeking of attention and excitement as her way to defend against the depression that was present when she stopped. Sharon's mother regarded her as a special person; as an object. There was certainly a great deal of vicarious projection onto Sharon of some of the mother's earlier split object representation. In that sense Sharon was seen both very positively and in a negative sense of being a bad object. In this sense the symbiosis and indulgence was always interspersed with negative comments, cutting remarks and rejection. Sharon's perception of all this was that she was a valued physical object but did not have much inside.

Sharon at times responded as an extension of her mother's ego and as such she felt somewhat invincible; at the same time the situation could be reversed in that she perceived her mother as an extension of herself and thus bore great responsibility. This in part created depression and a rush to get away from that feeling. She wanted to create enough distance to treat her mother as a peer, as a sister, and as a confidant. At times Sharon would remark, "I wish my Mom was older," or "I wish my Mom would grow up so I could really leave."

Family Pattern

The family represents a pattern that changed over time, unlike most families of the severely disturbed adolescent. It was certainly symbiotically close, but seemed to diminish as the relationship transferred to the more stable stepfather. It did, however, continue to be an indulgent pattern that lead Sharon into some delinquent trends, which were not overt at the time of entry into residential treatment. It is interesting that she recognized this when she stated that she would end up in a correctional setting if she did not get some help. This sort of insight was always interspersed with her usual insistence that she was perfectly "normal" and should be let out immediately.

The family pattern also included the unpredictable and violent element from the natural father, although the effect of this was diminished after the stepfather entered the family. In other words, the family pattern represents Low Rejection, along with some Severe Rejection elements.

Perception of Acceptance and Rejection

Sharon clearly perceived her mother's acceptance as being fairly consistent. She perceived her natural father, whom she accused of sexual abuse, in a very ambivalent rejection way. Even the mother's acceptance, though, was clearly not total. Sharon could get anything from her mother, but there was always a price attached in that she would also get some of the same devaluative remarks that one might get from a sister.

Resolution

Initially Sharon was a highly resolved adolescent (although the resolution was fragile) as most symbiotic Low Rejection adolescents are, because she had very few opportunities to try out her resolution to the stress. As she was confronted about the destructive qualities of her resolution she gradually became quite unresolved. She no longer looked supremely confident and her depression became much more obvious. She came to realize that her resolution to the problem was probably not going to work, partly because of her young age, and partly because of her need to put herself in a highly dependent relationship with someone, after she ran away. It was in these relationships that she was usually abused. She was willing to compromise, to consider other ways of achieving independence and separation from her mother, and to use the relationship with the therapist productively.

Sharon's sexual acting out was certainly a part of her defending against depression, and indirectly a part of her resolution, but there was more of a basis for it than that. The symbiotic attachment meant the need to be close, to be loved, and to be dependent. To some extent she was treated in a somewhat sensuous and erotic fashion by both her mother and natural father. Since her father had been an alcoholic and a very dependent person himself she felt very conflicting guilt and anger feelings about him. Her sexual acting out in a very self-destructive manner occurred after the alleged sexual abuse.

Treatment

Treatment continued in a residential setting for approximately 8 months, whereupon Sharon was released back to her mother and stepfather. She felt that she would rather try it at home while waiting for an opening to occur in a foster home, although she knew that she could never be successful at home for any length of time. I felt that giving her a trial in the community was appropriate because she needed to test her own controls over her behavior outside of a secure setting. Contacts with her therapist continued during this period.

It is often easy to establish a therapeutic relationship with symbiotic borderline adolescents, even as young as Sharon. They are very needy, frightened, and craving a dependent relationship. In particular, understanding the dynamics of how they feel becomes crucial because they are outwardly tough and inwardly vulnerable. They appear capable and intact, but ordinarily they sense how much of a front that really is. Confronting them about their defenses can produce some dramatic effects that are therapeutically positive. As with most Low Rejection adolescents, limit-setting and confrontation become very important. Once the therapeutic alliance has been formed the therapist can play an important part in setting these limits simply through their influence. You must, however, have earned that right by establishing trust and promoting a reasonable degree of independence and responsibility.

The depth of the borderline dynamics may not be known in Sharon's case until she reaches later adolescence, because of the still primitive level of the separation-individuation. However, a degree of integration or whole object relations seemed to be in the process of forming as she moved out of the symbiotic stage.

Case #15 Tod

Tod was a 15-year-old youth in treatment because of menacing with a knife and persistently being out of control in the community. There was a clear pattern of increasing lack of control over his own behavior and a desperate quality to his acts. He represents a Low Rejection pattern with inappropriate limit-setting and indulgence, but with no symbiosis. The particular pattern of threatening behavior came about because he did not have a delinquent resolution as a way of coping with stress. He was easily frustrated and frightened which would result in a high level of aggression, but he was not severely aggressive relative to other adolescents discussed.

Developmental History

Tod's early development was uneventful, although he was considered hyperactive from the beginning of school. From the time that he was 12 months old, and his brother was born there was much competition for mother's attention with inconsistent and insufficient limits placed on his behavior. There was some alcohol abuse and fighting between the parents, but the children were never abused and their physical needs were met.

Tod's father was a well-educated businessman and executive who had great difficulty displaying his own anger and frustration. His reaction to the conflict was to hold in his feelings for long periods and not talk to Tod. At times he would explode in verbal abuse and anger and then feel guilty for this outburst, and once again become indulgent. When Tod was 11 his father and mother divorced and he and his younger brother went to live with the father. The separation itself did not seem to be all that traumatic for Tod, although it did occur at a critical separation-individuation period; rather it seemed to be some relief to everyone that the fighting had ended. For approximately two years the three of them lived together with indulgence (which increased), arguing, silence, guilt, acting out, and then indulgence again in a pattern that gradually escalated. Contact with the mother continued on a regular basis and was fairly positive. Father remarried a woman with two boys about three years younger than Tod. She was not going to put up with the boys running the household in any way they wanted. This created even greater frustration and aggression in Tod.

Family Pattern

The family pattern was accepting for the most part and thus can be categorized as Low Rejection. Of even greater importance, though, is the indulgent atmosphere, the lack of limit-setting, and inappropriate model of dealing with frustration and anger. There was no reinforcement of inappropriate acting out, therefore a delinquent resolution was never strongly formed. In this respect the parents were consistent between their stated values and their own behavior. If there had been the delinquent and violent model, the aggressive behavior that Tod displayed would no doubt have been more severe.

PERCEPTION OF ACCEPTANCE AND REJECTION

More than any other severely disturbed adolescent we have discussed, Tod would insist that both his parents cared about him and accepted him. He felt that the problem was his behavior and when that was under control he could probably live with either one of them if he chose. It is interesting, though, that he had the most negative feelings toward his father, who had indulged him the most. However, he was secure enough in his perception that he could begin to sort out his own feelings about his parents and come to see in a fairly objective way what had gone on in the family. He was able to begin a process of distancing himself from his parents which was not a rejection as much as it was a normal process of separation and individuation through adolescence.

Resolution

Tod had no strong resolution to the stress when he came into the treatment program except to have a temper tantrum, cry or threaten if he felt that anything was standing in his way. His justification for his behavior was always that people were out to get him and he had to protect himself; he never felt that he was demanding anything unfairly. The anger always came from frustration centering around situations where someone was trying to curtail his behavior; it rarely stemmed from being thwarted at obtaining some material object in a delinquent fashion.

It was the lack of a resolution that made treatment relatively easy in Tod's case; if a delinquent resolution had been in effect, treatment may have been impossible with his indulgent history. It was the fact that his resolution was so poorly formed, and therefore provided a very poor defense, that made the frustration and aggression so frequent. Secure treatment where his acting out could be firmly controlled was necessary despite the relative psychological intactness that he possessed. There was very little splitting or other characteristics of the borderline personality. There was depression present, whether you confronted Tod or not; thus it was not abandonment depression. It stemmed more from discouragement with himself, his own behavior, and failure to control his own frustration and anger.

Treatment

Much of Tod's treatment consisted of confrontation around his daily behavior. His frustration tolerance was gradually built up to the point where he would become angry, but would not strike out at those around him. His difficulty in relating to peers was also a focus of treatment. In one to one therapy he began to identify his sources of anger in the reactions of his parents, and to look for other ways of expressing his feelings. Both parents were brought in for sessions.

The difference between Tod's family and that of most families of severely disturbed adolescents is that they both possessed whole object relations and had no psychotic characteristics. It was thus possible to carry out family sessions on a fairly straightforward communication model, with considerable effectiveness that would not result in a borderline family. A fair amount of open communication between he and his parents developed.

Tod never returned to live with his father because he could see that the situation with his stepmother would present too many difficulties for him. Instead he went to live with his mother and after a few months moved out on his own.

REFLECTIONS

This writing project began over two years ago in response to the need for reading material in the workshops I was asked to conduct. The book reflects my own growth and development over an important period of my professional life. In reflecting on the finished product it seems clear that there are inconsistencies that have resulted from my uncertainty as to objective and purpose. I doubt that editing will entirely rid the manuscript of these inconsistencies.

From my perspective now I would be quicker to emphasize the psychopathic aspects of many of the cases. It has become evident that the capacity of the adolescent to detach from the object, as it were, is even greater than I had at first supposed. They are then, for all practical purposes, psychopathic individuals. A related phenomenon that deserves greater emphasis is the relationship between parenting disruptions during the latter part of the first year and later psychopathic resolutions, and sexual aggression in particular.

The factor of Low Rejection itself, particularly in the area of violence, is even more complex than I had first imagined. More than in any other acceptance-rejection category one must think broadly in terms of subgroups. For example, it has become apparent that the perception of absolute acceptance (which is in fact a denial of rejection) of the mother plays a very important role in many violence cases (particularly those of a sexual nature). Indeed, it may be proper to conceptualize symbiotic attachment in terms of this unreasonable acceptance that seems not to be questioned and is not contingent upon the individual's behavior. Many acts of violence are preceded by an almost cathartic release of this acceptance. There is a sudden verbal barrage of long pent up hatred and rejection of the object (the mother) followed closely by aggression toward objects that may be said to be symbolic. While such behavior may be seen as a psychopathic resolution, it is intricately related to object relations theory and probably to the borderline process.

In retrospect, I can see that at times I was confused in how broadly I wanted to define the borderline process of ambivalence. To be sure the borderline condition derives from the withholding of libidinal warmth of the mother figure during the early developmental phase of separation-individuation. Problems occurring at other periods are not basically borderline in nature, although there may be a good deal of ambivalence in the perception and acting out. Even though the period of preadolescence has many similarities to the earlier separation-individuation period, in and of itself, it does not produce the borderline dynamics. What it produces is emancipation problems that might correctly be termed "reaction to adolescence." The adolescent will not perceive the same degree of ambivalence as the borderline and there is no abandonment fear resulting from the early lack of libidinal supplies from the mother. Confusion may come about because the second separation-individuation period of early adolescence becomes a replay of the earlier period for the child who already has borderline propensities. Separations from the parent, and other disruptions then will exacerbate borderline conditions but will not cause them in and of themselves.

While some of what I have written in this book may be considered original, and even radical from some perspectives, things have a way of coming full circle. The term psychopathic is very old and currently unfashionable. There are many who reject the term "out of hand" because it has a derogatory and pessimistic connotation. I have some concern that those who use my model in viewing the acting out adolescent will consign such labeled individuals to no treatment. This is certainly not my intent. While I believe it is imperative that we understand the nature and extent of such firm resolutions, and thus the futility of many of our intervention efforts, I would not wish us to stop our attempts at finding better approaches. As a matter of fact, my current research interest involves the more violent and psychopathic adolescents. I am specifically concerned with finding ways of penetrating the thus far impenetrable shell and I would hope that others would maintain a realistic but optimistic approach to all adolescents. It is perhaps analogous to the situation of the learning disabled child: It is the teacher who does not know how to teach, not the child who cannot learn. Only such a view will keep us all from falling into the complacency of thinking that we know enough.

With regard to the acceptance-rejection model itself, it can be viewed as a method of assessing detachment. There is a high correspondence between the adolescent's perception of acceptance and rejection and the actual resolution or distance from the object that exists. It should be noted though that the correlation is far from perfect when you get to the unreasoning acceptance of the psychopathic individual with an underlying borderline dynamic. This individual is ordinarily very difficult to detect until after some aggressive act. It may be that the acceptance-rejection model will be of particular relevance here because such an individual will ordinarily respond to direct questioning around acceptance in some very characteristic ways. They will deny negative affect toward the mother figure and insist on total unwavering acceptance. This response differs from other adolescents where a more reasoned blending of positive and negative attributes is much more characteristic.

I think the book can be summed up best by saying that it urges the reader not to be mislead by the more superficial aspects of acting out. It urges the readers to open their eyes and examine their own perception, their own detachment from understanding the painful realities of loss and abandonment. In our sometimes frightening fast-paced existence it is easy to fake relationships and go about our professional business via acceptable behavior patterns. This allows detached individuals to behave as though they are relating to the adolescent; in fact, they are not and may be a destructive influence. The response of some to such a confrontation would be that they are "paid to do, not to see." Conversely, the effective therapist probably operates on a conservation of energy approach and does not go around "relating" at every opportunity. Thus, his detachment and openness is deliberate and is used to the benefit of other people as well as for his own defense mechanism.

And finally, while I believe that the concept of the borderline personality is a powerful one, so pervasive that we have just begun to fathom its ramifications, I would hope the reader would not use it with indiscretion. I urge that no label be given an adolescent until all four factors in the holographic model are thoroughly understood by the therapist. Only in this way will we be able to provide ultimately effective intervention and treatment with the greatest conservation of limited psychological, economic, and professional forces.

REFERENCES

Abt, L. E. and Weissman, S. L. (Eds.). *Acting Out.* New York: Jason Aronson, 1976.

Ackerson, L. *Children's Behavior Problems I.* Incidence of Genetic and Intellectual Factors. Chicago: University of Chicago Press, 1931.

Anderson, R. Thoughts on fathering: Its relationship to the borderline condition in adolescence and to transitional phenomena. In S. Feinstein and P. Giovacchini (Eds.), *Adolescent Psychiatry Vol. VI.* The University of Chicago Press, 1978.

Bandler, R. and Grinder, J. The Structure of Magic I. Palo Alto, Calif.: *Science and Behavior Books,* 1975.

Bandura, A. and Walters, R. *Adolescent Aggression.* New York: Ronald Press, 1959.

Bateson, G., Jackson, D., Haley, J., and Weakland, S. Towards a Theory of Schizophrenia, *Behav. Sci.,* 1956, *1*:251–264.

Bender, L. and Curran, F. Children and adolescents who kill. *J. Crim, Psychopath.* 1940, *1*:297.

Benjamin, J. D. The innate and experiential in child development. *Lectures on Experimental Psychiatry,* H. Brosin, (Ed.). Pittsburgh: University of Pittsburgh Press, 1961.

Berger, M. M. (Ed.) *Beyond The Double Bind.* New York: Brunner/Mazel, 1978.

Berkowitz, D., Shapiro, R., Zinner, J. and Shapiro, E. Concurrent family treatment of narcissistic disorders in adolescence. *International Journal of Psychoanalytic Psychotherapy*, 1974, *3*: 379–396.

Blos, P. *On Adolescence.* New York: Free Press, 1962.

Blos, P. The second individuation process of adolescence. *Psychoanalytic Study of the Child*, 1967. *22*: 162–186.

Blos, P. *The Adolescent Passage.* New York: International Universities Press, Inc., 1979.

Bowlby, J. *Maternal Care and Mental Health.* Geneva: World Health Organization, 1951.

Bowlby, J. *Attachment: Attachment and Loss Vol. I.* New York: Basic Books, 1969.

Bowlby, J. *Separation: Anxiety and Anger Vol. II.* New York: Basic Books, 1973.

Bowlby, J. *Loss: Sadness and Depression Vol. III.* New York: Basic Books, 1980.

Bradley, S. J. The relationship of early maternal separation to borderline personality in children and adolescents: A pilot study. *Am J. Psych.*, 1979, *136* 4A.

Buhler, C. The Social Behavior of Children. In C. Murchison (Ed.) *Handbook of Child Psychology.* (Revised Edition). Worcester Mass.: Clark University Press, 1933.

Clarke, A. M. and Clarke, A. D. B. *Early Experience: Myth and Evidence.* London: Open Books, 1976.

Cooper, B. M. and Ekstein, R. Borderline adolescent girls in rebellion against the father. In S. Feinstein and P. Giovacchini, (Eds.), *Adolescent Psychiatry Vol. VI.* Chicago: The University of Chicago Press, 1978.

Dollard, J., Miller, N., Doob, L., Mowrer, O., and Sears, R. *Frustration and Aggression.* Yale University Press, 1939.

Easson, W. M. and Steinhilber, R. M. Murderous aggression by children and adolescents. *Arch. Gen. Psychiat.*, 1961, *4*: 1–9.

Ekstein, R. and Wallerstein, J. Observations on the Psychology of Borderline and Psychotic Children, Psa. *Study Child*, 1954, *9*: 344–369.

Ekstein, R. *Children of Time and Space.* New York: Appleton-Century-Crofts, 1966.

Ellis, A. *Humanistic Psychotherapy: The Rational-Emotive Approach.* New York: Julian Press, 1973.

Erikson, E. H. *Childhood and Society.* New York: Norton, 1950.

Erikson, E. H. *Identity, Youth and Crisis.* New York: Norton, 1968.

Erikson, E. H. *Dimension of a New Identity.* New York: Norton, 1974.

Esman, A. H. (Ed.). *The Psychology of Adolescence.* New York: International Universities Press, 1975.

Fairbairn, W. R. D. Psychoanalytic Studies of the Personality. London: Tavistock Publications, 1952. Published under the title of *Object Relations Theory of the Personality.* New York: Basic Books, 1954.

Feshbach, S. Aggression. In P. H. Mussen (Ed.), *Carmichael's Manual of Child Psychology Vol. 2.,* New York: Wiley, 1970.

Fraiberg, S. Introduction to Therapy in Puberty. In R. Eissler, A. Freud, H. Hartman, and E. Kris (Eds.), *The Psychoanalytic Study of the Child Vol. 10.* New York: International Universities Press, 1955.

Frank, J. D., *Persuasion and Healing.* New York: Schocken Books, 1974.

Freud, S. *An Outline of Psychoanalysis.* New York: Norton, 1949.

Fromm-Reichman, F. Notes on the mother role in the family group. *Bulletin of the Menninger Clinic,* 1940, *4*:132–145.

Garfield, S. L. and Bergin, A. E. (Eds.). *Handbook of Psychotherapy and Behavior Change.* New York: John Wiley & Sons, 1978.

Giovacchini, P. The adolescent process and character formation. In S. Feinstein and P. Giovacchini (Eds.), *Adolescent Psychiatry Vol. 2.* New York: Basic Books, 1973.

Giovacchini, P. The borderline aspects of adolescence and the borderline state. In S. Feinstein and P. Giovacchini (Eds.), *Adolescent Psychiatry Vol. VI.* Chicago: The University of Chicago Press, 1978.

Glasser, W. *Reality Therapy.* New York: Harper & Row, 1965.

Goldfarb, W. Psychological deprivation in infancy and subsequent adjustment. *Amer. J. Orthopsychiat.,* 1945, *15*: 49–56 (a).

Goldfarb, W. Effects of psychological deprivation in infancy and subsequent stimulation. *American Journal of Psychiatry,* 1945, *102*: 18–33 (b).

Gordon, D. *Therapeutic Metaphors.* Cupertino, Calif.: Meta Publications, 1978.

Grinker, R. Sr., Werble, B., and Drye, R. *The Borderline Syndrome.* New York: Basic Books, 1968.

Gunderson, J., Kerr, R., and Englund, D.. Families of Borderlines: A comparative study. *Archives Gen. Psychiatry, Vol. 37.,* 1980, *1*: 27–33.

Gunderson, J. and Singer, M. Defining borderline patients: An Overview, *Amer. J. Psych.,* 1975, *132*: 1–9.

Harlow, H. F., Harlow, M. K., and Hansen, E. W. The maternal affectional system of Rhesus monkeys. In H. Rheingold (Ed.), *Maternal Behavior in Mammals*. New York: John Wiley & Sons, 1963.

Hesse, H. *Narcissus and Goldmund*. New York: Farrar, Straus and Giroux, 1968.

Jacobsen, E. *The Self and the Object World*. New York: International Universities Press, 1964.

Johnson, A. M. Sanctions for superego lacunae of adolescents. In K. Eissler (Ed.), *Searchlights on Delinquency*. New York: International Universities Press, 1949.

Johnson, A. and Szurek, S. The genesis of antisocial acting out in children and adults. *Psychoanalytic Quarterly*, 1952, *21*: 323–342.

Kagan, J. Resilence and continuity in psychological development. In A. M. Clarke and A. D. Clarke (Eds.), *Early Experience: Myth and Evidence*. London: Open Books, 1976.

Kagan, J. *The Growth of the Child*. New York: W. W. Norton & Co., Inc., 1978.

Kaplan, L. J. *Oneness and Separateness: From Infant to Individual*. New York: Simon and Schuster, 1978.

Kernberg, O. Borderline Personality Organization. *J. Amer. Psychoanal. Assoc.*, 1967, *15*: 641–685.

Kernberg, O. The Treatment of Patients with Borderline Personality Organization. *International Journal of Psychoanalysis*, 1968, *49*: pp. 600–619.

Kernberg, O. *New Developments in Psychoanalytic Object Relations Theory*. Presented at the 58th Annual Meeting of the American Psychoanalytic Assn., Washington, D. C., 1971.

Kernberg, O. *Borderline Conditions and Pathological Narcissism*. New York: Science House, 1975.

Kernberg, O. *Object Relations Theory and Clinical Psychoanalysis*. New York: Aronson, 1976.

Kernberg, O. The diagnosis of borderline conditions in adolescence. In S. Feinstein and P. Giovacchini (Eds.), *Adolescent Psychiatry Vol. VI*. Chicago: The University of Chicago Press, 1978.

Kernberg, O. F. Technical considerations in the treatment of Borderline Personality Organization. In J. LeBoit and A. Capponi (Eds.), *Advances in Psychotherapy of the Borderline Patient*. New York: Aronson, 1979.

Imsey, L. R. and Arnold, L. W. Precipitating factors in the female borderline syndrome—A dichotomy. *Diseases of the Nervous System,* 1977, *38*: 413–318.

King, C. H. The ego and the intergration of violence in homicidal youth. *Amer. J. Orthopsychiatry,* 1975, *45*: 134–145.

Lamb, D. *Psychotherapy with Adolescent Girls.* San Francisco: Jossey-Bass, 1976.

Lax, R., Bach, S., Burland, J., *Rapproachmont: The Critical Phase of Separation-Individuation.* New York: Aronson Press, 1980.

LeBoit, J. and Capponi, A. *Advances in Psychotherapy of the Borderline Patient.* New York: Aronson, 1979.

Leowald, H. Ego and reality. *International Journal of Psycho-Analysis,* 1951, *32*: 10–18.

Levy, D. M. The Hostile Act. *Psychological Review,* 1941, *48*: 356–361.

Lewis, D. O., Shanok, S., Pincus, J., and Glaser, G. H., Violent Juvenile Delinquents: Psychiatric, Neurological, Psychological and Abuse factors. *Journal of Child Psychiatry,* 1979, *18*: 307–318.

Lidz, T., Cornelison, A. R., Fleck, S., and Terry, D. The intrafamilial environment of schizophrenic patients II. Marital schism and martial skew. *American Journal of Psychiatry,* 1957, *114*: 241–248.

Lidz, T., Fleck, S., and Cornelison, A. R. *Schizophrenia and the Family.* New York: International Universities Press, 1960.

MacFarlane, J. W. Perceptives on personality consistency and change from the guidance study. *Vita Humana,* 1964, 7: 115–126.

Mahler, M. *The Psychological Birth of the Human Infant.* New York: Basic Books, 1975.

Mahler, M. S. *Infantile Psychoses and Early Contributions. Vol. I.* New York: Jason Aronson, 1979. (a).

Mahler, M. S. *Separation-Individuation. Vol. II.* New York: Jason Aronson, 1979. (b).

Masterson, J. F. The psychiatric significance of adolescent turmoil. *Amer. J. Psychiat.,* 1968, *124*:11.

Masterson, J. *Treatment of the Borderline Adolescent: A Developmental Approach.* New York: Wiley, 1972.

Masterson, J. *Psychotherapy of the Borderline Adult: A Developmental Approach.* New York: Brunner/Mazel, 1976.

Masterson, J. The borderline adolescent: An object relations view. In S. Feinstein and P. Giovacchini (Eds.), *Adolescent Psychiatry Vol. VI.* Chicago: The University of Chicago Press, 1978. (a).

Masterson, J. F. Transference acting out and working through. In Masterson, J. F. (Ed.), *New Perspectives on Psychotherapy of the Borderline Adult.* New York: Brunner/Mazel, 1978. (b).

Masterson, J. and Costello, J. *From Borderline Adolescent to Functioning Adult: The Test of Time.* New York: Brunner/Mazel, 1980.

Masterson, J. F. and Rinsley, D. R. The borderline syndrome: The role of the mother in the geneisis and psychic structure of the borderline personality. *Int. J. Psycho-Anal.,* 1975, *56*: 163–177.

Meade, M. *Coming of Age in Samoa: A Psychological Study of Primitive Youth for Western Civilization.* New York: Morrow, 1928.

Meade, M. *Growing up in New Guinea.* New York: Morrow, 1930.

Meade, M. *Sex and Temperament in Three Primitive Societies.* New York: Morrow, 1935.

Meiselman, K. C. *Incest: A Psychological Study of Causes and Effects with Treatment Recommendations.* San Francisco: Jossey-Bass, 1979.

Murphy, L. B. and Moriarty, A. *Vulnerability, Coping and Growth: From Infancy to Adolescence.* New Haven: Yale University Press, 1976.

Nielsen, G., Engle, T., and Latham, S. *Through the Looking Glass: A Short-term follow-up study of adolescents released from secure treatment.* Paper presented at Oregon Psychological Association, Spring Conference, 1979.

Offer, D. and Offer, J. *From Teenager to Young Manhood.* New York: Basic Books, 1975.

Offer, D., Marohn, R. and Ostrov, E. *The Psychological World of the Juvenile Delinquent.* New York: Basic Books, 1979.

Patterson, G. Families: Application of Social Learning to Family Life. Champaign, Ill.: Research Press, 1971.

Plutchik, R. *Emotion: A Psychoevolutionary Synthesis.* New York: Harper & Row, 1980.

Pringle, M. and Bossio, V. Early Prolonged separation and emotional maladjustment. *J. Child Psychiat.,* 1960, *1*: 37–48.

Provence, S. and Lipton, R. *Infants in Institutions.* New York: International Universities Press, 1962.

Ribble, M. *The Rights of Infants: Early Psychological Needs and Their Satisfaction.* New York: Columbia University Press, 1943.

Rinsley, D. The adolescent inpatient: Patterns of depersonification. *Psych. Quart.,* 1971, *45*: 1–20.

Rinsley, D. Diagnosis and treatment of borderline and narcissistic children and adolescents. *Bulletin of the Menninger Clinic,* 1980, *44*(2): 147–170.

Robins, L. *Deviant Children Grown Up*. Baltimore: The Williams & Wilkins Co., 1966.

Rohner, R. *They Love Me They Love Me Not*. Snider, N.Y.: Hraf Press, 1975.

Russell, D. A Study of juvenile murderers. *J. Offender Therapy*, 1965, *9*: 55–86.

Rutter, M. *Maternal Deprivation Reassessed*. Middlesex: Penquin Books, 1972.

Saroyan, W. *Sons Come & Go, Mothers Hang In Forever*. New York: McGraw-Hill, 1976.

Scarf, M. *Unfinished Business: Pressure Points in the Lives of Women*. New York: Doubleday, 1980.

Searles, H. F. The countertransference with the borderline patient. In J. Leoit and A. Capponi (Eds.), *Advances in Psychotherapy of the Borderline Patient*. New York: Aronson, 1979.

Shapiro, E. R. Research on family dynamics: clinical implications for the family of the borderline adolescent. In S. Feinstein and P. Giovacchini (Ed.), *Adolescent Psychiatry Vol. VI*. Chicago: The University of Chicago Press, 1978, (a).

Shapiro, E. R. The psychodynamics and psychology of the borderline patient: A review of the literature. *Am. J. Psychiatry*, 1978, *135*: 11 (b).

Skinner, B. F. *Verbal Behavior*. New York: Appleton-Century-Crofts, 1957.

Skinner, B. F. *Cumulative Record* (Revised edition). New York: Appleton-Century-Crofts, 1961.

Sollenberger, R. T. The effect of male hormone on behavior with special reference to adolescence. *Psychol. Bull.*, 1938, *35*: 666.

Szurek, S. Genesis of psychopathic personality trends. *Psychiatry*, 1942, *5*: 1–16.

Tanay, E. Psychiatric study of homicides. *Amer. J. Psychiat.*, 1969, *125*: 1252–1258.

Thomas, A. and Chess, S. *Temperment and Development*. New York: Brunner/Mazel, 1977.

Thomas, A. and Chess, S. *The Dynamics of Psychological Development*. New York: Brunner/Mazel, 1980.

Thompson, W. R. and Grusec, J. E. Studies of early experience. In P. H. Mussen (Ed.), *Carmichael's Manual of Child Psychology, Vol. 1*. New York: John Wiley & Sons, Inc., 1970.

Vaillant, G. E. *The Adaption to Life*. Boston: Little, Brown, 1977.

Volkan, V. D. The "Glass Bubble" of the Narcissistic Patient. In J. LeBoit and A. Capponi (Eds.), *Advances in Psychotherapy of the Borderline Patient.* New York: Aronson, 1979.

Wallerstein, J. S. and Kelly, J. B. *Surviving the Breakup: How Children and Parents Cope with Divorce.* New York: Basic Books, 1980.

Wolman, B. Treatment of Schizophrenia. In B. Wolman (Ed.), *The Therapist's Handbook.* New York: Van Nostrand Reinhold, 1976.

Wynne, L. C., Rycoff, I. M., Day, J., and Hirsch, S. I. Psuedomutuality in the family relations of schizophrenics. *Psychiatry,* 1958, *21*: 205–220.

Yarrow, L. J. Separation from parents during early childhood. In M. L. Hoffman and L. W. Hoffman (Eds.), *Review of Child Development Research Vol. 1.* New York: Russell Sage, 1964.

Zinner, J. and Shapiro, E. Splitting in families of borderline adolescents. In J. Mack (Ed.), *Borderline States in Psychiatry.* New York: Grune & Stratton, 1975.

Zinner, J. Combined individual and family therapy of borderline adolescents: Rationale and management of the early phase. In S. Feinstein and P. Giovacchini (Eds.) *Adolescent Psychiatry Vol. VI.* Chicago: The University of Chicago Press, 1978.

APPENDIX

A. Family Pattern Ratings

These factors can be useful in rating the family pattern. This represents the "observer's" perception of the family in terms of parenting style or manner in which they interact with the adolescent. After the adolescent has gained knowledge of the family dynamics, I also use these factors to assess the congruency between their perceptions and my perception by having them rate independently. Ratings should be done in terms of a seven-point scale from low to high. Connecting the rating on "Rejection" with that on "Acceptance" with a straight line and using the degree of "Acceptance-Rejection" as a measure of variance will produce a graphic portrayal of the Two-Factor Model.

Rejection
Physical Abuse
Sexual Abuse
Neglect
Physical Separation

Inappropriate Control
Chaotic Style
Dependency
Engulfment
Abandonment Threat
Acceptance/Rejection
Permissive
Nurturance
Acceptance

B. ACCEPTANCE–REJECTION INTERVIEW EVALUATION

The following questions may be useful in determining the degree of relative acceptance and rejection that the adolescent perceives. The questions, because of the obvious sensitivity, should be asked (never administered in written form) only in the context of a clinical interview. The questions should be phrased such that the adolescent responds in terms of a number from one to seven. (One means "Not At All," and seven means "Very Much.")

1. How much do you think your mother (natural, step) really wants you to live with her?
2. How much do you think your father (natural, step) really wants you to live with him?
3. How much do you really care about your mother (natural, step)?
4. How much do you think your mother (natural, step) really cares about you?
5. How much do you really care about your father (natural, step)?
6. How much do you really want to live with your father (natural, step)?
7. How much do you really want to live with your mother (natural, step)?
8. How much do you think your father (natural, step) really cares about you?

C. DEVELOPMENTAL RECORD

These questions are helpful in gathering developmental information about an adolescent from parents and other sources. It should be done in the context of an informal interview where questions can be followed up for more specific information where appropriate. The information should always be recorded in terms of the age period in which it occurred or applied such that one has a chronological view of the significant developmental factors.

1. Significant injury to mother during pregnancy.
2. Difficult birth.
3. Anoxia at birth.
4. Prematurity at birth.
5. Inadequate nutrition during pregnancy.
6. Mother drug/alcohol abuse.
7. Father not living in home.
8. Family members described as having borderline or below intelligence.
9. Father is common-law husband to child's mother.
10. Disturbances in motility.
11. Delayed or atypical reflexive behavior.
12. Rejecting mother.
13. Emotionally unstable father.
14. Emotionally unstable mother.
15. Physical abuse by parent.
16. Severe physical neglect.
17. Extended physical separation from one or both parent figures (specify which).
18. Inadequate nutrition.
19. Traumatic physical injury.
20. Allergic reactions.
21. Extended period of hospitalization.
22. Child considered hyperactive.
23. Delayed developmental milestones.
24. Child is enuretic/not toilet trained.
25. Sibling born.
26. Mother thought to have psychiatric disturbance.
27. Father thought to have psychiatric disturbance.

28. Change in residence of family.
29. Child adopted.
30. Child placed in foster home.
31. Child cared for by grandparents.
32. Frequent or extended use of babysitters.
33. Child has neurological examination.
34. Mother described as overprotective of child.
35. Mother inconsistent in responding to child.
36. Mother works out of home.
37. Parent convicted of felony.
38. Delayed language development.
39. Child sexually abused.
40. Yelling or emotional outburst used as frequent method of discipline.
41. Ignoring or rejecting, a frequent response from parents.
42. Child alternates living with separated parents.
43. Child removed from home (ward of court).
44. Child diagnosed as having brain damage.
45. Siblings older than child.
46. Siblings younger than child.

D. CLINICAL AND FAMILY CHARACTERISTICS ASSOCIATED WITH ACCEPTANCE-REJECTION PATTERNS

Clinical and Family Characteristics Associated with Total Rejection

1. Has given up hope of being reunited with parents except as fantasy.
2. A generally flattened affect (mild to moderate depression).
3. Frequent psychosomatic complaints.
4. Frequent bursts of anger that quickly subside.
5. Frequent disregard of physical appearance.
6. Poorly structured fantasy that is not elaborate, or complex, and is very superficial.
7. A disregard for self to the extent of exposing oneself to dangerous situations.

8. Minor self-destructive behavior used partly as way of manipulating environment.
9. The general absence of severe psychiatric disturbances.
10. Infantile behavior.
11. The presence of anxiety or neurotic behavior.
12. Makes superficial attachments to adults but experiences little separation problems from these attachments.
13. Little abandonment fear.
14. Attention-getting is the primary mode of dealing with the environment.
15. Like a sieve; no matter what is put in very little seems to remain for long.
16. Has some unusual physical characteristic having to do with posture, gait, appearance, etc.
17. Is recognizable to nearly anyone as being "different."
18. Has very poor judgment, i.e., perceptual.
19. Functions poorly in groups.
20. Cannot internalize negative feelings, but must react upon immediate environment.

Clinical and Family Characteristics Associated with Severe Rejection

21. Has rageful feelings toward mother.
22. Threatened loss of mother used as early parenting pattern.
23. Aberrant or self-destructive sexual behavior.
24. Females tend to be aggressive and masculine acting.
25. Unusual attraction to adults of opposite sex.
26. Males tend to be individualistic and more feminine in behavior.
27. A history of arson.
28. Sexual role confusion.
29. Sexual aggression.
30. Interest in bizarre, occult, or demonology.
31. The adolescent perceives severe rejection from parent.
32. Profess to want nothing to do with the family.
33. Periodic severe depression.

34. There appears to be a superficial outer shell of "tough-ness" or "togetherness."
35. Adolescent is basically infantile in feelings.
36. Primary method of operating in the environment is through game playing and manipulation.
37. There is a great degree of fear and paranoia, which is kept controlled and masked.
38. Anger outbursts are not frequent, but potentially severe when they appear.
39. An interest and skill in nonverbal artistic methods of expression.
40. Early development has been abusive or anxiety-producing such as to instill a great fear of the parents.
41. Often described as a "time bomb" just waiting to explode.
42. Under therapeutic questioning will admit to attachment to parents.
43. Is of vindictive nature and tries to get even.

Clinical and Family Characteristics Associated With Ambivalent Rejection

44. Family is socially isolated.
45. Family has unusual interest in animals.
46. Adolescent perceives relationship with parent as being primarily ambivalent.
47. Relationship with parent is highly variable.
48. Anger periodically projected toward parents.
49. Parents are brought up in conversation frequently.
50. Alternates between emotions of love and hate.
51. Relationship with mother is highly symbiotic.
52. Frequently expresses desire to return to family.
53. Claims parents treat them differently when in treatment settings.
54. Adolescent claims other adults are fooled by parents.
55. Family visits often.
56. Grandmother has been very influential with adolescent or family.
57. History of self-destructive or suicidal behavior.
58. History of running from the family.

59. Is in frequent telephone contact with the family.
60. Projects much of their problem onto the family.
61. Severe physical aggression or homicidal behavior fantasized toward members of family.
62. Frequently shows rapid and extreme emotional swings.
63. Claim no one understands them.
64. Acting out behavior often related to family contacts.
65. History of sexual promiscuity.
66. Sexual fantasies involving other family members.
67. Family is matriarchal.
68. Problem is multigenerational.

Clinical and Family Characteristics Associated With Low Rejection

69. Adolescent views parent as almost entirely accepting and basically supportive.
70. Fearful of new situations.
71. Frequently influential with peers and tends to be argumentative.
72. Has low frustration tolerance.
73. Is frequently threatening and aggressive when frustrated, but rarely does serious damage.
74. Is often described as hyperactive or as a behavior problem.
75. Is recognized by most people as being basically "psychologically intact."
76. Can use language in an age-appropriate and engaging way.
77. The parenting pattern has not been very abusive.
78. Parental separations during the period of pre-puberty or early adolescence.
79. Parents have been permissive in their limit setting.
80. Parents are willing to follow through on therapeutic suggestions.
81. Has a delinquent history.
82. Delinquent behavior has been goal oriented.
83. No physical separations from parents.
84. Father was alcoholic.
85. Father violent at times.
86. Adolescent thought to be sociopathic or antisocial.

INDEX